C000109064

MESSIANIC JUDAISM

Dan Cohn-Sherbok was born in Denver, Colorado, educated at Williams College, and ordained a Reform rabbi at the Hebrew Union College-Jewish Institute of Religion, in Cincinnati, Ohio. He received a Doctorate in Divinity from the Hebrew Union College-Jewish Institute of Religion, and a Doctorate in Philosophy from Cambridge University. From 1975 he taught Jewish theology at the University of Kent at Canterbury.
He is currently the first Professor of Judaism at the University of Wales. He is the author and editor of over 50 books including *The Jewish Faith*, *Atlas of Jewish History*, *Modern Judaism*, *The Future of Judaism* and *Understanding the Holocaust*.

Messianic Judaism

DAN COHN-SHERBOK

CONTINUUM
London and New York

Continuum
The Tower Building   370 Lexington Avenue
11 York Road   New York
London SE1 7NX   NY 10017–6503

First published 2000; paperback reprinted 2000

© Dan Cohn-Sherbok 2000

All rights reserved. No part of this publication may be reproduced or transmitted
in any form or by any means, electronic or mechanical, including photocopying,
recording or any information storage or retrieval system, without permission in
writing from the publishers.

British Library Cataloguing in Publication Data
A catalogue record for this book is available from the British Library.

ISBN 0-304-70132-7 (hardback)
    0–8264–5458–5 (paperback)

Library of Congress Cataloging-in-Publication Data
Cohn-Sherbok, Dan.
    Messianic Judaism / Dan Cohn-Sherbok.
        p. cm.
    Includes bibliographical references and index.
    ISBN 0-304-70132-7 (hb)—ISBN 0-8264-5458-5 (pb)
        1. Jewish Christians. 2. Missions to Jews—History. 3. Jewish Christians—
    History. I. Title

    BR158.C645 2000
    289.9—dc21   99-050300

Typeset by Kenneth Burnley, Wirral, Cheshire.
Printed and bound in Great Britain by Biddles Ltd, *www.biddles.co.uk*

Contents

Acknowledgements   viii
Introduction   ix

Part I: History and beliefs of Messianic Judaism   1

1 Early Jewish Christianity   3
   The disciples of Jesus   3
   The continuing tradition   5
   Jewish Christians in the Middle Ages   8
   Jewish Christians in the modern period   11

2 The emergence of Hebrew Christianity   15
   Early origins   15
   Israelites of the New Covenant   18
   The faith of the Israelites of the New Covenant   21
   The evolution of Hebrew Christianity   24

3 The Hebrew Christian Alliance of America   27
   The origin of the Hebrew Christian Alliance of America   27
   Conflict and controversy about the Alliance   30
   The growth of the Hebrew Christian Alliance   32
   The development of the Alliance   35

4 Missions to the Jews in the early twentieth century   38
   Missions in the United States   38
   Missions in Poland, Hamburg and Danzig   41
   Missionaries and Jewish believers   43
   Missionary activity after the war   46

5 Growth of the Messianic movement   49
   The Hebrew Alliance after the First World War   49
   From Holocaust to the post-war period   51
   Hebrew Christian churches   54
   The youth movement   57

6   Messianic Judaism in transition   60
    Jews for Jesus   60
    The Six Day War and its aftermath   63
    From Hebrew Christian Alliance to Messianic Judaism   66
    Reactions to the Messianic movement   68

7   Contemporary Messianic Judaism   72
    Messianic congregational organizations   72
    Modern Messianic Judaism   75
    Jewish and Christian reactions   79
    Messianic congregations   82

Part II: Messianic Jewish observance   87

8   Sabbath   89
    The Sabbath and Messianic Judaism   89
    Shabbat evening   90
    Sabbath morning service   93
    Havdalah   99

9   Pilgrim festivals   101
    Passover   101
    Counting of the *omer*   105
    Shavuot   107
    Sukkot   109

10 New Year and Day of Atonement   112
    New Year   112
    Day of Atonement   117

11 Festivals of joy   125
    Simhat Torah   125
    Hanukkah   127
    Purim   130
    New Moon   131
    Advent   133
    Independence Day   137

12 Life cycle events   140
    Naming ceremony   140
    Circumcision   142
    Redemption of the First Born   145
    Bar Mitzvah and *Bat Mitzvah*   148
    Marriage   150
    Death and mourning   153

13   Personal lifestyle   156
         Mezuzah   156
         Dietary laws   157
         Mikveh   159
         Tzizit   161
         Tefillin   163
         Head covering   165

Part III: The authenticity of Messianic Judaism   167

14   Messianic Judaism and the Jewish people   169
         Messianic Jewish theology   169
         The Jewishness of Messianic Jews   172
         Messianic Judaism and the Jewish tradition   175
         Messianic Jewish mission   178

15   Messianic Judaism and its critics   182
         Critique of Messianic Judaism   182
         Former Messianic Jews   185

16   Messianic Judaism and Israeli law   191
         Jewishness and conversion to another faith   191
         The Brother Daniel case   192
         The Shalit case   194
         The Dorflinger case   195
         The Dahaf Report   196
         The Beresford case   198
         Messianic Judaism and Jewish status   200

17   Models of Messianic Judaism   203
         Orthodox exclusivism   203
         Non-Orthodox exclusivism   205
         The pluralist model   209

         Notes   215
         Bibliography   221
         Glossary   224
         Index   227

Acknowledgements

I would like to acknowledge my indebtedness to a number of important books from which I have obtained information as well as source material. Of particular importance is a major study of Hebrew Christianity through the centuries: H. Schonfield, *The History of Jewish Christianity* (Duckworth, 1936). Two seminal studies of the history of Messianic Judaism have also been of immense value: Robert I. Winer, *The Calling: The History of the Messianic Jewish Alliance of America 1915–1990* (The Messianic Jewish Alliance of America, 1990), and Ruth I. Fleischer, *So Great a Cloud of Witnesses* (privately published, 1996). I am indebted as well to David A. Rausch, *Messianic Judaism: Its History, Theology and Polity* (Edwin Mellen, 1982), which provides an overview of the Messianic movement. In depicting Jewish observance, I am indebted to Barney Kasdan, *God's Appointed Times* (Lederer Publications, 1993) and *God's Appointed Customs* (Lederer Publications, 1996), as well as Jeremiah Greenberg, *Messianic Shabbat Siddur* (Messianic Revival Ministries, 1997), John Fischer and David Bronstein, *Siddur for Messianic Jews* (Menorah Ministries, 1988), and John Fischer, *Messianic Services for the Festivals and Holy Days* (Menorah Ministries, 1992). I am also indebted to Dan Juster, *Jewish Roots* (Destiny Image Publishers, 1995), David Stern, *Messianic Jewish Manifesto* (Jewish New Testament Publications Incorporated, 1997), and Bentzion Kravitz, *The Jewish Response to Missionaries* (Jews for Judaism, 1996). In discussing the status of Messianic Jews, I am indebted to Walter Riggans, 'Messianic Judaism and Jewish–Christian Relations: A Case Study in the Field of Religious Identity' (unpublished PhD thesis, University of Birmingham, 1991) and Carol Harris-Shapiro, *Messianic Judaism* (Beacon Press, 1999). I am grateful to those authors and publishers who have allowed me to quote extensively from their books.

Note: Throughout this book I have used a number of different translations of Scripture since Messianic Jews themselves use various Bible translations in their liturgy as well as in explaining the nature of the movement. With regard to the transliteration of Hebrew, I have generally used the most familiar forms.

Introduction

Some time ago my wife and I spent several months in the United States interviewing a cross-section of the Jewish community for a book we were writing entitled *The American Jew*. In the process we heard about a small synagogue where individuals calling themselves 'Messianic Jews' held religious services. One of those who told us about them was the director of an anti-cult organization. Sitting on the porch of his house drinking mandarin tea while a squirrel overhead pelted us with small pieces of bark, he told us about his experiences with this new religious movement.

What is terrible about the Messianic Jews, he said, is that they are extremely deceptive: 'At the core of their theology is their belief that Jesus was God, but they won't tell you that straight away. They only say he is the Messiah.' Despite such criticism, he believed it was a mistake to characterize the Messianic movement as weird or strange. 'Unfortunately,' he continued, 'the movement is growing. They will tell people they are the most rapidly growing group in Judaism . . . we think there are approximately 200,000 Jews who are caught up in it at the moment . . . So to take it as a passing, unimportant phenomenon would be a very large mistake . . . as I go around, I am amazed by the number of people in the Jewish community who have been touched by it: it may be a cousin; or people go to a circumcision, and it turns out to be a "Messianic" synagogue, or someone's sister's child is being married in a "Messianic" synagogue.'[1]

Given the importance of this new movement, we were anxious to meet a representative figure. The following week we arranged an interview with the local Messianic rabbi. His congregation was located in an industrial area on the outskirts of the city; they had a converted warehouse which consisted of offices, classrooms, storage and a large sanctuary. The sanctuary had an Ark in the eastern wall which contained a *Torah* scroll. There was a purple curtain with an embroidered Star of David hanging in front of the Ark. In the storage area of the building a group of congregants was packing food parcels for Russian Jews who had come to live in the area, and several of the men wore *kippahs* (skullcaps) and *tzizit* (fringes).

We spoke to their leader in a small office. The bookcases were full with Old Testament theology, a *Talmud*, Hebrew prayer books and a dictionary of Yiddish slang. On the wall was a large photograph of the Wailing Wall. The rabbi himself was a large, curly-haired man in his forties. His hair and beard were light brown, and he wore a yellow sports shirt. He told us that as a child he was adopted and grew up in a religious home. At the age of 12 he wanted to be a rabbi, and his parents sent him to the Jewish academy in Chicago. However, he did not have a good enough Jewish background or proficiency in Hebrew. As a result, he left after several months.

Returning home, he helped out in the local synagogue, and one of his teachers in school took an interest in him. She was a Christian and asked what the Jewish people believed about the Messiah. He explained that it was something Jews really did not talk about much. For a number of years they remained in contact, and she sent him religious literature. After graduating from college, he went on to graduate school, where he obtained a degree in social work, and eventually got a job in the Division of Child Welfare.

During this time, he was active in the local synagogue, but after considerable study he eventually secretly professed his belief that Yeshua (the Hebrew name for Jesus) is the Messiah. Despite such a conviction, he served as the President of the Conservative Jewish congregation in the town where he lived. Leading this double life, he met an elderly Messianic Jew who told him that it was not necessary for him to give up being a Jew even though he believed in Yeshua. He asked him to come to one of the Messianic Jewish services. Eventually he made a public profession of his faith; this resulted in him losing his job. After accepting Yeshua, he refused to party with his staff, drink, or smoke marijuana. He was told he had become a religious fanatic, and his job was terminated. In time, however, he became the rabbi of the synagogue to which he had been introduced.

Showing us around the synagogue, he explained that about 400 people come every week, including visitors. As the rabbi, he prepares young people for *Bar Mitzvah* and *Bat Mitzvah*, and leads services for all the festivals. The congregation has its own *mikveh* (ritual bath), and the biblical food laws are rigidly followed. In this regard, he was anxious to point out that rabbinical practices are followed only if they conform with Scripture. Messianic Jews regard Christmas and Easter as pagan festivals so they are not observed. He agreed that the movement is anxious to recruit Jews; but he was deeply disturbed by the Jewish community's reaction to Messianic Judaism as well as the attitude of most churches:

> Generally the Rabbinical Association doesn't like us, and to be honest, neither do some of the established Churches. We get as much opposition to our faith from the mainline Churches as from the rabbinic community. They've taken the position we're neither Jews nor Christians: if we were Jews we wouldn't pretend to be Christians, and if we were Christians, then we wouldn't pretend to be Jews. It's amazing. We seem to be caught between a rock and a hard place. [2]

Intrigued by this new movement, once we returned from the United States I contacted Messianic Jews living in England, and my wife and I were invited to their annual national conference. On arrival, we were greeted by smiling, friendly believers who directed us to the bookshop and market stall. Hebrew folk music played in the background as we perused stalls loaded with Jewish ritual objects including *shofars* (ram's horns), prayer shawls, pictures of the Wailing Wall, *mezuzahs* (boxes with prayers attached to doorways) and *menorahs* (candelabra). On other tables there were stacks of books dealing with Messianic Judaism as well as various aspects of Jewish belief and practice. Milling around us were delegates to the conference: many of the women displayed large Jewish stars around their necks, while the men wore skullcaps and fringes.

After lunch, we attended a series of lectures dealing with various aspects of Messianic Judaism. At one dealing with Messianic Jewish music, the speaker stressed the importance of including traditional Jewish melodies in religious services. He played several Hebrew and Yiddish songs, and explained how these could be integrated into Messianic worship. Later in the day, my wife and I attended the afternoon service. To our surprise it turned out to be a prayer meeting with little connection to the traditional Jewish liturgy. There were no prayer-books, neither were Hebrew prayers recited. Instead the participants improvised, lifting up their hands to God.

In the evening, all the delegates gathered together in a large hall. In the front a band consisting of a violinist, pianist, drummer and several singers played exceptionally loud music as members of the audience flooded forward to the stage. Joining hands, they sang and danced, praising the Lord. Everyone else stood, lifting their hands in thanksgiving. This religious service, I was later told, was typical of Messianic worship. At the end of the service, members of the congregation lined up at the front to receive a blessing from the rabbis. Praying fervently, the rabbis placed their hands on the faithful who collapsed backwards, overcome by emotion. This, I learned, is called being 'slain by the Spirit'.

Anxious to learn more about the movement, my wife and I travelled to Harrisburg, Pennsylvania, for the annual International Messianic Jewish Conference which takes place at Messiah College. Driving up to the College, we spotted a yellow tent with a gigantic sign: 'Jews for Judaism'. Bearded figures waved furiously at our taxi – we later learned that this group was at the conference to protest against Messianic Judaism. In their view, Jews cannot possibly accept Jesus and remain Jewish.

On the first day of the Conference, we went to the first session:'Why I am not a Christian'. The speaker, a bespectacled Messianic rabbi wearing a skullcap, told us that although he believes that Yeshua is the Messiah, he is emphatically not a Christian; instead, he is a fulfilled Jew. After this talk, my wife and I went to the marketplace, much like the stalls at the National Conference in England. It contained a vast array of books and religious objects. In the evening we attended the religious service in the college sports hall.

Along one side was a replica of the Wailing Wall in Jerusalem; in front a rock band plus violinist. When the music began, the entire audience stood up. Raising their hands in prayer, they sang uproariously. In the front a mass of people came forward to dance quasi-Israeli folk dances. This was interspersed with a variety of speakers whose words were constantly interrupted with shouts of 'Praise the Lord'. Again, at the end of the service, the Messianic rabbis lined up in front as the devout stood in line to receive a blessing.

On the next day we headed off to the 'Jews for Judaism' tent where we were lectured about the iniquities of the Messianic movement. Our informants insisted that Messianic Jews are evangelical Christians deceiving innocent Jewish people away from their ancestral heritage. In the afternoon, we went to hear another Messianic rabbi talk about the enemies of the movement. He harangued his audience with quotations from Scripture: they responded 'Amen' and 'Praise the Lord'. The next day we went to a healing service. We followed a large crowd to the college chapel where a spiritual healer was holding forth. The chapel was packed and we were told to stand if we had any physical difficulties. Lots of prayers were said and various miraculous healings appeared to have taken place.

When we returned from the Conference, I was convinced of the need for an objective account of this important development in modern Jewish life. Despite the criticisms made by 'Jews for Judaism' and others, this new movement has captured the hearts and minds of thousands of pious individuals from the Jewish community, as well as Gentiles who have accepted Yeshua as their Lord and Saviour. Its membership numbers over a quarter of a million individuals – no doubt the high rate of intermarriage between Jews and Christians in contemporary society has greatly contributed to such growth. Messianic Judaism provides a home for those couples who seek to integrate Jewish living with belief in Jesus.

This study thus traces the development of Messianic Judaism from its origins in ancient times. Beginning with an account of the early history of Jewish Christianity, the book continues with a depiction of the Hebrew Christian renaissance in Europe and continues with a discussion of the development of Hebrew Christian Fellowship organizations. The book then surveys the rise of Christian missions to the Jews, and the impact of the Six Day War on Jewish believers in Christ. This is followed by a discussion of the creation of Messianic organizations, the rise of 'Jews for Judaism', and the emergence of the modern Messianic movement. The second part of the book deals with Messianic belief and practice: here the essential features of Messianic Jewish theology and observance are presented in detail. The final part of the book assesses Messianic Judaism's claim to represent an authentic interpretation of the Jewish faith and proposes three models for understanding the place of Messianic Judaism within the Jewish community.

PART I

History and beliefs of Messianic Judaism

In the view of Messianic Jews, the first Messianic congregation originated in Jerusalem after the ascension of Yeshua. This group was initially a sect within Judaism. Living in the Holy Land, these Jewish believers lived a Jewish lifestyle while trusting in Yeshua as their Messiah and Lord. After the destruction of the Temple in 70 CE, they were perceived as outsiders. Fleeing to the city of Pella in Transjordan, they remained loyal to Yeshua until the *Bar Kochba* revolt against the Romans in the second century. In the following centuries Messianic Jews were overwhelmed by the Gentile Church. In the view of the Christian community, only those in the Church could be saved; as a consequence, Church leaders became bitter opponents of Judaism, and Jewish believers were compelled to conform to the Gentile-oriented Church.

In subsequent centuries only rare individuals sought to remain faithful to the Jewish tradition while accepting Yeshua as Saviour. During the nineteenth century, however, an awakening took place among the Jewish people. From the middle of the century numerous missionary organizations sought to draw Jewish believers to Yeshua. In Europe such figures as Joseph Rabinowitz paved the way for the rebirth of Messianic Judaism among the Jewish people. Others within the Hebrew Christian movement attempted to draw Jewish believers into the Christian fold. As a result, a number of congregations were formed to serve the needs of the Hebrew Christian community.

Following the Six Day War, a major shift took place among Hebrew Christians. Increasingly, Jewish believers were anxious to form Messianic Jewish congregations where they worshipped Yeshua in a Jewish manner. Emerging out of their Hebrew Christian beginnings, Messianic Jews saw themselves as living fulfilled Jewish lives. Today there are over 150 Messianic congregations worldwide, with approximately 250,000 adherents. There are currently three major organizations which serve as the overarching structure for the Messianic community: the Union of Messianic Jewish Congregations (UMJC), the International Alliance of Messianic Congregations and Synagogues (IAMCS), and the Fellowship of Messianic Congregations (FMC), as well as two minor groups, the Association of Torah-Observant Messianics and the International Federation of Messianic Jews. Together these bodies unite Messianic Jews in dedication to Messiah Yeshua.

1 Early Jewish Christianity

The disciples of Jesus

Following Jesus' death, his messiahship was proclaimed by Jewish followers, the Nazarenes, who continued to follow a Jewish lifestyle. Together with fellow Jews they worshipped in the synagogue and kept the law. According to Acts, these believers resided in Jerusalem. Under Simon bar Yona (Peter), this group proclaimed the arrival of the long-awaited deliverer of the nation. It appears that several *parnasim* or deacons were appointed to distribute alms – possibly this led to the creation of a Nazarene synagogue. In time, however, the Jerusalem community scattered so that they preached the Gospel everywhere. As a result, new adherents of the faith were drawn from Samaritans and provincial Jews. Other disciples went as far as Phenice, Cyprus and Antioch, preaching the faith. Paul, too, was called from Tarsus by Barnabas and resided in Antioch, where the Nazarenes were called Christians. As a result of their success, the civil authorities joined with the religious establishment to suppress the movement. One of their leaders, James the son of Zebedee, was seized by Herod Agrippa and beheaded. Although Peter was imprisoned, he managed to escape.

During this period, it appears there was no division between the Nazarenes and the Jewish community. As with mainstream Judaism, the Nazarenes established an organizational structure including officials, a president, deacons, and a precentor; three of these individuals formed a tribunal for judging legal cases. This local council was responsible to the higher court in Jerusalem, to which serious cases were referred. This structure also provided for itinerant preachers who were empowered to spread the Good News. During this period James was regarded as the chief functionary, who ruled over the Hebrew Christians as well as the churches that had been founded to spread the Good News.

At this stage in the history of the Church, the Antioch community sent out a mission consisting of Paul and Barnabas to Asia Minor in order to spread knowledge of Jesus among Jews and Gentiles. Returning to Antioch, they reported that many had been attracted to the faith. Nonetheless, the status of the Gentiles presented a problem. Were they converts to Judaism or half-proselytes obliged to keep only the Noachide laws (laws binding on all human beings)? When the question was referred to Jerusalem, the council presided over by James concluded that God sought to receive Gentiles even though they had not converted to Judaism. It was agreed that James, Peter and John should minister to Jews, whereas Paul and Barnabas should labour among Gentiles. As Acts relates:

> The brethren, both the apostles and the elders, to the brethren who are of the Gentiles in Antioch and Syria and Cilicia, greeting. Since we have heard that some persons from us have troubled you with words, unsettling your minds, although we gave them no instructions, it has seemed good to us, having come to one accord, to choose men and send them to you with our beloved Barnabas and Paul, men who have risked their lives for the sake of our Lord Jesus Christ. We have therefore sent Judas and Silas, who themselves will tell you the same things by word of mouth. For it has seemed good to the Holy Spirit and to us to lay upon you no greater burden than these necessary things: that you abstain from what has been sacrificed to idols and from blood and from what is strangled and from unchastity. If you keep yourselves from these you will do well. (Acts 15:23–29)

Setting sail on a second journey, Paul created a number of centres of believers declaring that the just shall live by faith. Concerned that Paul was disregarding the law, the Jerusalem Christians warned against forsaking the faith of their ancestors. Aware of such dissension, Paul returned to Jerusalem, landing at Tyre. On his arrival in Jerusalem, the apostles stated:

> You see, brother, how many thousands there are among the Jews of those who have believed; they are all zealous for the law, and they have been told about you that you teach all the Jews who are among the Gentiles to forsake Moses, telling them not to circumcise their children or observe the customs. What then is to be done? They will certainly hear that you have come. Do therefore what we tell you. We have four men who are under a vow; take these men and purify yourself along with them . . . Thus all will know that there is nothing in what they have been told about you but that you yourself live in observance of the law. (Acts 21:20–24)

Prior to the destruction of the Temple, most Nazarenes sought refuge in the neighbourhood of Pella. According to Irenaeus, these Jewish Christians practised circumcision, and persevered in the observance of the law.[1] As followers of Christ, they believed that Jesus was the son of Joseph and Mary and was appointed to the office of the Messiah because of his Davidic descent and holy life. This office was confirmed at his baptism by the descent of the Holy Spirit and the declaration: 'Thou art my son, this day have I begotten you.' In addition, the early Christians believed that Jesus had laid down his life for the salvation of the nation, was buried, rose from the dead, ascended into Heaven, and would come again to reign in glory.

Separating themselves from the Gentile Christians who adopted a more supernatural interpretation of Jesus' life, the Jewish Christians viewed themselves as the true heirs of the Kingdom of God. Calling themselves 'Ebionites', they stressed that they were poor in wealth but rich in faith. The Gentile Christians responded that they were poor in knowledge of Christ. Proud of their lineage, the Jewish Christians emphasized their direct relationship with Jesus. As Hegesippus relates, under Domitian's persecution of the Jewish people, the grandsons of Jude the brother of Jesus were arrested and brought before the emperor: 'He put the question, whether they were of David's race, and they confessed that they were. He then asked them what property they had, or how much money they possessed.'[2]

In the persecution under Trajan, Simon the son of Cleophas, who was a cousin of Jesus and successor to James as president of the Jewish Christian community, died as a martyr. Another Jewish Christian, Justus, succeeded Simon as president, and from the second century CE leadership passed from the relatives of Jesus. Until the Jewish revolt against Rome in the second century CE, thirteen Jewish Christian bishops of Jerusalem are recorded: Justus, Zaccheus, Tobias, Benjamin, John, Matthias, Philip, Seneca, Justus II, Levi, Ephraim, Joseph, and Judas.[3]

In 133 CE the Jewish nation rebelled against Rome as a result of Hadrian's policy. Under Simeon bar Kochba, Jewish fighters engaged in a hopeless battle. Jewish Christians, however, refused to take part in this struggle. Refusing to accept Simeon bar Kochba as the long-awaited Messiah, they remained loyal to their faith. Once the Jewish forces were defeated, the Romans decreed that Jerusalem was to become Aelia Capitolina, and all Jews were forbidden to enter the city. Gentile Christians, however, were permitted to reside there, and the Church constituted itself under a Gentile bishop, Marcus. Excluded from their ancient home, the Jewish Christians became a minority sect separated from the Gentile community of believers. Nazarenes were also barred from worshipping in synagogues, and a prayer against heretics was added to the daily liturgy.

The continuing tradition

During the latter half of the second century and continuing into the third century, relations were strained between the Jewish and Gentile Christian communities. The early Church had produced the canon of the New Testament, whereas the Nazarenes remained faithful to their own Hebrew Gospel. Antagonistic to Judaism, a number of Early Church Fathers developed an *Adversos Judaeos* tradition. In response, Jewish sages recounted scurrilous tales about Jesus. In this conflict both sides cited Scripture to demonstrate the truth of their claims.

Although little is known about the development of Jewish Christianity from the middle of the second century CE until the rise of Islam in the sixth century, Epiphanius records that communities existed throughout

Coele-Syria, the Hauran, Batanea, the Decapolis and as far away as Mesopotamia.[4] He writes further that the Nazarenes had synagogues and elders like the Jews, and engaged in similar religious practices.[5] However, it appears that they altered the act of circumcision and observed the weekly fasts in a different fashion. Possibly this was due to their exclusion from the Jewish community. Awaiting the return of the Messiah, they worked as agricultural labourers.

By the end of the second century, the Jewish Christian community began to divide into two distinct groups. According to Origen, there were two sects of Ebionites – one believed that Jesus was born of a virgin, whereas the other asserted that he was born like other human beings.[6] Some of the Jewish Christians, particularly in Syria, were willing to accept some of the dogmas of the Gentile Church. There the Church accepted the antiquity of the Nazarenes and embraced a number of their independent traditions about Christ. Dismayed by this development, other sections of the Jewish Christian community became increasingly exclusivistic, separating themselves from the Christian community.

In the fourth century the Emperor Constantine converted to Christianity. This led to an era of persecution of both the Jewish and Jewish Christian communities. Jews in Palestine fled to Persia and Mesopotamia, and the Jewish academies of Sura and Pumbeditha gained ascendancy over the Palestinian academies located in Tiberias and Sepphoris. The Church regarded Nazarenes as heretics; at this stage a new type of Jewish Christian emerged, having little relationship with the older Nazarene community. Pre-eminent among these Jewish believers was Epiphanius, Bishop of Constantia in Cyprus. Born of Jewish parents in Palestine, he became a Christian, founded a monastery near his native home, and later became bishop. In his *Panarion*, he denounced a wide range of Christian and Jewish sects.

During the century, Christian persecution of the Jewish community intensified, and all Jewish converts were required to desist from any form of Jewish practice. Before accepting the true faith, a Jew was compelled to denounce the Jewish people and renounce any form of Jewish observance. Either he, or his sponsor if he were a child, was compelled to declare:

> I renounce all customs, rites, legalisms, unleavened breads and sacrifice of lambs of the Hebrews, and all the other feasts of the Hebrews, sacrifices, prayers, aspersions, purifications, sanctifications and propitiations, and fasts, and new moons, and Sabbaths, and superstitions, and hymns and chants and observances and synagogues, and the food and drink of the Hebrews; in one word, I renounce absolutely everything Jewish, every law, rite and custom.[7]

As a result of such anti-Jewish attitudes, the Nazarenes were separated from both the Jewish community and Gentile Christians. Influenced by Gnostic theology, they developed a distinct Christology. According to Epiphanius, they believed that:

Jesus was begotten of the seed of man, and was chosen; and so by the choice he was called son of God from the Christ that entered into him from above in the likeness of a dove. And they deny that he was begotten of God the Father, but say that he was created, as one of the archangels, yet greater, and that he is the lord of angels and of all things made by the Almighty.[8]

With the rise of Islam, little is known about the history of the Jewish Christian community, with the exception of various converts. Throughout the Middle Ages, Jews were frequently compelled to convert to Christianity: these forced converts should be distinguished from those Jews who embraced Jesus as their Messiah and Saviour. One of the earliest pious converts to Christianity was Julian, Archbishop of Toledo. Of Jewish origin, he was educated at a religious institution in Toledo, eventually becoming Archdeacon of the Cathedral there. In 680 he was appointed Archbishop of Toledo. Among his writings was *De Comprobatione Aetatis Sextae Contra Judaeos*, which was composed in 686 at the request of King Ervigio. The aim of this work was to refute the Jewish insistence that the Messiah was not to come until 6,000 years after creation. Julian's argument was based on the chronology of the Greek Septuagint version of Scripture which was viewed by the Church to be a purer text than that of the Massoretes.

The conquest of Spain by the Moors established peace between Jews and their neighbours. In England, William Rufus convened a meeting of Jewish scholars and Christian bishops in London. Holingshed's *Chronicles* of this period illustrate the nature of Jewish Christianity at this juncture:

The king being at Rouen on a time, there came to him divers Jews who inhabited the city, complaining that divers of that nation had renounced their Jewish religion, and were become Christians; wherefore they besought him that, for a certain sum of money which they offered to give, it might please him . . . to constrain them to abjure Christianity, and to turn to the Jewish Law again. He was content to satisfy their desires. And so, receiving their money, called them before him; and what with threats, and putting them otherwise in fear, he compelled divers of them to forsake Christ, and to turn to their old errors. Hereupon, the father of one Stephen, a Jew converted to the Christian faith, being sore troubled for that his son turned a Christian presented unto him sixty marks of silver conditionally that he should enforce his son to return to his Jewish religion . . . the young man answered: 'Your grace doth but jest . . . Truly I will not do it; but know for certain that if you were a good Christian, you would never have uttered such words; for it is the part of a Christian to reduce them again to Christ which are departed from him, and not to separate them from him which are joined to him by faith.'[9]

Another figure of the early Middle Ages, Moses Sephardi (Petrus Alfonsi), was born in 1062 in Huesca, and baptized in 1106. Among his writings was a work consisting of a series of dialogues between himself before and after his conversion in which he sought to persuade the Jewish people to accept Christ. The Middle Ages witnessed a convert of a different nature, Nicholas Donin of Paris, who laid charges of blasphemy against the *Talmud* before Pope Gregory IX in 1238. This resulted in a disputation in Paris between Donin and Rabbi Jehiel of Paris, together with several other Jews. As a consequence, copies of the *Talmud* were seized and burnt.

Later in the century another disputation took place between the convert Pablo Christiani and Nahmanides before James I of Aragon. Stemming from Montpellier, Christiani had become a Dominican monk. After seeking to missionize among his own people in Provence, he sought to persuade Jews in Aragon to accept the Christian faith. With the consent of the king, the debate took place in Barcelona from 20 to 24 July 1263. The subject of the debate concerned whether the Messiah had yet appeared, whether he is to be conceived as divine, and whether Jews or Christians possess the true faith. Despite Nahmanides' eloquence, the Dominicans declared that they had been victorious. The following year Christiani obtained a Bull from Pope Clement IV for the *Talmud* to be censored.

In the same century another Jewish Christian, Abner of Burgos, sought to justify his action in an essay, 'Epistle on Fate'. Later, at Burgos, a Jewish Christian, John of Valladolid, engaged in a disputation with Moses ha-Cohen of Tordesillas in which he sought to demonstrate the messiahship and divinity of Christ. Previously he had been on a preaching tour through the Castilian provinces to persuade Jews to embrace the Christian faith. In the next century, another disputation was held at Tortosa, which took place before Benedict XIII. At this disputation Joshua ben Joseph ibn Vives Al-Lorqui (Geronimo de Santa Fé) engaged in debate with Jewish representatives. As a consequence, James II of Aragon issued a decree that Jews should be present at missionary meetings overseen by Dominicans.

Jewish Christians in the Middle Ages

Even though Jews were persecuted in the Middle Ages, a number of prominent Jewish officials were allowed to hold high office, particularly those who had converted to Christianity. Baptism served as the means whereby such individuals were able to attain acceptance into general society. Pre-eminent among such Jewish Christians was the Pierleoni family of Italy. In the eleventh century, Baruch, a Jewish banker from Rome, became a Christian and latinized his name to Benedictus Christianus, marrying the daughter of a Roman nobleman. Subsequently, his son Leo de Benedicto Christiano became an important figure in Roman political life. His son, Petrus Leonis, attained the rank of consul, and became the leader of the papal party.

When Henry V arrived in Rome, Petrus was at the head of the papal legation which sought to bring about a reconciliation between the Pope and the emperor. In addition, he helped in the liberation of Pope Gelasius II and played an important role in the election of Calixtus II. In 1128, he died after having witnessed his son made Cardinal Pierleoni, and his daughter married to King Roger of Sicily. Two years later Cardinal Pierleoni was elected Pope as Anacletus II, despite anti-Jewish attitudes. Later, a brother of Anacletus, Jordan Pierleoni, was elected Senator; and later, as Patricius, became head of the Roman Republic. At this time another brother, Leo Pierleoni, served as papal delegate at Sutri together with Petrus, a nephew. Subsequently John Pierleoni was appointed Elector by Pope Innocent III.

Another family of Jewish Christians who gained eminence were the Carthagenas in Spain founded by Rabbi Solomon Halevi. Born in Burgos, he married in 1376; when he was 40, he began to study the Christian faith. Several years later he was baptized along with his family and took the name of Paul de Santa Maria. Later he took a Doctorate of Divinity in Paris; after a visit to London, he was appointed Archdeacon of Trevino, and later Bishop of Carthagena. He eventually was appointed Keeper of the Royal Seal by King Henry III of Castile and member of the Council of Regency. In 1414 he was appointed Archbishop of Burgos. Describing his background in a testament for his son, he wrote:

> I was . . . brought up in Jewish blindness and incredulity; while learning Holy Scripture from unsanctified teachers, I received erroneous opinions from erring men, who cloud the pure letter of Scripture by impure inventions, as such teachers have been wont to do. But when it pleased Him whose mercies are infinite to call me from darkness to light, and from the depth of the pit to the open air of heaven, the scales seemed as it were to fall from the eyes of my understanding . . . Day and night I sought help from Him, and thus it came to pass that my love for the Christian faith so much increased, that at length I was able openly to confess the belief which my heart had already received.[10]

In his *Dialogus Pauli et Sauli Contra Judaeos, sive Scrutinium Scripturarum*, he predicted that the Jewish people would eventually accept Christ:

> As for the remnant of Israel, which shall remain at the coming of Christ, we firmly believe that when the delusion of Antichrist has been made manifest, they will turn in truth to the Messiah, and for his sake endure much persecution, continuing to the end steadfast in the faith . . . Thus at last shall the whole nation of Israel be brought to the faith in Christ.[11]

One of Halevi's sons, Don Alfonso de Carthagena, became Deacon of Santiago and Segovia, Archdeacon of Compostella, and later Bishop of Burgos. Together with his brother, he represented Spain at the Council of Basle in 1431. Another brother, Don Gonzalo Garcia de Santa Maria, became Archdeacon of Briviesca, Bishop of Astorga, Bishop of Placentia, and Bishop of Siguenza. Little is known of Jewish Christians in the Eastern

Church with the exception of Gregory Abu'l Faraj who became Bishop of Gubos in 1246, and later Maphrian of the Eastern Church.

During this period a home for converts was established in Southwark in London. Subsequently two other homes for Jewish converts were created in London and Oxford. Henry III's charter for the London house declared:

> We ... have granted, and by this our charter confirmed for us and for our heirs to the house which we caused to be built in the street which is called New Street, between the old and new temple of London, for the maintenance of the converted brethren, and those to be converted from Judaism to the Catholic faith, and for the aid of the maintenance of these brethren that dwell in the said houses, the houses and the lands.[12]

Several hundred Jews lived in these dwellings from the time of their foundation, becoming members of the Church.

In Spain, the number of Christian converts became a distinct group – the New Christians or Marranos. Under King Ferdinand and Queen Isabella the Inquisition came into full force, seeking to purge these Jewish Christians who were suspected of remaining loyal to the Jewish faith. In 1478 a Papal Bull was promulgated which established the Castilian Inquisition; four years later the first tribunal came into operation in Seville.

Once the Inquisition was established, the tribunal requested that heretics give themselves up – this 'Edict of Grace' lasted for 30 days. Those who came forward were obliged to denounce all other Judaizers; in compensation they were spared torture and imprisonment. Their sins were atoned for by flagellation, by wearing the *sambenito*, and by the confiscation of their belongings. In addition, they were denied the right to hold office, practise a profession, or wear formal dress.

At the next stage of the Inquisitorial process, Catholics were asked to name any suspects. An edict was promulgated which outlined various ways to recognize such individuals: Judaizers celebrated Jewish holidays, kept the dietary laws, consumed meat during Lent, omitted the phrase 'Glory be to the Father, and to the Son, and to the Holy Ghost' at the end of Psalms, cooked with oil, and so forth. Once suspects were identified, the Inquisitors sought to obtain a confession. To achieve this end, torture was used. Individuals who confessed saved their lives – those who persisted in denying the accusations made against them were burned at the stake.

The first tribunal was established in Seville where the majority of Marranos attempted to placate the Inquisitors by manifestations of Christian dedication as well as offerings and gifts. Nonetheless, for seven years the Inquisition purged 5000 individuals who were punished and accepted reconciliation with the Church; 700 others were branded heretics and burned. In 1483 Tomas de Torquemada became Inquisitor for all of

Spain, and tribunals were instituted in other provinces. From 1486 to 1490 some 4850 Marranos were reconciled to the Church and fewer than 200 were burned.

Many Spanish Marranos who sought refuge from the Inquisition fled to Portugal. These crypto-Jews, unlike their Spanish counterparts, imitated the Christian way of life and complied with all Catholic rites, including attending Mass and Confession. However, they selectively observed various Jewish rituals and traditions such as *Yom Kippur* and the Fast of Esther. In 1536 the Inquisition was established in Portugal, tracking down Marranos in cities, villages, forests and mountains. As in Spain, these Jewish Christians went to their deaths with bravery. During this onslaught a number of Marranos fled abroad, but many remained behind to practise Judaism in secret.

However, among these individuals knowledge of Judaism seriously declined. In an *auto da fé* in 1705 an archbishop declared the following regarding these New Christians:

> O degraded remnants of Judaism, unhappy fragments of the Synagogue! the last spoil of Judaea! opprobrium of the Catholics! abhorrence and laughing-stock of your fellow Jews! it is to you I address myself, ye misguided men! You are the abhorrence and laughing-stock of the Jews; for your ignorance is such that you know not how to observe the very Law you profess. You are the opprobrium of the Catholics; for, being born within the pale of its Church, your voluntary apostasy has banished you from its bosom . . . You are the wretched fragments of the Synagogue; for all its former greatness is come to an end in your present misery. Finally, you are a degraded remnant of Judaism, the wretched off-shoots of Israel, who since the destruction of your country, have spread throughout Europe to infect whole nations by your presence.[13]

Jewish Christians in the modern period

As in the Middle Ages, Jews in post-medieval society were regarded with contempt. In 1516 a converted Jew, Johannes Pfefferkorn, published a pamphlet, 'Der Judenspiegel', which denounced the *Talmud*. Advocating the suppression of Jewish books, he obtained from Emperor Maximilian the consent to seize and destroy all copies of the *Talmud*. In response, the Christian humanist, Johann Reuchlin, defended Jewish sources, and attempted to demonstrate that the *Talmud* and kabbalistic sources confirm the truths of Christianity. This conflict erupted into a widespread debate between Christian humanists and others, and all European men of letters sided with Reuchlin.

Initially Martin Luther condemned the persecution of the Jews and advocated a tolerant policy towards them. Concerning the controversy between Reuchlin and Pfefferkorn, he criticized the confiscation of the *Talmud* and rabbinic literature. In his pamphlet, 'That Christ Was Born a

Jew', he adopted a sympathetic stance toward the Jewish faith. Yet when his early missionary efforts failed to win the Jewish people to Christ, he grew hostile and in 1542 he published his pamphlet 'Against the Jews and Their Lies'. In this work Luther attacked both Judaism and the Jewish people.

According to Luther, the Jews are an unwanted pestilence, repeatedly expelled by those among whom they live. Venomously he described what should be done with this foreign pestilence:

> First, their synagogues should be set on fire, and whatever does not burn up should be covered or spread over with dirt so that no one may ever be able to see a cinder or stone of it. And this ought to be done for the honour of God and of Christianity in order that God may see that we are Christians, and that we have not wittingly tolerated or approved of such public lying, cursing and blaspheming of his Son and his Christians . . . Secondly, their homes should likewise be broken down and destroyed. For they perpetrate the same things there that they do in their synagogues . . . Thirdly, they should be deprived of their prayer books and *Talmud*s in which such idolatry, lies, cursing and blasphemy are taught. Fourthly, their rabbis must be forbidden under threat of death to teach any more . . . Fifthly, passport and travelling privileges should be absolutely forbidden to the Jews.[14]

Despite such sentiments, Jewish Christians during this period were actively engaged in disseminating Jewish learning. Among those who were active participants in this renaissance of Jewish literature were Paul Nunez Coronel, Alfonso de Zamora and Alfonso d'Alcala who aided Cardinal Ximenes in preparing the Complutensian Polyglot Bible. A former rabbi of Safed, Dominico Irosolimitano, taught Hebrew at Rome after accepting the Christian faith. Another Jew from Safed, Giovanni Baptista Jonas, converted in Poland in 1625 and became Professor at the University of Pisa and subsequently a Vatican librarian. In addition to producing a Hebrew translation of the Gospels, he compiled a Hebrew–Chaldee lexicon.

In the first half of the sixteenth century the German Jew Paulo Riccio became Professor of Philosophy at the University of Pavia, and helped Christians gain a greater knowledge of Jewish literature. Johannes Isaac Levita Germanus was baptized in 1546 and served as Professor of Hebrew in London and subsequently in Rome. Another figure of this period, John Immanuel Tremellius, became a Christian and taught Hebrew at Strasburg. Later, he became Regius Professor of Hebrew at Cambridge. Among his works was a Latin translation of the Bible from Hebrew and Syriac. In the same century an Italian Jewish Christian, Mark Raphael, aided Henry VIII with his matrimonial difficulties. Another important Jewish Christian of this period was Rodrigo Lopez, who served as Physician to Queen Elizabeth.

The next century witnessed the arrival of a self-proclaimed Messianic pretender, Shabbatai Zevi. Born in Smyrna into a Judeo–Spanish family, Shabbatai received a traditional Jewish education and later engaged in the study of the *Zohar*. After leaving Smyrna in the 1650s he spent years in various cities in Greece, as well as in Constantinople and Jerusalem. Eventually he became part of a kabbalistic group in Cairo and travelled to Gaza where he encountered Nathan Benjamin Levi who believed Shabbatai was the Messiah. In 1665 his messiahship was proclaimed and Nathan sent letters to Jews in the diaspora asking them to repent and recognize Shabbatai Zevi as their redeemer. Eventually Shabbatai journeyed to Constantinople, but on the order of the Grand Vizier he was arrested and imprisoned. He was later brought to court and given the choice between conversion and death. In the face of this choice, he converted to Islam and took on the name of Mehemet Effendi. Such an act of apostasy scandalized most of his followers, but he defended himself by asserting that he had become a Muslim in obedience to God's commands. Many of his followers accepted this explanation and refused to give up their belief.

Subsequently various Shabbatean sects emerged throughout the Jewish world, including that established by Jacob Frank in the eighteenth century. Born in Podolia in 1726, Frank lived in Salonika and Smyrna, but returned to Podolia in 1755. Believing himself to be the incarnation of Shabbatai, Frank announced that he was the second person of the Trinity and gathered together a circle of disciples who indulged in licentious orgies. During this time disputations took place between traditional Jews and Frankists; subsequently Frank expressed his willingness to become a Christian but wished to maintain his own group. Although this request was refused by Church leaders, Frank and his disciples were baptized. The clergy, however, became aware that Frank's trinitarian beliefs were not consonant with Christian doctrine, and he was imprisoned for thirteen years. Frank then settled in Germany, where he continued to subscribe to a variant of the Shabbatean kabbalistic tradition.

In the eighteenth century the English thinker John Toland drew attention to the distinction between Jewish and Gentile Christianity:

> From the history of the Nazarenes, and more particularly from the evident words of Scripture, I infer in this discourse a distinction of the two sorts of Christians, *viz.* those from among the Jews, and those from among the Gentiles: not only that in fact there was such a distinction (which nobody denies) but likewise that of right it ought to have been so (which everybody denies) and that it was so designed in the Original Plan of Christianity. I mean that the Jews, though associating with the converted Gentiles, and acknowledging them for brethren, were still to observe their own Law throughout all generations; and that the Gentiles, who became so far Jews as to acknowledge One God, were not however to observe the Jewish Law.[15]

In the next century Christian missions to the Jews led to the recreation of Jewish Christianity. Such steps were initially taken by Joseph Samuel Frey and Ridley Herschell who inspired the London Society and the British Society for Promoting Christianity among the Jews. By the end of the century there were nearly 100 such bodies labouring among Jews in various parts of the world. As a consequence nearly a quarter of a million Jews were converted. One of the most important missionary agencies was the Hebrew Christian Testimony to Israel, which was established in 1893 by David Baron and C. A. Schönberger in the east of London. Their aim was to draw Jews to Christ and demonstrate that Jesus and Israel are inseparable. As Baron stated:

> What we continually press upon the Jews is that we believe in Christ as the Son of Man and Son of God, not in spite of, but because we are Jews. We believe that Jesus is the Divine King of our people, the sum and substance of our Scriptures, the fulfiller of our Law and our Prophets, the embodiment of all the promises of our covenant.[16]

2 The emergence of Hebrew Christianity

Early origins

Although there were numerous Jewish converts to Christianity through the centuries, there were few attempts to spread the Gospel among the Jewish people. In 1809, however, the London Society for Promoting Christianity Amongst the Jews (LSPCJ) was established, and a number of Christians were actively involved in missionary activity. In 1813 the Children of Abraham was created under the auspices of the LSPCJ. Simultaneously, in the second decade of the nineteenth century the first translation of the New Testament was made in Hebrew.

As a result of such missionary activity, a number of distinguished Jewish figures were drawn to the Christian faith, including Bishop Samuel Isaac Schereschewsky, missionary to China and translator of the Bible into Mandarin and other dialects; Dr Alfred Edersheim, scholar and author; Solomon Ginsburg, missionary to Brazil; Dr David Baron, founder of the Hebrew Christian Testimony to Israel; Dr Bernard Betelheim, missionary to Japan; Isidor Lowenthal, missionary to Afghanistan; Joseph Wolff, missionary to the Jews in the Middle East; and Rabbi Dr Leopold Cohn, founder of the American Board of Missions to the Jews.[1]

Pre-eminent among such Jewish converts was Michael Solomon Alexander, who was born at Schönlanke in Posen. After receiving a traditional Jewish education, he settled in England in 1820, serving as a rabbi in Norwich and later at Plymouth. Under the influence of the Revd B. B. Golding, a curate of Stonehouse, he converted to Christianity. Once ordained as a deacon and subsequently a priest, he became a missionary of the London Jews' Society. Simultaneously he was Professor of Hebrew and Rabbinic Literature at King's College, London. In 1841 King Frederic William IV of Prussia proposed that a joint episcopal representative be established at Jerusalem. On 5 October 1841 Parliament passed a bill to establish a bishopric in Jerusalem.

Given the desire that a Jewish Christian should occupy this position, Alexander was appointed to this new see on 7 November 1841; the next morning he celebrated Holy Communion in the Episcopal Jews' Chapel before setting sail for Jerusalem. In accordance with instructions from Constantinople, a declaration was made in the mosques in Jerusalem that whoever touches the Anglican Bishop will be viewed as having touched the apple of the Pasha's eye. In 1845 Alexander died on a trip to Cairo. His remains were brought back to Jerusalem where they were buried in an English cemetery. In a letter to his wife, a group of Jewish Christians in Jerusalem expressed their devotion to his memory:

> Next to yourself and your dear family, we consider ourselves the chief mourners; for we feel both collectively and individually that we have lost not only a true Father in Christ, but also a loving brother and a most kind friend. The suavity and benignity of his manner, which so greatly endeared him to all, and which gained him the highest and most entire filial confidence of every one of us, tend much to increase the keen sense we feel of our loss. The affectionate love he bore to Israel, which peculiarly characterized him, could not fail to render him beloved by every one who had the privilege of being acquainted with him; while his exalted piety, and most exemplary life and conversations, inspired the highest esteem. He was a burning and a shining light; and when he was raised to the highest dignity in the Church, he conferred the most conspicuous honour on our whole nation, but especially on the little band of Jewish believers.[2]

In the quest to bring Jewish believers to Christ, England played a pivotal role. On 9 September 1813 a group of 41 Jewish Christians established the Beni Abraham association at Jews' Chapel. These Jewish Christians met for prayer every Sunday morning and Friday evening. In addition they daily visited any sick member to pray and read the Bible to him. In 1835 this group became known as the Episcopal Jews' Chapel Abrahamic Society; its aim was to visit Jewish converts and inquirers. The Hebrew Christian Prayer Union, founded in 1882 by Dr H. A. Stern, also sought to unite Jewish Christians in spiritual fellowship. Every Sunday prayer was offered privately by each member, and there were general worship meetings as well. From 1883 to 1890 its membership increased from 143 to 600. In addition, branches were established in Germany, Norway, Romania, Russia, Palestine, and the United States.

In 1865 an attempt was made by Dr C. Schwartz, minister of Trinity Chapel, Edgware Road, London, to unite all Jewish Christians with the creation of the Hebrew–Christian Alliance, In a declaration of its principles, this group stated that its objects were:

1. To promote a social and frequent personal intercourse among Christian Israelites by meeting together at stated periods.
2. To stir up and stimulate one another in the endeavour of uniting with, and caring for, our brethren.
3. To search the Scriptures together relating to Israel and Israel's king.

As an indication of this group's benevolent intentions, the Hebrew–Christian Alliance adopted as its motto the first verse of Psalm 133: 'Behold, how good and how pleasant it is for brethren to dwell together in unity.' In the following year Dr Schwartz launched the first Jewish Christian journal, *The Scattered Nation*. Later in the year, a circular letter was sent to all Jewish Christians announcing that a meeting of all Jewish Christians was scheduled for May:

> Dear Brother,
> It has occurred to us that it would be desirable and profitable that as many Israelites who believe in Jesus as can be brought together should meet in London on the 23rd of May.
> Our object is to become acquainted with one another, and to be built up in our holy faith. There are special ties which bind us together as descendants of Abraham, and we believe that this conference for prayer and consultation might issue in a permanent union of Jewish Christian brethren in this land.
> We do not come before you with any definite plan for action, but would simply say that, as there exists an Evangelical and a Jewish, an Hebrew–Christian Alliance also might be formed.
> We trust that you feel with us the desirableness and importance of such a meeting, and that we may reckon on your presence and on your prayers.[3]

Eighty Jewish Christians met together at the Conference, convinced that this was the first gathering of converted Jews to be held since the days of the early Church. At the meeting, Revd A. M. Meyer argued that the creation of a Hebrew–Christian Alliance was in no sense a threat to Jewish identity:

> Let us not sacrifice our identity. When we profess Christ, we do not cease to be Jews; Paul, after his conversion, did not cease to be a Jew; not only Saul was, but even Paul remained, a Hebrew of the Hebrews. We cannot and will not forget the land of our fathers, and it is our desire to cherish feelings of patriotism . . . As Hebrews, as Christians, we feel tied together; and as Hebrew Christians, we desire to be allied more closely to one another.[4]

The next year a public meeting was held at Willis' Rooms, King Street, St James, under the presidency of Dr Schwartz. At this gathering it was resolved that although the members of the Alliance belonged to different Churches, they were united in Christ. As such, they declared before the Jewish community that they had found in Jesus the Messiah to whom the Law and the prophets bear testimony. It is in his blood, they stated, that they had found peace, and looked for his coming in glory as the hope of Israel. Eventually the Hebrew Christian movement was established in the United States under the Presidency of the Revd S. B. Rohold.

Israelites of the New Covenant

Alongside the developments that were taking place in Great Britain, Christian missionaries were also active in Europe. In 1882 the first Jewish Christian mission was established by Joseph Rabinowitz. Born on 23 September 1837 in Resina on the Dniester, Rabinowitz was the son of David ben Ephraim. Due to the death of his mother, he grew up in the family of his maternal grandfather, Nathan Neta, until he was 11. During this formative period, he was influenced by Hasidism. At the age of 13 he was betrothed, marrying six years later. It was through his future brother-in-law that he became acquainted with Christianity: he lent the youth a Hebrew copy of the New Testament, remarking that possibly Jesus of Nazareth was the Messiah.

Astonished by this suggestion, Rabinowitz was determined to study Scripture. Eventually he returned to Orgeyev with his grandfather where he practised law. In addition, he was actively involved in communal affairs, and frequently contributed to Jewish newspapers. In addition, he gave a series of lectures at Kishinev, arguing for a reform of the tradition. In 1878 he wrote an article in the newspaper *Haboker Or*, in which he encouraged the rabbis to ameliorate the conditions of Russian Jews through agricultural training. Later, due to an anti-semitic outbreak he travelled to Palestine with the intention of establishing a Jewish colony.

On arrival in Jerusalem, Rabinowitz was deeply troubled by the poverty of its Jewish inhabitants. Before his departure, he ascended the Mount of Olives; viewing the Mosque of Omar in the distance, he asked himself what had been the cause of Jewish suffering through the ages. Filled with a vision of God's glory, Rabinowitz concluded that the key to the Holy Land is in the hands of Jesus. Returning to Kishinev, he gathered together numerous adherents of his doctrines. This new movement, calling itself 'Israelites of the New Covenant', was set forth in twelve articles of faith modelled on Maimonides' *Principles of the Jewish Faith*:

1. I believe with a perfect faith, that the Creator, blessed be His name, is the living, true and eternal God, who hath made by His Word, and His Holy Spirit, heaven and earth, all things visible and invisible; that He is One, and all is from Him, through Him and to Him.
2. I believe, with a perfect faith, that the Creator, blessed be His name, is not corporeal, that we cannot apprehend Him by the corporeal senses, and that there is no likeness to Him.
3. I believe, with a perfect faith, that the Creator, blessed be His name, has made a covenant with our father, Abraham, to be his and his children's God, and to give him and his descendants the land of Canaan for an eternal inheritance, and that the sign of this covenant is circumcision of the flesh, a sign of an eternal covenant.
4. I believe, with a perfect faith, that the Creator, blessed be His name, has,

according to his promise, brought out the children of Israel from Egypt, with a strong hand through Moses, His chosen one, and commanded them (us) to keep holy the Sabbath and the Passover, as a law for ever.

5. I believe, with a perfect faith, that the Creator, blessed be His name, raised up prophets in our midst from among our brethren, and that all their words are true, and not one of them shall remain unfulfilled.

6. I believe, with a perfect faith, that the Creator, blessed be his name, raised up prophets in our midst from among our brethren, and that all their words are true, and not one of them shall remain unfulfilled.

7. I believe, with a perfect faith, that the Creator, blessed be His name, promised to David, the son of Jesse, of Bethlehem, that He would make his name great, and that his throne and kingdom should endure for ever and ever.

8. I believe, with a perfect faith, that the Creator, blessed be His Name, rewards those who observe His commandments and punishes those who transgress them.

9. I believe, with a perfect faith, that the Creator, blessed be His name, in His infinite mercy, has raised up in the house of his servant David, a Horn of salvation, the Righteous Zemah, the Saviour, the Lord Jesus Christ of Bethlehem, and that He reigns over the house of Jacob forever, and of his kingdom there shall be no end.

10. I believe, with a perfect faith, that according to the will of the Creator, our Messiah, Jesus, was persecuted and crucified; that He poured out His soul unto death for our salvation; that He rose from the dead, and now sits at the right hand of the Father.

11. I believe, with a perfect faith, that in accordance with the counsel of the Creator, our forefathers hardened their hearts and rejected their Messiah, Jesus, and that this was permitted in order to provoke other nations to jealousy, to bring salvation to the whole world; that the Gentiles also might believe in our Jesus through the preaching of His messengers of peace, whom we rejected and drove from our midst, so that the whole world might be filled with the glory of the Lord, and that He might be the King of the whole earth.

12. I believe, with a perfect faith, that when it shall please our heavenly Father, there will be a resurrection from the dead even as our Lord rose from the dead and became thereby the first-fruits of the resurrection:
   For Thy salvation have I waited, O Lord, I have waited,
   O Lord for Thy salvation have I waited.[5]

By 1865 Rabinowitz had formulated an order of service for his congregation for the morning service on the Sabbath based on a mixture of Jewish and Christian elements:

The Cantor says in a loud voice:
Repent, for the Kingdom of Heaven is at hand (Matthew 3:2).

The Congregation's confession of sin:
Come and let us return unto the Lord . . . (Hosea 6:1 followed by a set confession of sin).

The Lord's Prayer.

The Cantor:
Bless the Lord, the only (God)!

Congregation:
Blessed be the Lord, the blessed one!

Recitation of Psalm 33:
Rejoice in the Lord, O ye righteous . . .

Then (expanded) Shema Israel:
Hear O Israel: The Lord our God is one Lord. And thou shalt love the Lord thy God with all thine heart, and with all thy soul, and with all thy might. And thou shalt love thy neighbour as thyself (Deuteronomy 6:4–5; Leviticus 19:18).

On weekdays Psalm 103 is recited:
Bless the Lord, O my soul . . .

On Sabbath days Psalm 92 is recited:
It is a good thing to give thanks unto the Lord . . .

The Cantor is handed the New Testament and says:
Out of Zion shall go forth the law (*Torah*) and the word of the Lord from Jerusalem (Isaiah 2:3).

The Cantor is handed the Torah *scroll and says:*
This is the law which Moses set before the children of Israel (Deuteronomy 4:44).

The Cantor reads from the Law of Moses and the New Testament. The Torah *scroll and the New Testament are returned to their places. He says:*
And when it (the Ark of the Covenant) rested, he said: 'Return, O Lord, unto the many thousands of Israel' (Numbers 10:36).

Common Prayer for the Czar.

Sermon upon God's Holy Word.

Afterwards, Psalm 40:4–6 is recited:
Blessed is that man that maketh the Lord his trust . . .

The Sabbath hymn *Lekah Dodi*.

The Aaronic Blessing.[6]

While there are a number of Jewish features of this service, the liturgy has been reworked to include a range of Christian elements. The confession of sin was grounded in a recognition that Jesus has come to forgive sins and redeem the world; the *Shema* was expanded to reflect the Christian understanding of Jesus' teaching about the commandments; both the Hebrew Bible and the New Testament were viewed in the service as containing God's revelation to the Jewish people; the sermon preached in the service took its inspiration from the words of both the Hebrew Scriptures and the New Testament. It is noteworthy that while there are echoes of the Jewish liturgy in Rabinowitz's worship service, there are obvious omissions from the synagogue liturgy such as the *Amidah*, the *Kaddish*, and the *Alenu* prayers.

The faith of the Israelites of the New Covenant

In addition to the Twelve Theses, Rabinowitz composed a series of articles of faith based on the Thirty-nine Articles of the Church of England; these were designed to function in the life of the congregation he founded:

1. There is but one true and living God, not corporeal, without divisions, who cannot be apprehended by the bodily senses, of great goodness, power and wisdom beyond comprehension, who creates forms, makes and upholds everything by His Word and by His Holy Spirit. All things are from Him, all things in Him, and all things to Him.
2. The true God has, according to His promise to our forefathers, to our prophets, and to our king David, the son of Jesse, raised unto Israel a Redeemer, Jesus, who was born from the virgin Mary, in Bethlehem the City of David, who suffered, was crucified, dead and buried for our salvation, rose again from the dead, and liveth, and sitteth on the right hand of our heavenly Father; from thence He shall come to judge the world, the living and the dead. He shall be king over the house of Jacob for ever, and of His dominion there shall be no end.
3. According to the counsel and foreknowledge of God, our ancestors have been smitten with hardness of heart to sin and rebel against the Messiah, the Lord Jesus, in order to provoke to jealousy the other nations of the earth, and to reconcile all the children of men, through their faith in Christ, by the ministry of His holy Evangelists and Apostles, in order that the knowledge of God should cover the earth; and the Lord be King over the whole world.
4. Through faith alone in Jesus the Messiah all men may be justified without the works of the law. There is but one God, who shall justify the circumcised Jews by faith, and the uncircumcised Gentiles through faith; and there is no difference between Jew and Greek, between bond and free, between male and female; for they are all one in Christ Jesus. By faith in Christ we fulfil the law, and that faith is a wonderful balm to our soul, and full of comfort.
5. The Holy Scriptures contain everything necessary for our salvation. No one is bound to accept anything not found in them, nor made binding by them, as articles of faith, or as things necessary to salvation. By 'Holy Scriptures' we mean the books of revelation Old and New Testament which have always been accepted by the Church as inspired by the Holy Spirit.

6. The Scriptures of the New Testament do not contradict those of the Old Testament, for in both life everlasting is offered unto mankind through the Messiah, who alone is the Mediator between God and man. The law which was given by God through Moses was to lead us to Christ, that we might be justified through faith in Him. But we are the seed of Abraham according to the flesh, who was the father of all those who were circumcised and believed, we are bound to circumcise every male-child on the eighth day, as God commanded him. And as we are the descendants of those whom the Lord brought out of the land of Egypt with a stretched out arm, we are bound to keep the Sabbath, the feast of unleavened bread, and the feast of weeks, according as it is written in the law of Moses, whilst the (Gentile) Christians celebrate them only in commemoration of the resurrection of the Messiah from the dead, and the outpouring of the Holy Spirit from heaven.

7. The *Mishnah* and *Talmud* are not to be used for establishing any doctrines, but regarded only as an everlasting monument of the spirit of deep slumber which God has permitted to fall upon us; so that the *Shulkhan Arukh* became a net, a snare, and a stumbling-block to us, and has darkened our eyes so that we failed to see the ways of the true and life-giving Faith.

8. Original sin is the cause of the corruption of every natural man born of blood and the will of the flesh, which always inclines towards evil. The lusts of the flesh war against the spirit, rendering it hard to accept the law of God.

9. Man in his natural condition is unable to do good works, to walk uprightly, or to call upon God, unless there first be given to him the grace of God, which is treasured up in Christ, who is the Word of our Heavenly Father, and begotten of the Father from all eternity.

10. The good works of the sons of men are the signs of a true and living faith in the heart, as the tree is known by its fruit; and they are acceptable before God in Christ; but nevertheless they are unavailing to blot out transgressions, or to avert the severity of God's judgment.

11. The works done prior to the bestowment of the grace of Christ and the reception of the Holy Spirit are insufficient to secure, as a reward for merit, grace and righteousness for those who practice them; for undoubtedly they are defiled by the nature of sin, and there is no merit in deeds which originated with men, and who think they are doing more than is required of them . . .

12. Christ alone was sinless in body as well as in spirit; but we, although baptized and born anew in Christ, still fail in many things; and if we say, we have no sin, the truth is not in us.

13. Every sin, whether committed intentionally or unintentionally, is forgiven when the sinner repents with his heart and soul; and even after we have fallen into sin, we may by the grace of God rise and amend our ways. But a sin against the Holy Ghost is one which remains unforgiven.

14. It was the secret counsel of God, and His will before the foundation of the world was laid, to save those from the curse and from judgment whom He

chose in Christ, and to bring them through Christ unto everlasting salvation . . .

15. The visible Church of Christ is the congregation of believers among whom the Word of God is preached in purity, and the holy ordinances observed in every detail according to the charge of Christ by the holy Evangelists.

16. The Church is at liberty to introduce rules and observances. She is, however, not at liberty to introduce anything contrary to the Word of God, or to interpret one verse of Holy Scripture in such a manner as to contradict another. Neither is she at liberty to impose any doctrine outside the Old and New Testament Scriptures, as necessary to salvation.

17. Without the permission of the Authorities neither a general nor special assembly is to take place; for the Government is ordained by God, as we are told in the Holy Scriptures, and in her hands God has placed all the concerns of the country, temporary as well as spiritual, to hold in check by the power of the sword of the State those who are bent on doing evil.

18. It is forbidden for any one to officiate as minister unless he is authorized by the congregation and by the laws of the Country.

19. The liturgy as well as the whole of the service must be conducted in a language understood by the people; and as the most of the sons of Israel in Russia understand Hebrew, 'the holy tongue', and the German jargon, therefore, it is decided that the service be conducted in these languages.

20. The sacraments instituted by Christ serve as faithful witnesses of the grace of God, and His goodwill towards us; and it is through them that He is working in us in a mysterious and wonderful way . . . The Sacraments are two: Baptism and the Lord's Supper . . .

21. As the minister is not ministering in his own name but in the name of Christ and on the strength of being sent by Him, it is our duty to listen to his proclamation of the word of God, and to receive at his hands the sacraments . . .

22. Baptism is a sign of the new birth. By means of water baptism, the baptized one is placed and planted in the Church, the Church of Christ. By means of water baptism there is the washing and cleansing from all evil; the baptized ones testify before all that they know their sins are forgiven and that they are the children of God. It is therefore quite right that little ones should be led into the Church by baptism.

23. The Lord's Supper is a sign that we remember the death of our Lord the Messiah, till He come, and by partaking of that heavenly bread and wine we unite all our physical and spiritual powers with the body and blood of Christ . . .

24. He who breaks intentionally any of the rules of the Church, although it is not against the word of God, is to be reprimanded as one who acted against the order of the Church; and against the permission of the Government. It is within the power of the general, as well as in that of a special assembly, to revise and to alter any Church rules which have only been framed by the wisdom of man . . .

25. We acknowledge that false and thoughtless swearing is, according to our

> Lord Jesus Christ, and His apostle James, forbidden; but still we are of
> opinion, that according to the religion of Christ, it is not forbidden, but
> allowed to take an oath in matters touching the Government . . .[7]

The evolution of Hebrew Christianity

Rabinowitz's endorsement of a Jewish lifestyle, combined with an acceptance of Jesus' messiahship, was shared by another Jewish Christian,
I. Lichtenstein, a Hungarian rabbi. Previously he had viewed Christ as
the cause of Jewish suffering through the ages, yet once he read the
New Testament his opinion was completely altered:

> I was surprised, and scarcely trusting my eyes, I took a New Testament out of its
> hidden corner; a book which some forty years ago I had in vexation taken from a
> Jewish teacher, and I began to turn over its leaves and to read. How can I express
> the impression which I then received? Not the half had been told me of the
> greatness, power, and glory of this book, formerly a sealed book to me. All
> seemed so new to me, and yet it did me good like the sight of an old friend, who
> has laid aside his dusty, travel-worn garments, and appears in festal attire.[8]

Once he began to use New Testament quotations in his sermons, his congregants accused him of heresy. Forced to resign his post, he preached the
Gospel even though he refused to be baptized.

In opposition to Rabinowitz and Lichtenstein, some Gentile Christians
maintained that these Jewish followers of Christ had distorted Jesus'
message. Anxious that these believers might form their own Hebrew
Christian organization, they sought to persuade Jewish Christians to
remain within the Church. At meetings this potential schism was frequently discussed. Such figures as Mark John Levy pressed for the Church
to allow its members to embrace Jewish customs. In an address given to the
General Assembly of the Episcopal Church of the United States, he stated
that it is desirable:

> That the Church does not require its Jewish members to forsake their own
> people, but leaves them in their Christ-like liberty to have their children circum-
> cised according to God's covenant with Abraham, should they so desire, and to
> observe all the other customs inherited from their fathers, provided it be clearly
> understood that neither Jew nor Gentile can be saved through the works of the
> Law, but solely through the sacrifice and atonement of Jesus Christ, our Lord and
> Saviour.[9]

Arguing along similar lines, Philip Cohen in South Africa, Theodore Lucky
in Galicia, and Paulus Grun in Hamburg argued that there should be a
separate alliance of Jews who had accepted Christ. According to Cohen,
there were important reasons why Jewish Christians should embrace

Jewish practices: a love of their tradition and the belief that Jewish Christianity can only be effective if it adopts a Jewish character.

In a speech at a Jewish Christian conference in Stanislau, Lucky emphasized the need for Jewish Christians to remain faithful to their traditions:

> I do not demand from my fellow-believers the complete and strict observance of all Jewish customs at any price . . . I do not judge his conscience, nor is he to let me be a conscience to him in the matter of meats, or of the Sabbath, all of which are only a shadow of that which we have the substance in Christ. On the other hand, another says, 'Because I believe in Christ therefore I give up the Sabbath.' Well, he is no less acceptable to God on that account, and I do not despise him for it nor condemn him. But I am sorry for him, and it hurts me to the depth of my heart because he too is a child of Israel and should help us to build up the walls of Jerusalem.[10]

Responsive to these sentiments, some Gentile Christian leaders acknowledged that Hebrew Christians needed to form their own communities. At the London Missionary Conference in 1903, Canon G. H. Box stated:

> I venture to beseech Jewish Christians to take this question into their prayerful consideration. I know full well that many of them are affectionately attached to Gentile Christian communities, and that it will be fairly difficult to find a common basis. But I would ask them at least to set this unity before them as their goal. And should a homogeneous Hebrew Christian Church be formed centring round a liturgy which is informed with a certain adaptation to the national and historic Jewish spirit, may those who cannot give their full and hearty allegiance to such a Church at least refrain from putting hindrances in the way of its free development.[11]

Similarly the Revd Th. Lindhagen urged fellow Christians to heed this initiative at the International Jewish Missionary Conference held in Stockholm in 1911:

> It cannot be denied that up to now the relation of Jewish Christians to their people has been far from altogether satisfactory. The reproaches which have been levelled against them are unfortunately only too well grounded. It is quite true that there are Jewish Christians and missionaries to the Jews who make an altogether vicious use of Paul's word to the Galatians, 'There is neither Jew nor Greek' . . . It is equally true that the Gentile Church has helped to estrange Jewish Christians from their own people through calling them 'proselytes' . . . In this respect a thorough-going change of policy and practice is necessary . . . That the ideal of an autonomous Jewish Christian Church is closely connected with these aspirations regarding the right attitude of Hebrew Christians to their people is self-evident.[12]

Anxious to ensure that Jewish Christians in the United States acknowledge the importance of Jewish customs, Mark Levy convened a group of Jewish believers in Boston on 22 May 1901. This gathering – the Boston Conference of the Messianic Council – agreed that a national conference take place to organize the Hebrew Christian Alliance of America. Under the leadership of Arthur Kuldell and Louis Meyer, a circular was sent out in November 1902 to all Messianic Jews living in the United States; after receiving 437 replies, the committee began to formulate plans for such a gathering to take place at Mountain Lake Park, Maryland. It was decided that Jewish Christians from throughout the world be invited as well. The conference was held from 28 to 30 July 1903 with Arthur Kuldell as president. Reflecting on these events, he wrote:

> At a conference in Boston we were drawn to each other very closely in the Lord, and decided to call a conference at Mountain Lake Park for the purpose of forming an Alliance of Hebrew Christians. Even though the writer was the chairman of the movement, yet the vast amount of work that had to be done preparatory to this conference was upon the willing and able shoulders of our departed brother as secretary.
>
> Louis Meyer was pastor of a small church at that time, and he had more time than the writer. The conference at Mountain Lake Park at the beginning of this century was a success, but we were not yet ripe for an Alliance.
>
> The ideal of the writer was a Hebrew Christian Union or Alliance with Hebrew Christian business men, professors and pastors at the forefront, and missionaries in the background. The reason was because of the prejudice with which the Jewish heart was filled against the missionary, and yet another reason which need not be stated.
>
> The Hebrew Christian pastors and professors and business men did not rally around the writer, and pastor Louis Meyer soon learned to his sorrow that the time for an Alliance, with the material at hand, was premature and he resigned. Thus the matter was held in abeyance until about seven years ago.[13]

3   The Hebrew Christian Alliance of America

The origin of the Hebrew Christian Alliance of America

As Kuldell noted, it was not until 1913 that further steps were taken to create an international body of Jewish Christians. One of those who attended the Mountain Lake Conference in 1903 was Maurice Ruben. Of European origin, Ruben had become a believer in Pittsburgh and was committed by his family to an insane asylum. After securing his release, he bore testimony to his faith and became convinced that an assembly of believers should be established. In 1913 he convened a conference of Hebrew Christians in Pittsburgh to commemorate the fifteenth anniversary of the New Covenant Mission. Those who attended this gathering agreed that the Hebrew Christian Alliance of America should be formally established and asked Kuldell to send out an invitation to Jewish believers to form this body.

On 22 May 1914 a planning meeting was held at the headquarters of the Presbyterian Church in New York which developed a constitution and By-Laws Committee. At a second meeting at the Williamsburg Mission to the Jews in Brooklyn, Arthur Kuldell was appointed Corresponding Secretary and Mark Levy Recording Secretary to prepare for the conference which was to take place the following year. Although Kuldell was to reside in New York prior to the meeting, he was unable to comply, and the responsibility for organizing the conference fell upon Mark Levy.

From 6 to 9 April 1915 delegates met at the Assembly Hall of the United Charities Building in New York to ratify a Constitution for this new body:

Article I. Name
1. The name of this organization shall be The Hebrew Christian Alliance of America.
2. The Alliance shall have its headquarters in Greater New York.

Article II. Objects
1. To encourage and strengthen Hebrew Christians and to deepen their faith in the Lord Yeshua the Messiah.

2. To propagate more widely the Gospel of our Lord and Saviour, Yeshua, by strengthening existing Jewish missions, and fostering all other agencies to that end.
3. To provide for evangelical Christian churches of America an authoritative and reliable channel (of) how best to serve the cause of Jewish evangelization.

Article III. Membership
1. Every evangelical Hebrew Christian of good standing shall be eligible for membership.
2. Local branches formed in accord with the object of the Alliance, and holding its character, are eligible (for) membership and are entitled to a delegation according to the provisions of the By-Laws.

Article IV. Executive Committee
There shall be an Executive Committee of fifteen including the officers. This Committee shall be elected by the Alliance at its annual meeting, to serve for a period of one year, and to continue in office until their successors are installed. In case of resignation or death of a member of the Executive Committee, his successor shall be appointed by the Chairman of the Executive Committee until the following annual election. The Executive Committee of fifteen shall constitute the Board of Managers in whom shall be vested the powers of the Alliance.

Article V. Officers
The officers of the Alliance shall consist of a President, and a first, second and third Vice-President, a Recording Secretary, a General Secretary, and a Treasurer. They shall be elected annually by the Alliance.

Article VI. Annual Meeting
There shall be an annual meeting of the Alliance in the Spring of every year.

Article VII. Special Meetings
At a written request of seven members of the Executive Committee, the General Secretary may call a special meeting, notice of which is to be given to every member at least three weeks in advance before said meeting.

Article VIII. Quorum
A Quorum of the Executive Committee shall consist of five members, including at least three officers of the Alliance.

Article IX. Amendments
The Constitution may be amended by a vote of two-thirds of the members present at the Annual Meeting. Notice of the proposed amendments shall be sent to its members not less than three weeks before said meeting.[1]

During the Conference Sabbati Rohold, a Palestinian Talmudist from a line of Orthodox rabbis, was elected President. Other officers included A. Lichtenstein, First Vice-President; Harry Zeckhausen, Second Vice-President; Julius Magath, Third Vice-President; Mark Levy, General Secretary; Joseph Lewek, Recording Secretary; Maurice Ruben, Treasurer. Determined that believers should engage in evangelism, the Conference issued a resolution calling for new methods to be adopted in order to spread the message of the Gospel to fellow Jews:

> Recognizing the failure of present day Judaism in America as a religious and regenerating force, as admitted by leading Jewish rabbis and the Jewish press in general, and believing implicitly in the power of the Gospel of Yeshua, we as a Hebrew Christian Alliance of America, shall aim to make known this message to the millions of Jews in our midst. It is therefore resolved:
> 1. To unite Jewish believers into a corporate testimony, and to urge upon them in the name of the Lord Yeshua to give up their minor differences.
> 2. To mutually uplift each other and to raise the spiritual standard of the Jewish believers, that they might be worthy representatives of the Lord Yeshua to the Jew and the Gentile alike.
> 3. To encourage Jewish believers to come out openly and boldly in their confession of the Messiah.[2]

During the Conference representatives of the Federal Council of Churches of Christ offered their support for this initiative. In response the Conference urged that the Federal Council encourage its members to observe an Annual Day of Prayer for Israel. In addition, it was resolved that for Jewish believers the Day of Atonement be set aside as a day of prayer for the Holy Land. The following day delegates resolved to create a centre for Jewish believers as well as establishing a Chair of Jewish Studies at Kennedy College in Connecticut.

Two years after the Conference, Arthur Kuldell described the achievements of this meeting in an article, 'The Spiritual Aims of the HCAA':

> The very existence of the Alliance is a challenge to the Church. She often excuses her indifference to Israel's salvation on the plea that 'you cannot convert a Jew', but here is an Alliance of men and women from Israel . . . Its chief aim and ultimate goal is to reach the American Jewry with the Gospel, to bring before them the true claims of Yeshua the Messiah and to endeavour by every means possible to effectively dispel their erroneous ideas about the Messiah of God . . . The Alliance is not a lodge. It is not a society organized for the purpose of aiding its members to the exclusion of others. It is not here to defame and slander the Jew behind his back. It is an organization that breathes the spirit of Messiah. It is actuated by the tenderest love for Israel. It is solicitous for their true spiritual and abiding welfare, looking at their deep needs with the eyes of the prophets, offering the divine remedy with the love of a mother, longing for their

restoration with the heart of the saviour. Our theology might be misunderstood and misconstrued, our methods might be spurned and derided, but our love for them will abide and will win.[3]

Conflict and controversy about the Alliance

The creation of the Hebrew Christian Alliance of America provided a framework for Jewish believers to unite together. In 1916 a Second General Conference was held in Philadelphia; at this gathering Sabbati Rohold, the President of the Alliance, reflected on the creation of this body. In his view, the Alliance had previously existed in the hearts and minds of Jewish believers. 'They also realized the true condition of the Jewish believers and what ails them', he stated. 'Yet they felt the seeming hopelessness of their condition; but at the same time they held the vision of a HCAA, the powerful force . . . to awaken Israel from their nineteen hundred year sleep.'[4]

Celebrating this new development in Hebrew Christian life, Joseph Landsman sent words of encouragement from England. News had reached him, he declared, that Jewish believers from England who now live in America created an Alliance. 'This stirred in me holy feelings and thoughts', he stated. 'With a rejoicing heart do I praise God. Jewish believers ought to be one with Gentile believers. But we have still another duty to perform, and that is . . . to gather together all the scattered and divided forces and unite them, so that united we may be better able to remove the stumbling block from before our own nation.'[5]

At the 1916 Conference, Sabbati Rohold was re-elected President, and a Missionary Committee was appointed to select a full-time worker for the Alliance. In addition, the Literature Committee established a Board of Editors responsible for publishing literature in various languages. The next year the Hebrew Christian Alliance *Quarterly* appeared containing a Yiddish supplement – its aim was to foster the conviction that by accepting Yeshua, Jewish believers do not cease to be part of the Jewish people. The same year Dr Emmanuel Greenbaum was appointed worker-evangelist whose job was to promote the work of the Alliance around the country.

Despite such an enthusiastic beginning, the HCAA was subject to repeated attack from Jewish leaders as well as from the established Church. The creation of an organization of Jewish believers conflicted with the beliefs of those Christians who maintained that the Christian community was the true Israel. In their view, no distinction should be made between Jew and Gentile in the body of Christ. In 1919 the *Organ of the New York Evangelization Society* challenged the legitimacy of the Alliance. Although the existence of the HCAA illustrated the desire of many Jewish believers for self-expression, divisions within the Church were undesirable:

There may be some justification for thinking that a Jewish message by a Jew is the proper method among Jews, because the message originally came through the Jewish race and is tinged with that people's peculiarities. But we doubt if such concessions to Jewish peculiarities as some Jewish brethren demand is at all required in reaching the Jew with the Gospel. We believe it is well to clothe the message for Jews in Jewish garb, but the main thing is the message not its vesture.[6]

Determined that there should be no middle wall of partition between Jew and Gentile, the article went on to caution Jewish believers not to see themselves as superior to Gentiles who accepted Christ:

> We trust our brethren will understand that we do not charge them with the spirit of separation. What is clear to us is that, given a separate society, unconsciously such a spirit develops . . . In spite of themselves the separate organization of Jewish converts tends to a consciousness of superiority, especially in the weaker and more carnal members. There is a strong tendency to division among the members of such organizations, and this seems to be the divine way of rendering null and void their efforts to do what we believe the word of God in spirit forbids.[7]

Such criticisms were typical of many in the Church. In their view, the efforts of Jewish believers to establish their own body undermined the foundations of Christian belief in Christ. Jew and Gentile, they affirmed, are no longer separate in the sight of God. It was the Church, not the synagogue, which had received God's blessings. Hence, any attempt to create divisions within the body of Christ was contrary to the Gospel. Citing Ephesians 2:14, they insisted that Paul's words must be heeded: 'For he is our peace, who has made both one, and has broken down the middle wall of partition between us.'

In response to such criticisms, the HCAA stressed the need for Jewish believers to unite together in service to Yeshua. In a statement published in the *Organ of the New York Jewish Evangelization Society* the following year, a committee of the Alliance asserted that the HCAA is neither a church nor a denomination. There was no intention on the part of Jewish believers to rebel against the Church. Rather, the aim of the Alliance was to evangelize the Jewish nation. It was agreed by missionaries that the only way of bringing the Jewish people to the true faith is by raising up native leaders and preachers. Hence, the desire for self-expression within the HCAA is due to missionary enthusiasm. The HCAA did not seek to create a wall of partition; rather the aim is to bring Jews to Christ.

In this spirit the HCAA sought to embark on a missionary campaign:

> We are calling four missionaries for Palestine, two or three for Russia, and several teachers for a Hebrew Christian training school. Hundreds of dollars have been contributed by poor Hebrew Christians themselves lately for the relief of their brethren here and everywhere.[8]

Echoing these sentiments, Sabbati Rohold defended the HCAA from attack. Accepting the need to remain humble, he stated that members were saddened by the lack of sympathy expressed by critics of the movement:

> Our hearts are truly sad to find that through friendly criticism the seed of doubt and mistrust is sown, and the question comes, Shall we be silent. Too much attention must not be given, but we must at the same time be loyal and faithful, and zealously guard the honour of our Lord. The HCAA has made it clear as daylight that it is absolutely against anything which savours a distinction between Jew and Gentile.[9]

Gentile believers, he continued, do not perceive the necessity for Jews to draw together in faith. Previously Jewish believers have felt stranded within Church circles and subject to discrimination. 'It is these unshepherded Hebrew Christians', he wrote, 'that have touched the bowels of our compassion. It is because of their bitter cry and claimant needs that the HCAA has come into existence.'[10] According to Rohold, the HCAA has been eminently successful in its work because of the influence of the Holy Spirit:

> Twenty Hebrew Christian Alliances . . . all came into existence by the bidding of the spirit of God. They have served nobly in their day and generation. Their influence for good is still operating and the spirit that prompted them is constraining us . . . Some of its leaders were of the noblest men of God, chosen vessels whom God has honoured and used to lead literally thousands to Messiah, and though dead, yet live for the glory of God . . . The real issue is not walls of partition, discords, and all the other things we have mentioned. The real issue is, can we trust the Lord for the Hebrew Christian as well as for the Gentile Christian? If he is to be trusted for one, he must be trusted for all. Faith, confidence, complete and unconditional trust in the Lord is necessary.[11]

The growth of the Hebrew Christian Alliance

In the quest to develop its ministry, the Alliance embarked on a fundraising campaign. In 1919 it resolved to collect a million dollars. Its plan was to establish a Hebrew Christian headquarters and training school, and to send forth evangelists to propagate the Gospel in America, Europe and Palestine. Further, the HCAA was anxious to offer material assistance to Hebrew Christians living in Russia, Poland, Eastern Europe and Palestine. Resolved to aid existing missions, the budget specified that $150,000 be allocated for the headquarters; $300,000 for educational building and equipment; $50,000 for evangelization in the USA; $300,000 for evangelism and relief in Russia; $100,000 for evangelism and relief in Palestine; and $100,000 for the purchase of land and the creation of a Messianic Jewish colony in Palestine.

Unlike Rabinowitz's programme for Russian Jewish believers, the

Alliance was initially uninterested in integrating Jewish elements into its interpretation of the faith. However, at the Third National Conference held in 1917, Mark Levy discussed this issue, recommending that Jewish believers should feel free to select from the tradition those aspects which they found spiritually significant. In 'Jewish Ordinances in the Light of Hebrew Christianity', he emphasized that the Gentile Church had denigrated Judaism through the centuries. The Emperor Constantine, he explained, had hated the Jews and induced the Council of Nicea in 325 CE to change the date of Easter. While the synagogue denigrated Jewish believers, the Church divorced itself from its historical past. No branch of the Church has sought to remedy this situation.

What is now required, he continued, is for Jewish believers to affirm loyalty to the Jewish past. Highlighting the importance of Jewish observance in the life of Messianic Jews, he argued that the biblical festivals – including the Sabbath, Passover, Pentecost, Tabernacles, and the Day of Atonement – have a threefold significance: a national application to Israel; an individual application to every believer; a corporate application to the Church:

> Confusion arises in the Church because we do not note this fact carefully and thus measure our doctrines by the yardstick of Israel's God-given customs. The Passover marked the beginning of Israel's national independence and had its . . . spiritual fulfilment, when Messiah, our Passover was sacrificed for us and rose again for our justification. For me personally, the feast was fulfilled when I accepted Messiah as the eternal Paschal Lamb and was made free from the bondage of sin and Satan. The three-fold fulfilment holds good in all the feasts. The Sabbath has its . . . application in Messiah's invitations, 'Come unto me all ye that labour and are heavy laden, and I will give you rest.' Its corporate fulfilment we commemorate on the day of his resurrection; but the words 'Sabbath' and 'rest' are from the same Hebrew root and have several applications. The Sabbath itself and the Day of Atonement are days of rest in a double sense, i.e., physical and spiritual. The Sabbath of the soul none can enjoy who are not at peace with God through the blood of the everlasting covenant. Every day should be a Sabbath for the believer . . . When the Feast of Tabernacles has its . . . fulfilment when the Messiah returns to glory, Gentiles and Jews will be compelled to keep the feast and send national representatives to Jerusalem at its annual celebration to worship the Lord of Hosts . . . The question of circumcision, too, is very clear. It is the seal of an unconditional covenant made by Almighty God with our Father Abraham and relates to the possession of the Promised Land, from the Nile to the Euphrates.[12]

In this paper Levy argued along similar lines to Rabinowitz and others – Jewish believers must be free to embrace the customs of the Jewish people. After delivering this speech, Levy proposed a resolution that the Alliance embrace the principle of freedom of worship:

Whereas Judah is on the eve of restoration to Palestine and many Hebrew Christians will return with our nation to the Holy Land, be it: Resolved, that the Hebrew Christian Alliance of America endorse the resolution that our Jewish brethren are left free to admit their children into the covenant of Abraham and observe other God-given rites and ceremonies of Israel, if they so desire, when they accept . . . Messiah, according to the clear teaching of the New Testament and the practice of Messiah and the Apostles; providing that it is distinctly understood that neither Jew nor Gentile can be saved by works of the Law, but only through the merits and mediations of our compassionate Messiah.[13]

In the discussion following the presentation of this paper, some delegates questioned whether Hebrew Christians should feel themselves to be under the law. In their view, faith in the Lord Yeshua is the true power of salvation, independent of any human actions. A vote was then taken, and the resolution was defeated. As Maurice Ruben observed in a synopsis of the discussion in the Alliance *Quarterly*: 'By this overwhelming decision the HCAA has closed the doors once and for all to all Judaizing propaganda, and the organization stands squarely on the pure evangelical platform, with the avowed aim, purpose, and object to preach the Gospel . . . to our Jewish people everywhere.'[14]

During this period, views similar to those of Mark Levy were advanced by John Zacker. Born in Russia, he became a follower of Christ in London and eventually settled in the United States. After joining the Alliance, he became Associate Editor of the *Quarterly* and Chairman of the Relations Committee. In a paper delivered at the Seventh National Conference of the Alliance in Buffalo in 1921, he defended the principles of the movement:

The relation of the Messianic Israelite to his race and church of adoption is as yet undenied. At this moment of Hebrew revival, we, too, must arise to the occasion and feel the effect. We belong to that race of which God made Abraham the father . . . We owe an allegiance to our history, respect and affection for our martyred fathers and a deep sense of appreciation of the genius of our race and our loyalty must have positive expression. We are members of the 'Covenant People' and let the world know that we think it neither desirable nor necessary to cease being such. The hatred and bigotry of Jewry because of our religious convictions must no more interfere with our loyalty to them than it did with the Prophets and Apostles of old . . . We do not wish to be understood as advocating clannishness, but rather consciousness of the rock from which we have been hewn . . . Shall Messianic Jews be mere onlookers? Nay! Israel is diseased, homeless and blind! We must bring the panacea, provide shelter and restore light. It is true that the Jews are our bitterest opponents and enemies; they seek our destruction and suppression! They are our brethren nevertheless. The difference between their spirit and ours is accounted for by our allegiance to Him.[15]

Subsequently Zacker established the first Hebrew Christian place of worship in the United States, the Hebrew Christian Synagogue of Philadelphia. However, possibly due to the death of his wife, Zacker withdrew from Alliance activities and served the Gentile Church.

The development of the Alliance

As the Alliance expanded, a number of eminent figures emerged who sought to involve the movement in a wide range of issues. Max Reich, for example, a German Jew by origin who had become a believer in England, was a Talmudic scholar. Travelling throughout the Western part of America at the end of the century, he shared his understanding of the Messiah with both cowboys and Indians. From 1921 to 1926, as well as from 1935 to 1945, he served as President of the Alliance. During this period he combated anti-Jewish propaganda in the Alliance *Quarterly*. In 1921 he wrote:

> The so-called 'Protocols of the Learned Elders of Zion' was one of the basest forgeries ever fathered on the Jewish people. Jewish believers will stand by their slandered nation at this time. We know the people of the Jews are innocent of any plotting against governments and of planning world domination. Jews in every country honour their flag . . . None love America more than her Jewish citizens . . . Jewish believers utterly detest the spirit that has made prominent men take up unproven accusations against their brethren, lending themselves to be tools in the hand of unscrupulous Jew-haters, who remain anonymous, bent on stirring up racial strife and religious bigotry.[16]

In addition, Reich supported the Alliance's quest to undo false teaching about the Hebrew Christians by holding seminars:

> Recently while at an open discussion of the book of Romans . . . I asked the question, 'When a Jew becomes a Christian does he cease to be part of Israel?' The whole company almost shouted with one voice, 'Yes.' I then pointed out that it was the unbelieving branches who were cut off of their own olive tree. The believing branches remain where they had their origin. The olive tree represents the spiritual Israel rooted in the soil of the natural Israel . . . Gentiles . . . must not crowd out the branches that have never been broken off, nor forget that if they abide not in the goodness of God, they also shall be cut off, and the natural branches, supernaturally preserved, be restored to their ancient place. The fact is that God has always recognized an inner and outer Israel. The effective Israel was never more than a remnant at any time. And the inner was the salt of the outer, preserving it from decay. Hebrew Christians cannot fulfil their mission to their people unless they remain a part of Israel.[17]

To strengthen the work of the Alliance, the movement began to raise funds to establish a Chair of Jewish Studies and Missions at Moody Bible

Institute. In 1923 Solomon Birnbaum was appointed to this post, and classes were held in a wide range of subjects including biblical studies, Hebrew, Yiddish and rabbinic literature. In the same year a Women's Auxiliary was created to raise the position of women within the movement. Five years later the Alliance issued a second publication, *The True Light* – this was intended to spread the Alliance's understanding of Yeshua as the Messiah.

Turning to Eastern Europe and Russia, the Alliance became actively involved in the promotion of the Hebrew Christian Church in Kiev. Under its pastor Peter Gorodishz, it had grown from five members to over 50 by 1921. Under the auspices of the HCAA, Pastor Gorodishz came to America where he gave talks about the plight of Jewish widows and orphans following the pogroms in his country. In 1923, at the Conference in Trenton, New Jersey, the Alliance received a report from D. J. Newgewirtz, Vice-President of the Alliance, about a proposal to hold an International Congress of Hebrew Christians. It was resolved to support such a plan and Mark Levy was authorized to travel to Europe to pursue this proposal.

On 9 October a meeting was held in London at the headquarters of the Prayer Union for Israel to consider the suggestion that an International Hebrew Christian Conference be held in 1925. Speaking at this meeting, Mark Levy emphasized that for some time there had been a feeling that the time had come to unite Jewish believers into an international organization. To facilitate this initiative, the Prayer Union for Israel offered use of its officer personnel as well as space. Speaking in support of such a conference, the President of the Hebrew Christian Alliance of Great Britain, Samuel Schor, stated that such a gathering would inevitably prove successful and would have important results. The meeting then passed a resolution that the conference take place in London in the spring of 1925.

In January 1924 Schor wrote to Levy about the progress of these plans:

> We have been thinking much of you and your visit to us last fall, there has been much prayer, and the result is that we have decided to go ahead with the International Conference . . . our brother Elijah Bendor-Samuel . . . is throwing himself heart and soul into the preliminary work. A circular has been drawn up which will, before the end of this month, find its way . . . into the papers in England . . . Germany, Sweden, Norway, etc. We will, of course, leave your friends in America to see that the conference is well to the fore in your papers.
>
> It seems to me that the time is fully ripe for Hebrew Christians to make themselves felt as a power for truth and righteousness all over the world.[18]

Some time later a letter was sent to Jewish believers throughout the world inviting them to attend:

Dear Brethren in the Lord our Messiah,

We, members of the Hebrew Christian Alliance of Great Britain and America send you hearty greetings. Since the days of the Apostles, Hebrew Christians have been scattered units in the diaspora, ostracised by our unbelieving brethren and lost among the nations. We believe, however, that the times of the Gentiles are being fulfilled and that the God of our fathers, according to His gracious promise, is about to restore Israel to her ancient heritage. We also believe that, as Hebrew Christians, though a remnant weak and small, we have a share in the building up of the Tabernacle of David that is fallen down. We deem that it is an opportune time to meet and confer together, seeking Divine guidance by prayer and the Word of God. We have therefore decided to hold . . . an International Hebrew Christian Alliance Conference in London, England.[19]

At this gathering Sir Leon Levison, who acted as Chairman, explained the need for an international association:

The International Alliance was needed to give brethren of Great Britain, the United States, those on the Continent of Europe, in Poland, Russia, Rumania, in Palestine a feeling that there was a centre which represented the body of Hebrew Christians, by which they could get in touch with wider issues. That would mean life to the persecuted, twice-despised, and twice-rejected Hebrew Christians. It would give Hebrew Christians a standing, enabling them to show both to the Jew and Gentile alike what they really were in rendering service to Yeshua.[20]

Once the resolution in favour of establishing the IHCA was accepted, Sir Leon was elected President and London was chosen as the base for its headquarters. Sir Leon provided a vision of its future:

The International would represent the whole of them (national alliances), and their relationship would be such that nothing would be done without a coordinating opinion which, as it were, would unite them. Each country would be affiliated with the International, and each individual member would be a member first of the Alliance in his own country. The Alliance in America, or the Alliance in Great Britain, or elsewhere, should not be in a position to say, 'We are a separate body.' That has been done away with, though each would have home rule; there was no intention to interfere with any country's internal affairs. Each Alliance would have to possess a charter . . . showing that the Alliance in each country was affiliated with the International.[21]

4 Missions to the Jews in the early twentieth century

Missions in the United States

While the Hebrew Christian Alliance underwent considerable growth in the United States, the mission to the Jews continued apace. As we have seen, in England and on the continent, missionary activity among the Jews became a central feature of church life in the nineteenth century. Christians in the United Kingdom in particular were actively engaged as missionaries throughout this period. Following the creation of the London Society for Promoting Christianity Amongst the Jews at the beginning of the century, various British groups were established, including the British Society for the Propagation of the Gospel Among the Jews, the Mildmay Mission to the Jews, the Barbican Mission to the Jews, the Hebrew Christian Testimony to Israel, the London City Mission, and the East London Mission to the Jews. By 1927 there were over 70 missionaries, and missionary bodies were established in cities in England, Scotland and Ireland with sizeable Jewish populations. These British societies, however, did not confine their efforts to the United Kingdom; on the continent there were missionary groups in France, Germany, Poland, Austria, Czechoslovakia, and Hungary; similar missions were also established in the Middle East and Asia.

In the United States, there was a wide range of missionary organizations as well. At the end of the nineteenth century the Zion Society for Israel, the Chicago Hebrew Mission, the American Board of Missions to the Jews, and the New Covenant Mission were founded. In 1906 Jewish Missions of the United Lutheran Church of America was established, followed by the New York Evangelization Committee of the Presbyterian Church in the USA, the American Baptist Home Mission Society, the Christian and Missionary Alliance, and the Home Mission Board of the Southern Baptist Church. These bodies supported 35 missionary bodies located throughout the United States.

Pre-eminent among such American organizations, the Presbyterian Church served as a major focus of Jewish missionizing. Although its work had begun in the nineteenth century, a National Advisory Committee on Jewish Evangelism was established in 1917 which sent the Revd E. Greenbaum and the Revd H. L. Hellyer to found a mission in Newark,

New Jersey. Known as the Bethany Neighbourhood Centre, it operated a summer camp for Jewish children and became the model for other missions around the country. The Centre was staffed largely by Jewish believers who had become Presbyterian ministers. Commenting on the success of these missions, the Revd Morris Zutrau, the director of the Daniel Community Centre in San Francisco, stated:

> During the six months we have had many heart-throbbing experiences. A seventy-two-year-old rabbi has been led to Christ by a rabbi I was privileged to lead to Christ two years ago. Through him several other rabbis and many intellectual Jews have been persuaded to read the New Testament and are considering its way of life. At camp Kent last summer twelve of our young people became Christians and at a San Francisco church where I was speaking a German Quaker came up to me after the service. He said 'It was of the Lord that I should come to this church this morning. I just came into contact with a Jewish man who is to meet me at my hotel this afternoon. Will you come and meet with him and me?' I was there. Other meetings followed and finally this fine young man made the great decision and God is greatly using him.[1]

At another mission, the Peniel Centre in Chicago, various ages and interests were catered for. On Friday evenings an open discussion took place on a range of religious topics led by the director, David Bronstein. In addition, an English and citizenship class for adults took place two nights each week. During weekday afternoons, children under 10 participated in organized play while older children engaged in various craft activities. Peniel also sponsored the Boy Scouts, the Girl Scouts, and athletic programmes. A mothers' party took place on one Saturday each month which was conducted by Esther Bronstein. The Peniel Centre also sponsored a summer camp which was highly successful.

As a result of the success of the Peniel Centre, a group of Jews petitioned the local Presbytery to establish a Hebrew Christian Church:

> There was a need of a Hebrew Christian Church to conserve the . . . Jewish Mission. Prior to this time a few isolated Jewish Christians had joined the Gentile churches and had adapted themselves to that fellowship. The majority who joined a Gentile church were unable to adapt themselves and dropped out of the church. Some never joined any church at all and were stunted in their spiritual growth. Others drifted away altogether from their faith in Christ.[2]

Persuaded by this argument, the Chicago Presbytery established the First Hebrew Christian Church of Chicago in 1934. Under the auspices of the Presbytery, the congregation adopted the Presbyterian style of worship, and had a choir, a women's prayer group, a men's Bible study group, and a Sunday School. David Bronstein served as pastor, assisted by four elders and four deacons. On the first Sunday of each month, the 'Sacrament of the

Lord's Supper' was celebrated. Commenting on its achievements, Bronstein wrote:

> The church has proven to be a united testimony to both Jew and Gentile that the Gospel has the power to save the Jew. Many Jews do not believe that a Jew can become a sincere Christian. The majority of Gentiles do not believe that a Jew can be converted. When they come to a service and witness a great number of Jews worshipping Christ as their Saviour, prejudice is melted. The unbelieving Jews regard this new experience as little short of a phenomenal occasion and many say that it is an experience that they never before imagined.
>
> As a testimony to the Jew, the church has developed also as a very fine agency for reaching the Jews for Christ. Jewish missions are sponsored by Gentiles. The Jewish Christian missionary is looked upon by the Jews as traitor to his race, who has hired himself out to the Gentiles . . . Their explanation is that the Gentiles pay a great sum to the missionary for each convert. Reaching the Jew through the First Hebrew Christian Church eliminates these objections. It is a group of Jews who believe in Christ and do not break away from the Jewish people.[3]

In addition to the activities of the Presbyterian Church, other independent Jewish missions were established in various parts of the United States. In New York the American Board of Missions to the Jews (ABMJ) was founded by Rabbi Leopold Cohn. Initially he had been associated with the American Baptist Home Mission Society, but in 1916 he resigned and established a mission without any denominational affiliation. Devoted to serving Jewish believers, Cohn wrote Yiddish tracts which he and his son, Joseph Cohn, delivered to the faithful. In addition, he sold Yiddish New Testaments. Like the activities at Peniel, Cohn's mission included a variety of activities and programmes for young people and adults including children's classes, mothers' meetings, Bible study, and English classes, and Friday evening services. In time a summer camp was organized in association with the ABMJ. When Cohn died in 1937, there were two ABMJ missions in the New York area and others in Europe.

Commenting on his father's success as a missionary, his son explained that Leopold Cohn had followed Paul's example:

> He followed the method introduced by Paul, 'To the Jew I became as a Jew'. Pork he would not touch, and it was not allowed at any time in our home. And so with the forbidden animals of the Bible, and the creatures of the waters. The Mosaic law was adhered to. When it came the time of Passover, we kept the feast in our home . . .
>
> This training in the home remained with me to the present hour, so that I too have never knowingly eaten pork, ham or bacon, lobster, crabs, clams or oysters. For all of this he was continually attacked, even by certain Jews who had already accepted Christ. The reason for my father's dietetic asceticism was not that he

felt himself under the law of Moses, but that by this method he was able to win Jews to Christ who could not have been won otherwise . . .

The result of this method was that my father in his own lifetime was able to report more actual conversions and baptisms than perhaps all the Jewish missions of America put together.[4]

Missions in Poland, Hamburg and Danzig

Missions to Jewish communities in Europe were organized along similar lines: an evangelist was sent to oversee the work of local Jewish believers. Direct contact with potential converts was undertaken by these Jewish workers, whereas the foreign missionary directed the activities of the centre, planned the programme of activities, and was responsible for the financial affairs of the organization. Frequently such individuals served as the chaplain to the British or other national community abroad.

In Warsaw the Revd Martin Parsons acted in such a capacity. Initially he had been a teacher at a theological college in England. On his arrival in Warsaw, he was met by the acting missionary, Revd H. C. Carpenter, whom he was to replace. Parsons was then taken to the Jewish mission building located near the university and shopping area of the city. This newly constructed building contained classrooms, lecture rooms, a reading room, an office and a chapel as well as a residence housing missionaries. Living at the mission were two Irish women who had taught the English classes, as well as the Revd Rudolf Brinker who later took over missionary work in Lvov.

When Parsons arrived, five Jewish believers were working as evangelists among the approximately 400,000 Jews living in the city. Their activities included distributing religious tracts and Bibles, preaching at the Yiddish service each Saturday, staffing the reading room in the evenings, and travelling to outlying areas during the summer months. In addition, these workers edited two bi-monthly magazines in both Yiddish and Hebrew which were distributed throughout Poland and beyond. Subsequently two sons of one of the workers in Lvov, Mr Jocz, joined the staff. The English workers at the mission were responsible for the English classes which attracted young Jews as well as Jewish businessmen. These Polish Jews were not particularly religious, but sought to learn English for business reasons or because they hoped to emigrate to Palestine, Europe or the United States. The mission also sponsored an English-speaking club for those who wished to practise their English skills.

In addition to his responsibilities at the mission, Parsons served as chaplain to the British community. On Sundays he conducted services, and arranged special services for festivals as well. He was also the official chaplain for births, marriages and deaths. These duties, however, were of secondary concern: it was the work of the mission which he regarded as of supreme importance. In his view, one of the major achievements of this period was the co-ordination of missionary activities by the four Jewish missions in Warsaw consisting of Moses Gitlin of the ABMJ, Sendyk of the Mildmay Mission, Miss Chistoffersen of the American European Mission, and Parson's branch of the CMJ. These four bodies met together for prayer and discussion, and went on retreats together. On one occasion a joint baptism service was organized between Parsons representing the Church of England and Moses Gitlin representing the Baptists. During this period these four groups sponsored a Bible school which trained twelve Polish students – ten were Jewish believers who had been won to the faith through the CMJ.

With the onset of war, however, the Warsaw mission was at risk. Some of the workers such as the Jocz brothers managed to escape the Nazi onslaught, but others were killed. In his memoirs Parsons reflected:

> When war broke out and we were in Ireland it was extremely frustrating to feel so cut off. The Mission Building was destroyed, and all our worldly possessions with it . . . Eventually most of our friends and fellow-workers perished in one way or another . . . But there is the undoubted fact that 'your labour is not in vain in the Lord'. When we met our old Warsaw friend in Israel he produced a photograph of a group of Hebrew Christians, about fifty strong, who had met in our church in 1939.[5]

Like the English missionaries, the Presbyterian Church of Ireland had sponsored Jewish missions from the middle of the nineteenth century. By 1927 they supported three missionary stations employing 60 workers. In Hamburg missionary work had begun in 1845 under the direction of Dr Samuel Craig. Pre-eminent among Jewish workers in this major port was the Revd Dr Arnold Frank. Originally from an Orthodox Jewish background, Frank became a Jewish believer in Hamburg; while working in a bank, he met the Revd J. D. Aston of the Irish Presbyterian Mission. Under his patronage, Frank completed his schooling in Ireland and attended the Presbyterian College. Ordained in 1884, he was sent back to Hamburg to serve under Aston.

During 54 years of service in Hamburg, Frank led hundreds of Jews to Christ and baptized them. Over 50 became ministers or missionaries. Under Frank's leadership, the Hamburg mission grew in strength, and the Jerusalem Church which had been founded previously built new premises which housed over 400 people. In addition, a modern hospital, a deaconesses' home, and a clinic were established, as well as a holiday retreat for deaconesses. From 1899 to 1936 Frank published a monthly magazine *Zion's Freund* which was distributed throughout Europe. By means of this magazine Frank was able to raise funds to enlarge the Hamburg mission.

With the rise of Nazism, Frank encouraged his flock to emigrate. As he explained:

The plight of the Jewish Christian was even worse since to the Jews he was an apostate and to all others a Jew . . . church members now found it dangerous to associate with one whose Christian faith was offset with Jewish blood . . . the Nazi propaganda had done its work all too well and there were congregations where Jewish Christians were not wanted and were advised to leave.[6]

In 1938 Frank was arrested and held by the Gestapo. Due to the Foreign Secretary's intervention, he was released and returned to Hamburg. Eventually he and his daughters left for London. In 1942 the Jerusalem Church was destroyed. After the war the assets of the Jewish mission were transferred to the Christian Reformed Church of Holland.

The Irish Presbyterian Mission also engaged in missionary work in Danzig. In 1922 Mr Benjamin Sitenhof was sent there to work among the local Jewish community. Earlier Sitenhof came to faith by reading a Polish New Testament; later his wife Yente also became a Jewish believer. In addition, Benjamin's sister, Dora, and her husband David were led to faith by David's father who had studied under Joseph Rabinowitz in Kishinev. Benjamin and his wife were baptized in Hamburg by Dr Frank, and later emigrated to London.

Located between Germany and Poland, Danzig served as a gateway to the West. Thousands of Jewish immigrants had gathered there on their journey from Europe to new lands. Working among these refugees in the temporary immigration camps, Sitenhof distributed tracts and gospels in Yiddish, Polish, and German. With the support of the Irish Presbyterians, Sitenhof was encouraged to build a mission centre in the city which contained a bookshop, auditorium, missionary apartments and a home for the destitute.

Missionaries and Jewish believers

For many missionaries, commitment to evangelizing the Jews was based on the belief that the restoration of the Jewish people would lead to the advent of the Messianic age. As a result of the First World War, a growing number of Christians believed that the time of the Gentiles was drawing to an end. In this context the scriptural reference to all Israel being saved was interpreted as referring to the return of the Jewish people to faith and their entry into the Church. For some Calvinists, particularly among the Presbyterians, it was necessary for the Jewish people to return to Zion before the Second Coming. Even though it was accepted that Jewish mission should be supported regardless of such prophetic views, such theological assumptions were of critical importance in the history of the missionary movement. Other missions, however, did not share such religious convictions. Rather than focus on Messianic redemption, these evangelists sought to bring Jews to a living relationship with Christ, and to testify to both Jews and Christians that Jesus and Israel are inseparable.

In their quest to bring Jews to Christ, Gentile missionaries were typically given the same preparation for Jewish missionary work as that received by pastors dealing with their local parish. In general these individuals received a classical education including Latin and Greek, though usually they did not learn Hebrew. In most cases missionaries were familiar with Christian theology, but had little knowledge of Jewish sources including rabbinic commentaries on Scripture, the *Mishnah*, the *Targums*, the Talmud and midrashic sources. Bereft of such knowledge, many found it difficult to explain the Christian faith to Jewish believers or refute the arguments of the rabbis against Christian teaching.

Most mission societies did little to correct these deficiencies; none offered a training programme. In most cases the Gentile missionary was simply left to oversee the work of the mission, whereas interaction with local Jews was left to Jewish workers who served the organization. While it might have seemed preferable to send Jewish missionaries to such localities, it was generally felt that Gentile missionaries, despite their ignorance of the Jewish tradition, were preferable since they did not raise prejudices among the local Jewish population. Gentile missionaries were thus perceived as adequate to the task.

Jewish believers, on the other hand, were knowledgeable about the Jewish faith. Many were trained in rabbinics, and after coming to faith, they were sent to a seminary related to the organizations through which they had been converted. Some, like Paul Jocz, Victor Buksbazen, Rachmiel Frydland and Arnold Frank, studied in Scotland or England and received ordination through the Church of England or the Church of Scotland. Others, like Jakob Jocz, studied with Pastor Joseph Landsman or at the Institutum Judaicum Delitzschianum in Leipzig which had been established by Professor Delitzsch.

In the United States the Moody Bible Institute offered courses in a Jewish Missions department which, as we have noted, was initially funded by the HCAA in 1923 and was directed by the Revd Solomon Birnbaum, a Baptist minister of Jewish origin. Alongside Scripture, Hebrew and Yiddish were taught and Christian apologetics were presented in the context of Jewish religious thought. Birnbaum was succeeded by Dr Max Reich in 1929 and later by Nathan Stone. In Los Angeles the Bible Institute offered a Jewish missions-style programme. Under Dr Henry Heydt a course of Jewish evangelism was also commenced at the Lancaster School of the Bible in Pennsylvania.

In addition to these formal courses, Jewish missionaries and believers were offered an informal form of education involving discipleship. Although such training did not replace a formal course of instruction, it did provide on-the-job training. Typical patterns of internship were offered within families, such as in the case of Leopold and Joseph Cohn, Benjamin Sitenhof and his sons, the Jocz brothers and the Bronstein family. Others who had become Christians through the missions continued their practical training while attending a Bible college or a university.

As far as patterns of church participation were concerned, it remained an open question whether Jews who had been missionized should simply join the existing church structure or form their own organizations. As we have seen, among Jewish believers there was a growing desire for Jewish independence. Mark Levy, for example, who had been a driving force in the creation of the International Hebrew Christian Alliance, was largely responsible for the American Episcopal Church's resolve to support a Hebrew Christian Church. In an address before the General Assembly of the Episcopal Church of the United States, he pleaded for the restoration of the original Hebrew Christian branch of the Church:

> The Church does not require its Jewish members to forsake their own, but leaves them in their Christ-given liberty to have their children circumcised according to God's covenant with Abraham, should they so desire, and to observe all other customs inherited from their fathers, provided it can be clearly understood that neither Jew nor Gentile can be saved through the works of the Law, but solely through the sacrifice and atonement of Jesus Christ, our Lord and Saviour.[7]

Others throughout the Jewish world joined in support of this approach including Theodore Lucky in Galicia, Paulus Grun in Hamburg, and Philip Cohen in South Africa. In *The Messianic Jew*, Cohen offered three important reasons for a change to take place:

1. Deep love of our own nation, for its history and traditions.
2. A fervent conviction that we who are Christians can best serve the cause of Christ by demonstrating to our people that we are still linked to the Jewish people.
3. The conviction that Jewish Christianity can only impress the Jewish mind by taking on a Jewish complexion.[8]

Advocating the retention of Jewish practices within a Hebrew Christian framework, Theodore Lucky spoke vehemently at a Jewish Christian Conference in Stanislau in 1903:

> I do not demand from my fellow-believers the complete and strict observance of all Jewish customs at any price. Here is a brother who says, 'We live in exile and are not our own masters, and though I would like to keep the entire ceremonial law, and all the more because I am a disciple of Jesus, I cannot do it. I am a soldier and I must eat barrack fare. I must rest on Sunday and work on the Sabbath for the sake of my daily bread.' Well, he is my brother nevertheless. I do not judge his conscience, nor is he to let me be a conscience to him in the matter of meats, or of the Sabbath, all of which are only a shadow of that of which we have the substance in Christ. On the other hand, another says, 'Because I believe in Christ therefore I give up the Sabbath.' Well, he is no less acceptable to God on that account, and I do not despise him for it nor condemn him. But I am sorry for him,

and it hurts me to the depth of my heart because he too is a child of Israel and should help us to build up the walls of Jerusalem.[9]

Missionary activity after the war

Following the Holocaust, missions to the Jewish people ceased to function in those cities where the Jewish population had been largely eliminated. In Warsaw, for example, only a few hundred Jews survived the war: most of the workers stationed there escaped before the outbreak of the war, while others died in the Warsaw Ghetto or in one of several concentration camps. Another obstacle to missionary activity was the existence of an iron curtain between Communist countries and the West. Many of the countries which had previously housed Jewish missions had become inaccessible.

In the United States, on the other hand, opportunities for missionary work were considerable. Those organizations which had previously created missions functioning in the USA sought to expand their activities; other bodies opened new offices. Simultaneously Israel, South America and South Africa were viewed with great interest by mission societies. In addition, missionary ventures continued in Great Britain, France, and other Western European countries.

Yet despite these programmes, change was urgently needed. In the United States and Canada, most Jews had become better educated. Living in a largely secularized society, Jewry had become less interested in religion. Many had forsaken the inner-city Jewish ghettos and moved to outlying areas where synagogues had been established for the growing numbers of suburban dwellers. Further, in America Jewish community centres functioned in metropolitan communities offering social activities devoid of any connections with Judaism. In this milieu, Jewish thinkers like Mordecai Kaplan called for a reconstruction of Jewish life centred around the notion of peoplehood.

Responding to these changes in Jewish life, the American Board of Missions to the Jews (ABMJ) under the leadership of Joseph Hoffman Cohn, the son of Rabbi Leopold Cohn, became a focus of missionary outreach. In Europe, Israel and South America as well as the United States and Canada, mission stations were established to serve the needs of the community. The ABMJ was also a training ground for some who later directed other missions, including A. B. Machlin, founder of the American Association for Jewish Evangelism (AAJE), Victor Buksbazen, director of the Friends of Israel Missionary and Relief Society, Jacob Gartenhaus, president of the International Board of Jewish Missions, and Moishe Rosen, leader of Jews for Jesus.

A number of other bodies also functioned in the United States, including the Chicago Hebrew Mission, later becoming the American Messianic Fellowship. The Lederer Foundation, created by Henry and Marie Einspruch, played an important role in disseminating literature about Messianic

Judaism in both Yiddish and English. The Million Testaments Campaign was organized by George and Rose Davis; this printed and distributed New Testaments in a number of languages including Yiddish and Hebrew, along with notes explaining the text in terms of Messianic prophecy.

In America a number of Protestant denominations supported missions to the Jews. The Lutherans, for example, funded several stations during this period; the Southern Baptists employed Jacob Gartenhaus as their sole missionary; the American, Conservative and General Association of Regular Baptists maintained several workers among the Jewish people; the Assembly of God churches also employed Jewish believers. The PCUSA also continued to support Jewish missions in the United States in Chicago, Philadelphia and Baltimore. Nonetheless, the PCUSA underwent a major change in theological perspective during this period. In 1927 the Director of the Christian Approach to the Jews of the Presbyterian Home Mission had declared:

> As Christ becomes better known to the Jewish people, they will come under the spell of his personality and make his life their very own. Then shall we see that devotion to Moses which has shed reknown on the Jewish people merged with a yet fuller devotion to Jesus . . . out of which will come fresh interpretations of the Gospels and spiritual quickening for the whole world.[10]

After the events of the Holocaust, universalism as well as the belief in dual covenant theology profoundly affected church teaching. In 1925, the Policy Statement of the PCUSA advocated mission to the Jewish nation:

> The removal of racial prejudice and the cultivation of a Christian attitude toward the Jews. The education of the church to an appreciation of the need and urgency of a Christian ministry among the Jews. The enlistment of some churches in every Synod and Presbytery in some form of definite service for their Jewish neighbours. The establishment of Neighbourhood Centres for Evangelism in large Jewish communities now unoccupied by any denomination. The enlistment and training of workers to understand the peculiar needs of the Jews and effectively reach them with the gospel.[11]

Nearly twenty-five years later, the PCUSA adopted a very different approach as evidenced by their policy statement:

> The Board seeks to combat anti-semitism by establishing neighbourly and friendly relationships between Jews and Christians. It promotes the Parish Approach to the Jews by including them in the normal ministry of the local church. It establishes and maintains Neighbourhood Centres in large Jewish communities. It seeks to educate church members to right attitudes towards their Jewish neighbours and to accept Christian responsibility for this needy people.[12]

Once the PCUSA became part of the World Council of Churches, the Jewish missionary programme receded in importance. In place of evangelism, the Presbyterian Church fostered dialogue between Christians and Jews.

In Great Britain there was also a shift in orientation. In the post-Holocaust period the quest to missionize among the Jews ceased to play a significant role in the life of the churches. The Mildmay Mission to the Jews and the Barbican Mission to the Jews, founded in the 1870s, merged to form the Christian Witness to Israel. The London Society for Promoting Christianity Amongst the Jews changed its name to the Church's Ministry Amongst the Jews, seeking support of those outside the Church of England. The Hebrew Christian Testimony to Israel became the Messianic Testimony to Israel. Yet, despite such alterations in terminology, outreach to the Jews continued to be a central goal. Missions to the Jews in Europe were organized by a wide range of agencies including some from Finland, Scandinavia, the United States and Great Britain. In Paris, Paul Ghennassia, a Jewish believer of Sephardic origin, spearheaded an outreach programme. Similar bodies were also in other cities in France, Belgium and Holland.

As far as education was concerned, the Moody Bible Institute continued to offer a basic programme of education. With the appointment of Dr Louis Goldberg, however, a new direction of missionary education was instituted. Aware that few American Jews were able to speak Yiddish, Goldberg eliminated Yiddish from the list of required subjects. In addition, greater emphasis was placed on modern Jewish practice, as well as instruction in apologetics. In general, missionary societies did not provide training programmes for workers – such training was largely provided by Bible colleges and seminaries. In the 1960s Moishe Rosen, formerly director of the ABMJ in Los Angeles, organized a training programme for workers, including the study of Jewish history, religious practice, religious traditions, literature, Messianic prophecy, and apologetics. This initiative later underwent an important transformation as young Jewish people gravitated to the Jesus People movement of the late 1960s and early 1970s.

5 Growth of the Messianic movement

The Hebrew Alliance after the First World War

From 1924 until the 1930s the General Secretary of the HCAA, Jacob Peltz, was actively involved in a wide range of activities on behalf of the Alliance. In the early 1930s, however, a change in policy took place among Jewish believers. As Jacob Peltz explained, initially it was assumed that the various mission boards would be able to meet the needs of the movement. Yet, in time it became clear that greater organization was needed:

> For many years the leaders of the HCAA were hopeful that the various denominations through their Home Mission Boards would meet the responsibility of evangelizing the Jewish people. As Hebrew Christians we were happy to be the servants and missionaries of the various church agencies in this enterprise. But the denominations are failing us; some Board leaders have lost interest and others are frankly opposed to Missions to Jews . . . As a result of very careful deliberations . . . a resolution was adopted unanimously at the 1932 Boston Conference which established a Gentile Advisory Committee and a special Committee of Hebrew Christians for the purpose of extending the work of Jewish Evangelism.[1]

In 1931 Elias Newman was appointed Pastor-Evangelist, his duties including evangelizing Jews in places where no other agency was at work; finding Hebrew Christians not yet affiliated to the HCAA; and assisting Jewish missions and evangelistic societies as well as presenting the spiritual needs of Israel before the Christian community. 'Twelve years ago,' he stated,

> when similar work fell to our lot, it was the sole duty of the evangelist to carry out this threefold commission. Now we are more fortunate than formerly in that we have a General Secretary whose chief duty is to present the needs of Israel, the duty of the Church of Messiah, suggesting the methods most advisable in . . . winning the Jewish people to their own Messiah and arranging for and taking part in Bible conferences having these vital things as the great aim in view.[2]

In a letter written for the *Quarterly* in 1933, the President of the HCAA, Dr Greenbaum, explained that further funds were needed to carry out the evangelistic aims of the Alliance. One of its objectives was to combat the rise of anti-Semitism in the years leading up to the Second World War. Aware that anti-Jewish attitudes had been absorbed into the Church, the HCAA issued a proclamation at its 1931 Annual Conference taking place in Erie, New York:

> In view of the increasing discrimination against our Jewish brethren in social, economic and intellectual spheres, we, the HCAA, an organization of Jews who have come to believe that Messiah is the solution of all Jewish problems, respectfully petition the Ecclesiastical Courts of the various Christian denominations represented in our membership, to take action against the increasing anti-semitism in America . . . to study the whole problem in light of the New Testament, to reaffirm to our Jewish brethren that Messiah and his Church are the friends and lovers of Israel, and not here enemies, to prepare such literature and courses for Sunday schools and other Church Schools that shall bring Christian youth to an understanding and appreciation of the Jew, his place and future in God's economy.[3]

Two years later, in an editorial in the *Quarterly* magazine, the HCAA acknowledged the growing hostility in Germany toward its Jewish population. Friends of Israel everywhere, it declared, will condemn German actions against the Jew. Its real aim is to divert public opinion from the real causes. Jews are being blamed for everything that happens in Germany, beginning with the military defeat during the First World War to the collapse of the Germany economy. Yet, the article concluded, German Jewry will stand up to Hitler and his cohorts.[4]

Anxious to combat the rise of anti-semitism, the HCAA issued a resolution in June 1933 at its annual conference acknowledging the existence of this problem and affirming its desire to control such sentiments:

> Whereas, once again a section of the dispersed household of Israel has been called upon to suffer the pain and ignominy of racial discrimination; and
> Whereas, it is impossible to inflict pain upon a part of a body without communicating the same pain to every other part; and
> Be it resolved, therefore that we, the HCAA, assembled at our nineteenth annual Conference in the city of Binghamton, NY, protest the un-Christian and cruel treatment meted out to our brethren by the present government of Germany; and
> Be it resolved, that we assure our fellow Jews everywhere that we share with them in this hour of our common sorrow that we long and pray for the speedy return of the captivity of Zion; and
> Be it further resolved that we call upon all branches of the Christian Church everywhere to continue their protests until the Spirit of Messiah prevails and the lamentable situation is corrected.[5]

In a letter dated 14 October 1933 to Dr Greenbaum, President of the HCAA, Sir Leon Levison, President of the IHCA, expressed his deep concern about the plight of Jewish believers in Germany. 'It is imperative', he stated, 'that we represent a united front since it is nobody's duty so much as ours to voice the feelings and sufferings of our Hebrew Christians in that country.' Previously, he stated, it was thought that the number of Hebrew Christians in the country amounted to about 20,000 to 25,000 individuals. But with the rise of Hitler, these numbers appear to be inaccurate. We find today, he stated, 'that as against 600,000 Jews in Germany there are one and three-quarter million Christians of Jewish descent who go back to the second, third and fourth generation. Moreover', he continued, 'there are a large number of families where either the wife or husband was a Jew and became a Christian. In all these cases, they are treated as Jews and are subject to vicious discrimination. Hence Jewish believers are treated in the most tragic fashion. And if they apply to Jewish Relief agencies, they are told they must abandon their belief in Jesus.'[6]

Anxious to help Hebrew Christians who were victimized by the Nazis, members of the Alliance sought to offer whatever assistance they could. Writing to the members and affiliates of the HCAA in the spring of 1938, Morris Zeidman, Honorary General Secretary of the Alliance, surveyed the plight of European Jewry:

> In Poland, Germany and Austria, sorrow is turning into despair. They can see no hope, not a gleam of light or kindness anywhere. Persecuted by the Church and State, there is nothing left for them but suicide. Imagine hundreds of thousands of Jews, our brethren in this hopeless situation . . . In the midst of this darkness and despair, the HCAA, as well as the International Alliance, are holding out a helping hand . . . WE MUST HELP. The HCAA must help. We must help, if we have to sacrifice a meal a day. Surely those of us who eat three meals a day can afford to spare the price of one meal for our persecuted brethren in Central Europe. By doing so, you may save a whole family from committing suicide . . . Do not think Jews alone are suffering, for thousands of our own Messianic Jews, fellow believers in Messiah are suffering persecution, hunger, shame, and spiritual ostracism.[7]

From Holocaust to the post-war period

Prior to the Second World War, a growing number of Jewish believers came to the view that Jewish practices should be integrated into a Messianic lifestyle. At the 1938 Conference in Baltimore, Annie Zeidman spoke of the need for Hebrew Christians to embrace the Jewish heritage. 'Is it desirable,' she asked, 'that the children of Hebrew Christian parents remain Hebrew as well as Christian?' Such individuals, she explained, are frequently criticized if they show any signs of retaining any characteristics of their Jewish back-ground. Yet, she stated, there is no reason to put aside the Jewish heritage:

Have we nothing to hand on to our children to make them hold up their heads and thank God that they are Hebrews? . . . Woven into the background of our lives runs a strong thread of tradition – how strong, we are often slow to realize. Because we are believing Hebrews, are our children then to have only broken threads. Pitiful indeed is the child without some bright gleam out of the past in his life fabric; and just as pitiful is the child who, being denied traditions of his own, stretches out little hands to the traditions of others.[8]

At the same conference the President of the Alliance, Max Reich, held out hope for the future of the movement. In his view, it was necessary for Hebrew Christians to have a clear understanding of their objectives:

If it is only to enjoy social opportunities this movement will run into the sand and come to an end . . . The American Alliance will soon celebrate its silver wedding, and I have no hesitation in saying that I believe, with all its limitations, the movement which gave it birth is of God . . . But the goal has not been reached. I still regard the Alliance not as an end but as a means to the end. There is a danger for us to magnify the means and lose sight of the end. And we must also distinguish in our minds between the divine idea and the men who try to work it out, often in weakness, and conscious of deep failure. I cannot imagine that our Alliance as we see it at present is God's last word for Hebrew Christians . . . We have only put up the scaffolding of the building that is to be . . . We ought to be agreed on certain principles . . . Every Hebrew Christian belongs to us and we belong to him. We form one fellowship.[9]

The events of the Holocaust had a profound impact on Jewry worldwide. The great European centres of Jewish civilization were destroyed by the Nazis. In their place the United States and Israel became the primary focus of Jewish life. During this period the Alliance lacked a coherent plan. Reviewing the post-war period, the President of the Alliance, Dr Arthur Kac, explained why a decline in activity occurred:

A temporary decline of the effectiveness of the Alliance had taken place in the decade following World War II. A number of factors were responsible for this decline. The confusion and dislocation caused by the war were certainly an important element in the situation. The gradual withdrawal from our midst of many of the pioneers of the Alliance by reason of old age and death also had a depressing effect upon our movement. Finally, a different concept of what constitutes the chief destiny of the Alliance gained some influence. According to this concept the Alliance was first and last a fellowship of Hebrew Christians for the purpose of encouraging one another and enjoying one another's company. Why Christians of Jewish extraction should maintain a separate fellowship was left unanswered by the proponents of this view.[10]

At this stage, the Alliance decided to establish a home for the aged. The Executive Committee commissioned Mrs Margaret Weisenberg to acquire funds for the project. By 1951 she had raised $1,000 and pledged another $10,000 to the project once the HCAA purchased a property. The same year a special committee was created to purchase a rest home. Acquired in 1953, the home, which was situated on 93 acres of land, was called 'The Haven of Grace'. The purpose of this institution was to provide for the needs of elderly Jewish believers. However, within one year, 'The Haven of Grace' had run out of money, and it was eventually subsidized by the Alliance until it was sold in 1966. Commenting on this development, Kac observed that the creation of an old-age home had been a mistake: 'We . . . did exactly what Yeshua told his disciples not to do. We put our light under a bushel . . . and thus our effectiveness was cut sharply.'[11]

By the mid-1950s, however, the Alliance began to recapture its previous vision. As Kac explained:

> In the middle fifties, we recaptured the vision of the fathers of the American Alliance. We returned to the original position of the founders, namely, that the prime end and aim of the HCAA is to confront the Jewish people with Yeshua. New branches of the Alliance were established; Regional Conferences in certain parts of the North American continent were initiated; our work in South America was reorganized and strengthened; we resumed our interest in the Hebrew Christian movement in the State of Israel; a whole new line of Hebrew Christian literature was created.[12]

At this point the Executive Committee of the Alliance invited the International Alliance to host its ninth conference to coincide with the fortieth conference of the American Alliance. From 18 to 25 September 1955, a World Congress of Hebrew Christians took place in Chicago during the Jewish High Holy Days. Delegates arrived from Australia, Austria, Canada, Denmark, France, Germany, Great Britain, Holland, Israel, South Africa and Switzerland as well as from throughout the United States.

In the mid-1950s the situation of local branches of the American Alliance had reached a critical point: only five were functioning and the majority were in a perilous state of decline. In an attempt to revive the movement, these branches were strengthened and new groups were established in New York City in 1956, Miami in 1957, Northern New Jersey in 1960, and Los Angeles in 1961. It was decided at this stage that the practice of holding an Annual Conference should be suspended. Instead, a National Conference would take place every two years with regional conferences taking place in the meantime. Defending this decision, Kac stressed the importance of regional conferences:

> The Regional Conference is a new development in the history of the HCAA. It has been evident for a long time that the Annual Conferences drew only a small

percentage of the Jewish believers affiliated with the HCAA. Distance and a number of other factors were responsible for this undesirable state of affairs . . . The two chief objectives of the regional conferences are: first, to develop and strengthen . . . fellowship in a particular area; second; to promote among the Jewish believers and Gentile Christians in a particular area the ideals and aspirations of the HCAA.[13]

In the late 1950s, the Alliance joined with other national bodies in a campaign sponsored by the IHCA for Jewish believers in Israel. The aim of this programme was to help these Jews to become self-supporting and develop a strong movement in the Holy Land. The specific objectives of this plan were to provide pastoral ministry for Jewish believers, establish places for worship, offer financial assistance when needed, and establish a home for the aged as well as a Hebrew Christian Kibbutz. At the 1960 IHCA Conference in Augsburg, Germany, it was decided to establish a Hebrew Christian Centre in Israel, and Rachmiel Frydland was appointed Secretary to Israel.

Hebrew Christian churches

Alongside the developments that were taking place within the HCAA, Hebrew Christian congregations were actively engaged in evangelistic activities. By 1955 there were Hebrew Christian churches in seven North American cities as well as London. These congregations engaged in outreach programmes and also served as centres for Jewish believers who wished to express their Jewish identity. In some cases, they provided second and third generation Jewish believers with a sense of continuity.

Later Hebrew Christian congregations were established in Chicago, Philadelphia, San Francisco and Baltimore. Each of these was led by an ordained Presbyterian minister who had received pastoral training at a Presbyterian seminary. Other missions within the PCUSA located in Detroit, Los Angeles, Brooklyn, Newark, St Louis, Omaha and Chester, Pennsylvania held regular services although these bodies were not officially designated as churches. Although some Jewish features were occasionally included in the liturgy, these services followed the general pattern of Presbyterian services.

Within these Hebrew Christian churches, the background of Jewish believers was accepted. Yet there was little attempt to encourage loyalty to the Jewish tradition. Many of these Jewish Christians married Gentile Christians, and their children generally lost any connection with Judaism. Among those who married other Jewish believers, their children frequently retained some connection with their Jewish background, but such sensitivities gradually faded with the next generation.

Even though those who belonged to Hebrew Christian churches were largely accepted by the Christian community, Jewish believers faced extraordinary hostility from Jewry. Regarded as apostates, these individuals were perceived as traitors to the faith. In general it was felt that these converts to Christianity had forfeited any connection with Judaism and had ceased to be Jews even though rabbinic Judaism declares that a person is Jewish regardless of any act of apostasy. Pressure was also applied from the Christian community on these converts to the faith to desist from retaining a Jewish identity. In the view of many Christians, once one had accepted Christ that person was no longer a Jew.

Pre-eminent among the Hebrew Christian congregations was the First Hebrew Christian Church, located at Chicago's Peniel Centre. Other churches included branches in Chicago, Philadelphia and Baltimore. In Detroit the Hebrew Christian Church of Detroit was an independent establishment founded by the Revd Arthur Glass and his wife Emma Finestone Glass. After having served in Argentina under the HCAA, Glass came to work with Jewish believers in Detroit. Ordained as a Baptist minister, he was a graduate of Moody Bible Institute's Jewish Missions Department. During the time he spent in Detroit, he established a congregation of about 60 believers, largely of Jewish descent.

In Toronto, Canada, the Revd Morris Kaminsky directed a Jewish centre and a Hebrew Christian church under the auspices of the Anglican Church. As an evangelist, Kaminsky became a father-figure to many who became part of his church. Under his influence, a number of major figures within the Messianic movement, including Martin Chernoff, Jerome Fleischer and Ed Brotsky, subsequently took on leadership roles. In London, Dr Paul Levertoff fostered a revival of Hasidic Christianity. As a Church of England minister in Stepney, he described his synagogue as a Hebrew Christian congregation. Meeting on the Sabbath, he used traditional Jewish music, and the service was conducted in Hebrew.

In Los Angeles, the Congregation of the Messiah Within Israel was founded by Lawrence Duff-Forbes. A forerunner of later Messianic congregations, this congregation called itself both biblical and Messianic and employed a style of worship distinct from Hebrew Christian churches. Based on the synagogue service, the congregation utilized a traditional form of liturgy. According to Duff-Forbes, the objective of this congregation was to lead the Jewish people to the worship of the God of Israel. Insistent on the glories of the Jewish tradition, Duff-Forbes sought to fortify the Jewish people through the biblical heritage. In order to promote this philosophy, Duff-Forbes published a range of literature including booklets, as well as a quarterly magazine. He also broadcast a radio programme and produced tapes dealing with religious issues. His synagogue held *Shabbat* services, offered adult Bible classes, and ran a *Yeshivat Yahudat Meshichi*, an academy of the Jewish Messiah with classes in Hebrew, Yiddish and Jewish history.

In 1955 Ed Brotsky of Toronto encountered Duff-Forbes at the 1955 World Congress of Hebrew Christians. Duff-Forbes invited Brotsky to come to

Los Angeles to work with him. For nine months Brotsky served as associate rabbi. Even though the congregation was disbanded in 1970, it exerted an important influence on Brotsky's interpretation of Judaism as well as that of Moishe Rosen, who at that time was serving with the ABMJ in Los Angeles.

Despite the success of these new developments, a considerable number of Jewish believers were critical of the notion of a separate church for Hebrew Christians. In their view, Jewish believers should become members of a local Bible-based Gentile church even if they sought to associate with other Jewish believers through a Hebrew Christian fellowship. This was the view of figures such as Arnold Fruchtenbaum, the author of *Hebrew Christianity: Its Theology, History and Philosophy*, who stressed the connection between Jewish believers and the Jewish community while endorsing the notion of fellowship between Jewish and Gentile believers:

> The Hebrew Christian is a loyal member of the Jewish community, although the community may not accept him. Knowing the exact nature of God's programme for the Messianic People draws him to a greater love for his own people in a way that most Jews cannot understand. His desire to share the truths of the Scriptures with them is the result of his love for the Jews and not the result of any antagonism towards them. On the other hand, the Hebrew Christian's alliance with the Jew does not make him blind to the fact that the Jewish community is not always right. Nor does it blind him to the fact that the basic cause of Jewish suffering is their disobedience to the revealed will of God and unbelief in the person of the Messiah. These things are countered by witnessing to the Jews.[14]

In the view of these Hebrew Christians, there should be no middle wall of partition between Jews and Gentiles despite the links between Jewish believers. Instead of separation into distinct Hebrew Christian groups, Jewish believers should become part of the Christian witnessing community in an attempt to evangelize the Jewish population. Gentile church membership, they believed, would provide a coherent basis for communal worship as well as outreach initiatives.

The difficulty with this approach was that it provided no basis for continuing loyalty to Judaism and the Jewish people. What was at risk was total assimilation. Within Gentile churches, there was no attempt for Jewish believers to retain their separate identity, nor to ensure that their children would continue to honour their ancestral faith. Rather, it was inevitable that within a few generations Jewish believers would be totally absorbed into the life of the church. Frequently the children of Jewish believers ceased to regard themselves as in any sense Jewish. The Hebrew Christian churches thus failed to ensure Jewish believers would continue to remain faithful to the traditions of their ancestors. Among Hebrew Christians, there was nothing which served as a basis for Jewish identity and separateness within the body of Christ.

The youth movement

In 1967 Arthur Kac formulated his plans for the movement. The aim of the HCAA should be, he stated:

> to make known to the Church its obligation to present the Gospel to the Jew. To develop a programme to confront the Jews in America with Yeshua. To maintain a vital relationship with Jewish believers in Israel. To implement these aims the HCAA purposed to strengthen local branches and regional conferences, extend financial aid to students, teach at conferences on the role of Israel, publish suitable literature, and establish a library.[15]

Such a restatement of the Alliance's objectives, however, did not embrace the rapid changes taking place within the movement. In 1963 at the HCAA conference in Detroit a youth committee was established with Joseph Pfefer as chairman. This was followed two years later at the 50th Anniversary Conference at Chattanooga, Tennessee by the establishment of the Young Hebrew Christian Alliance under the leadership of Manny Brotman who served as National Chairman of the Young Hebrew Christian Youth Organization (YHCYO).

In 1966 a pilot programme for the YHCYO and a national youth headquarters were created in Chicago; during this period, the *Young Hebrew Christian Reporter* was also published. At the Executive Committee meeting of the HCAA in 1966, it was reported that several meetings of the pilot programme had taken place in the Chicago area, and that youth branches had been established in Detroit and the New York City area. Anxious to encourage these developments, the Executive Committee agreed that YHCYO views should be printed in the *Quarterly* magazine, that the YHCYO should be represented at the Executive Committee of the HCAA, and that during the HCAA Conference a youth meeting should take place.

At a Midwest Regional Conference of the Alliance held at Winona Lake, Indiana from 3 to 4 September 1966, nearly half of the delegates were young people. Special youth meetings were held during the conference, and the YHCYO had a planning meeting for the 1967 Biennial Conference. In June 1967 elections were held for the Young Hebrew Christian Alliance of the HCAA (YHCA) at the Lancaster Conference where Manny Brotman was elected President. At the Conference Executive Committee meeting, Manny Brotman presented a constitution and bylaws for this youth body, but it was decided that the YHCA conference appoint a constitution committee which would act together with a committee appointed by the HCAA. This joint body would then present a report to the Executive Committee at the next HCAA conference. The HCAA agreed to contribute $500 to a YHCA fund, with a promise of further support if necessary.

At the 1968 meeting of the Executive Committee which took place in Cincinnati, a revised YHCA constitution was presented. Although the

HCAA formally recognized the YHCA as its official youth organization, this constitution was not given approval, and it was agreed that no more work should be done on the constitution until the 1969 Biennial Conference. By the end of the year further youth branches had been created in Cincinnati and Philadelphia, and the Constitutional Committee continued to meet. Manny Brotman was appointed Executive Director of the Young Messianic Jewish Alliance of America (YMJA), and empowered to act as a liaison between the YHCA and the HCAA.

At the June 1969 Biennial Conference in Asheville, North Carolina, about 40 young people were in attendance. This youth group held their own meetings at which branch reports were given, officers elected, and classes conducted. At the HCAA Conference Executive Committee meeting, it was agreed that all YHCA members over the age of 15 would be permitted to vote in the HCAA elections. In addition, the YHCA annual Executive Committee meetings were approved. In May 1970 the Executive Committee accepted the YHCA Constitution, with minor reservations concerning age limits for membership and voting rights.

In 1970 the YHCA held its first conference at Messiah College in Grantham, Pennsylvania. Approximately 45 young people attended, staging a gathering very different from conferences held by the HCAA. For the first time free-form prayer took place, and the name Yeshua was used instead of Jesus. One of the pressing concerns was the relationship of the Hebrew Christian community to the Jewish people. Commenting on the changes that had taken place among these young people, Manny Brotman recalled:

> We were all discovering the abundant Jewish life at the same time. The joy of celebrating a Passover, *Hanukkah*, and other holidays was a new experience. There was a birth of a Messianic community. The revival that was born in the youth movement didn't come from the adult Alliance. It came from the youth who were filled with the Spirit. They had a zeal and vision for evangelism. This invigorated the whole Alliance. From there, the Holy Spirit began to assemble together different people in different areas for leadership roles in the Alliance. Among them were the Finkelsteins in Philadelphia and the Chernoffs in Cincinnati.[16]

Commenting on this shift in the movement, Yohanna Chernoff, the wife of Martin Chernoff, discussed the changes taking place within the United States in the late 1960s. Alongside the radical social climate of the period, there was a spiritual awakening among young people:

> Thousands upon thousands of young drug addicts, dropouts, runaways, flower children, rebels with and without causes 'turned on' to Jesus, becoming Street Christians, Jesus People, Jesus Freaks, the Jesus Revolution, the Jesus Generation. They were swept up in whirlwinds of praise and prayer and held adoration

of the Son of God. As one, they fell in love with God's Anointed, Jesus of Nazareth, King of Kings, Lord of Lords, Saviour of the World. Among them, multitudes of Jewish youth 'turned on' to the same and only Saviour, Jesus the Messiah, King of the Jews, King of the Universe.[17]

Reflecting on the shift that was taking place in religious consciousness within the movement, she described a conflict which occurred at the June 1969 HCAA conference in Asheville, North Carolina, between the youth and older Hebrew Christians:

> A delightful though disturbing crisis occurred one day, when we were waiting in the cafeteria for lunch. Someone from our group said, 'Let's sing a song!' In response, we all began to sing, *Havenu, shalom aleichem*, an old Hebrew folk song, the older Hebrew Christians present would all surely remember from their childhood. And sing it we did, with energy, enthusiasm and joy. Abruptly, some of the old Hebrew Christians' Gentile wives accosted us. 'Why are you singing that? Don't you know you shouldn't sing Jewish songs!' Their sudden anger amazed us. What could be wrong with enjoying a simple, little song familiar to all Jewish people from ages past? After all, we were all still Jews. But the older Hebrew Christians were embarrassed and rushed to suppress our singing. How assimilated they were! How far removed from their own people![18]

The conflict between the aspirations of the young people to embrace the Jewish tradition and the desire of older Hebrew Christians to integrate into the Gentile churches brought about a fundamental shift in orientation within the movement. Describing the change that occurred within their own congregation, Yohanna Chernoff stressed that previous attempts by Hebrew Christians to form congregations of Jewish believers had largely failed. With only few exceptions, such as the First Hebrew-Christian Church of Chicago led by David Bronstein, there had been little attempt to integrate an acceptance of Jesus with a Jewish lifestyle.

Nonetheless, these early attempts were vitally important for future generations – they expressed a deep need within Jewish followers of Yeshua to remain Jewish and to have their own congregations. This was the vision which motivated Martin Chernoff. In 1970, she explained, she and her husband had relocated their congregation in Cincinnati. Continuing the tradition of these early congregations, she wrote:

> Our congregation felt that it was time for us to raise up as one body to make a statement. In effect, we agreed that 'We are Jewish believers in Yeshua as our Messiah. We have our own destiny in the Lord. We will no longer be assimilated into the church and pretend to be non-Jews. If Yeshua Himself, His followers and the early Jewish believers tenaciously maintained their Jewish lifestyles, why was it right then, but wrong now?'[19]

6   Messianic Judaism in transition

Jews for Jesus

Paralleling the growth of the youth movement within the HCAA, Jews for Jesus emerged in the early 1970s out of the Hebrew Christian movement. Initially its founder Moishe Rosen had worked as a Hebrew Christian missionary with the Jewish Missions of America (JMA). By the late 1960s, however, Rosen had become disenchanted with the gentilization of the Hebrew Christian movement; in addition, he believed that the JMA was not sufficiently interested in the needs and aspirations of young Jewish believers. Determined to reach the youth, he founded a JMA branch in a suburb of San Francisco. Together with his wife Marie and several other young adults, he encouraged Bible study and street and campus evangelization.

During this period, a rabbi working at a local college referred to this group as Jews for Jesus; later Rosen appropriated this name for the movement. In 1971 Rosen met Stella, a Jewish Christian, who began to work in the office as a writer and artist. During this period a growing number of Jews who were part of the Jesus movement were drawn to Rosen's organization. Anxious to ensure that Jewish believers were knowledgable about Christian belief, Rosen encouraged them to attend a local Bible college. From October 1972 a variety of new activities took place, and a growing emphasis on Jewish ethnic identity became an integral feature of the movement. In addition, a drama group began to do performances and street theatre, and a singing group embarked on a cross-country tour.

By August 1973 the JMA had become increasingly alarmed by the activities of Jews for Jesus and terminated Rosen's contract. In response eleven members of the movement who were paid by the JMA resigned in protest, and efforts were made to raise funds. The period between September and December 1973 was a turning point for Jews for Jesus; having severed their connection with the JMA, the movement was determined to survive on its own. Policy was established, work roles were regularized, and an organizational structure was put into place. In addition, Jewish outreach was extended beyond the Jewish community to the Gentile church. Rosen and his followers were determined to teach through drama, song and testimonials about what it means to be Jewish. During the first six months of 1974 the movement added vocational and volunteer staff, improved the methods of generating income, formalized work routines, and planned evangelistic campaigns.

In San Francisco, the office of Jews for Jesus was located in a two-storey office building in one of the suburbs. Situated near a freeway, the office consisted of two suites of seven overcrowded rooms. Most spaces were shared by several people, and only the leader, office manager and information officer had areas of their own. The office housed a variety of equipment including electric typewriters, an addressograph, tape-recording equipment, a printing press, and a folding machine. At this time most of the members lived in rented apartments nearby. In general, housing arrangements for single members were temporary, and little was spent on furnishing or decorations.

Members of Jews for Jesus strongly identified with the group rather than the Church. The ideology of the movement was based largely on the beliefs of American fundamentalist Christianity. Its corporate charter expresses its commitment to fundamentalist and conservative Christian beliefs:

- We believe in the Divine Inspiration, infallibility and authority of the Old and New Testaments.
- We believe in the Triune God and the deity of the Lord Jesus Christ, the only begotten Son of God.
- We believe in His sacrificial atonement at Calvary, His bodily resurrection from the dead, and His premillenarial second coming.
- We believe that the New Birth by faith and obedience to Christ places each believer in the Body of Christ of which the local congregation is an expression.
- We believe that it is necessary for the Christian to be separated from the worldly system of sin and to resist the person of Satan.
- Finally, we believe in the lost condition of every human being, whether Jew or Gentile, who does not accept salvation by faith in Jesus Christ, and therefore in the necessity of presenting the gospel to the Jews.[1]

In addition to these beliefs, the movement is committed to Christian values including an emphasis on spiritual growth with Jesus as the model. Even though members of the group interpreted this belief system in various ways, there was a common acceptance of the group's goals. In addition, Jews for Jesus were insistent that the Jewish component of the movement's ethnic identity should be a vital feature of the faith. Yiddishisms appeared frequently in conversation, and members were drawn to Jewish humour, Jewish food, and Israeli folk dancing. Members attended synagogue, and many practised traditional rituals such as lighting Sabbath candles and keeping kosher.

A central element of the movement's ideology was its commitment to evangelism. Critical of traditional missionary activity, the group developed its own techniques of missionizing. A high premium was placed on confrontation. Adopting the strategy of political radicals, members of the group attempted to attract attention to the cause by being highly visible and vocal. Frequently they wore costumes and identifying jackets and participated in street theatre. Learning from experience, they sought to present their message in an effective manner and use the opposition creatively. In an attempt to reach the general public, Jews for Jesus put up posters in conspicuous places, and passed out broadsheets in tourist areas, airports, campuses and shopping centres. Because of the desire to reach young people, members of the movement frequently engaged in missionizing on college campuses.

In addition to direct evangelism, the group sought media publicity as an indirect method of communicating its message. By using press releases describing performances and demonstrations, Jews for Jesus appeared in the evening news programmes on television as well as in newspaper articles. During demonstrations, members carried large placards, sang, played tambourines and chanted. The main objective of such public displays was to ensure that the group's name was constantly in the news. Of crucial importance in ensuring publicity for the movement was the desire to evoke a reaction from the Jewish community. When opposition to Jews for Jesus was expressed in editorials and articles, this ensured that the movement would be discussed and its message gain attention.

Another goal for the movement was to challenge the Church to reevaluate its relationship to Judaism. Frequently members taught what it means to be Jewish so that Gentiles would be able to appreciate the spiritual roots of the Christian faith. Such church evangelism was carried out by the Singing Group, the Drama Group, and speakers who preached in churches throughout the country. Yet despite such a commitment to the Jewish tradition, Jews for Jesus have been ambivalent about their relationship to the Jewish community. Because the movement has evoked a deeply hostile reaction from the Jewish establishment, it is difficult for Jews for Jesus to engage in positive dialogue with other Jews.

The strategy for dealing with such hostility was to stress the importance of free speech in a democratic society. As Rosen explained:

> Jewishness should not be a liability in a free society, and Jews have always had to struggle for acceptance and tolerance. Yet, having won freedom from oppression, there are many Jews who will not accord the same tolerance to others who want to express and promote their beliefs, simply because they are Jews who believe in Jesus.[2]

Some Jews, however, remained immune to such arguments. Anxious to suppress the activities of the movement, they put pressure on Christian campus groups to exclude Jews for Jesus speakers and tried to prevent the publication of articles about the group in local newspapers. Defending the activities of the Jewish Defense League in combating Jews for Jesus, a member stated:

The Jewish Defense League is going to hassle the Jews for Jesus until they quit. No Jew should be subjected to the personal affront of having contact with these people. It's an insult. We are trying to show all Jews that they don't have to put up with this obnoxious phenomenon. When we go to a demonstration, we kick some shins, we hassle them, rough them up some, take away their literature.[3]

Undeterred by such an offensive, Jews for Jesus was convinced that even such violence served as an effective means of gaining publicity. As Rosen explained:

If they want to fight Jesus People, let them fight us. The Messianist Jews don't get newspaper articles like we do. We didn't decide we'd frustrate the Jewish community, but we don't want to be ignored. When the brickbats are thrown, we're offering ourselves as the first target. The impact brings the focus of attention; then you can speak what you want to say.[4]

The Six Day War and its aftermath

One of the main factors which influenced the youth of the 1970s was the impact of the Six Day War. Commenting on the events of this struggle, Yohanna Chernoff recalled:

During the first weeks of June, 1967, with breath held in abeyance and hearts pounding, we rode out the war, holding special, all-night prayer meetings . . . Breathlessly, we hung on to each news report . . . We thrilled to accounts in Jewish newspapers of how even hard-hearted, atheistic Israelis reported miracles on the battlefield. There was no question about it: God had fought for Israel . . . we gave God all the glory for their amazing victory, and praised Him mightily with singing, with raising and clapping our hands, with tears of joy and laughter.[5]

In the wake of Israel's victory, the movement formally declared its dedication to the Jewish state. At the June 1969 conference in Asheville, North Carolina, delegates stated their conviction that the reconstitution of the State of Israel was a unique phenomenon in Jewish history:

Once again it demonstrates God's overruling intervention in the destiny of the Jewish people. Among Bible believing Jews and Christians . . . the land was promised by God to the Jewish people as an eternal possession . . . We identify ourselves fully with the Jewish people. Our faith in Yeshua the Messiah has deepened the meaning of our Jewishness, has intensified our love for our people and has enlarged our understanding of the nature of Jewish destiny. On this twenty-first anniversary of the rebirth of the State of Israel we, the delegates assembled at the 54th Conference, wish to convey to the government and people of Israel our hearty greetings. While much suffering may yet be in store for Israel we are certain that with God's help she will prevail.[6]

For many Messianic Jews the regathering of the Jewish people in the land of their ancestors was perceived as a fulfilment of prophecy in Scripture. Jewish believers were convinced that a new era of history had commenced, and a new generation of young Jews was drawn into the movement. The Alliance underwent enormous growth. As Robert Winer, formerly President of the HCAA, explained:

> It is hard for those who were not involved in the Alliance at this time to comprehend what it was like to be a part of the events that took place. The only way I can describe it was that there was a sense of excitement in the air, an incredibly intense energy level, and an awareness that one was in the midst of people deeply committed to seeing their people know the Messiah. The foremost thing in the minds and hearts of the people was the Messianic Vision. It was as if the voice of God was speaking to a group of diverse people the same message, 'The vision is for now. You must take this message to my people and to all Jewish believers. What has been suppressed for nineteen hundred years must now become a reality. Go; do not cease from this labour until all the earth knows this message.'[7]

Pre-eminent among those who encouraged the young people in their quest to create a Jewish lifestyle were Joe and Debbie Finkelstein. Having embraced Yeshua in the 1960s, they created a place for study and worship in their home in Philadelphia. Known as 'Fink's Zoo', their congregation pioneered a shift away from Hebrew Christianity. A significant number of Jewish and Gentile young people were converted through their efforts, and the Finkelsteins were insistent that these Jewish converts could still remain Jewish while accepting Jesus. In Cincinnati, Martin and Yohanna Chernoff similarly established a congregation, Beth Messiah, in their home, and their children Joel, David and Hope formed the core of a group of young Messianic Jews. In Washington Sandra Sheskin and her mother supported a local branch of the Alliance. In Chicago Manny Brotman gathered a number of young people together under the auspices of the Alliance's pilot programme for the Young Hebrew Christian Alliance.

These youths played a pivotal role at the YHCA Conference where a new type of worship and praise was expressed for the first time. Adamant that change was needed, these young people sought to distance themselves from Hebrew Christianity. In their view the use of church hymns drawn from a Gentile setting was inappropriate for Jewish believers. Instead, they wished to compose modern music in a contemporary style, often played on guitars. The older generation, however, was displeased with such change. Undeterred, the youth believed that the message of Yeshua should be stressed.

Distancing themselves from older members of the movement, the youth believed that different methods of evangelism should be used. Influenced by the techniques devised by Jews for Jesus, they promoted the use of pamphlets with humorous illustrations and dramatic themes proclaiming Yeshua. In addition, like Moishe Rosen's group, they participated in street theatre and outdoor concerts. Faced with the disapproval of the adults, they believed that the YHCA, rather than the movement as a whole, would be receptive to their approach.

Martin Chernoff, however, as one of the key figures of the HCAA, was sympathetic to the attitude of the youth. From 1967 to 1979 he had served on the Executive Committee of the Alliance; in 1971 he was elected President. Initially he had been an active participant in the Hebrew Christian movement, but as we have seen, in the early 1970s he and his wife had founded their own congregation which drew together a wide circle of young people. In his view, Jewish believers must combine a Jewish lifestyle with their commitment to Yeshua. Within the Alliance, such a stance evoked dismay. Yet he was regarded by many as a pioneer, seeking to influence the Alliance to adopt a Messianic stance.

Under Chernoff's influence a major shift took place within the movement: in the 1970s a growing number of young people were committed to maintaining a culturally Jewish lifestyle, in the mode advocated by Rabinowitz in the nineteenth century, and Levy and Zacker in the early half of the twentieth century. Such determination led these young people to press for the movement to change its name from the Hebrew Christian Alliance of America to the Messianic Jewish Alliance of America. At the Biennial Conference held in Dunedin, Florida in June 1973, a motion for this change was put before the delegates – even though it received 62 per cent of the vote, a two-thirds majority was required. At the 1975 Biennial Conference, a similar motion was proposed and passed. Reflecting on these events, Paul Liberman in an article 'Toward Our Destiny' explained why such a shift was needed:

It was not long, however, before many congregants began to feel that the term 'Hebrew Christian' had become outdated. It seemed almost to run contrary to our assertions of being indigenous and independent. After all, Americans normally expect that Christians of all types attend church and Jews of all types attend synagogues. Thus, it seemed of critical importance to be officially known to the world as Messianic Jews if our new style congregation was to succeed . . . Fortunately, God provided a way. Probably the most significant pivotal event was the election of Martin Chernoff as President. Seeing the intensity of dispute over the name change, the new President made a wise executive decision which permitted local chapters to identify as the Messianic Jewish Alliance. This cleared the way for the establishment of at least a half-dozen new Messianic congregations and a resulting doubling in conference attendance at the 1975 conference.[8]

From Hebrew Christian Alliance to Messianic Judaism

In the early 1970s a considerable number of members of the Hebrew Christian Alliance were committed to a church-based conception of Hebrew Christianity. The YHCA, however, was forging a new conception of the movement rooted in the counter-culture of the early 1970s. In particular, the Jesus People movement provided momentum for a revision of previously held notions about the lifestyle of Jewish believers. At the 1973 Conference Martin Chernoff was re-nominated President of the Hebrew Christian Alliance; with the support of a number of moderates he was elected despite the opposition of traditionalist members of the movement.

As previously noted, a constitutional amendment was proposed to change the name of the HCAA to the Messianic Jewish Alliance of America. Such a change was more than semantic; the majority of delegates were aware that such an alteration would initiate fundamental changes in the movement. When the amendment failed to obtain the required two-thirds majority, its supporters did not despair. The following year the YHCA held their own conference at Messiah College in Pennsylvania. This conference stressed the importance of a Jewish lifestyle and featured musicians and music groups which played Messianic music with a Jewish flavour.

Unlike many of the older members of the movement, these young people were determined to identify with their Jewish roots. In their view the acceptance of Yeshua should be coupled with a commitment to the cultural and religious features of the Jewish faith. Among the leaders of the youth was Manny Brotman who served as President and first Executive Director of the YHCA. Through his influence the earliest Messianic literature was produced which stressed the Jewishness of faith in Yeshua. Another important figure was Joseph Finkelstein, formerly President of the YHCA and Executive Director from 1972 to 1975. Through his influence many young Jews were brought into the movement; in addition Finkelstein organized a singing group, Kol Simcha, which wrote their own music and also introduced choreographed dance worship as well as testimonies from the singers. Other leaders, such as Arnold Fruchtenbaum and Barry Leventhal, encouraged the study of the Bible.

The 1975 HCAA Conference, chaired by Manny Brotman, was the largest held for years and combined a week of teaching with music and dance. At the business meeting, the issue of changing the name of the movement was debated and carried. Previously the Alliance had been composed of Jewish believers from various Christian denominations – some were from a Presbyterian background, others from a Baptist or an Anglican milieu. Most were unprepared for the revivalist emphasis championed by young believers. At this conference, charismatic forms of worship were introduced including raising of hands, clapping to the Lord, and singing in the Spirit. Even though the biblical background of these practices was acknowledged, a number of older members of the Alliance were dismayed.

Another issue which divided the movement was the question whether Jewish believers should live a Jewish lifestyle. Some members believed that it was desirable to follow Jewish traditions as long as they were in accord with Scripture, such as wearing a skullcap, a *tallit* (prayer shawl), *tallit katan* (undergarment with fringes), and *tefillin* (phylacteries). In addition, these members stressed the importance of *davening* (chanting daily prayers from the traditional prayer book), lighting candles on the Sabbath, and reciting the traditional *kiddush* prayer on the Sabbath and at festivals. Some followed kosher food laws and rested on the Sabbath day. In general those who were drawn to the tradition were not from Jewish homes, yet wished to identify with Jewish practice. To many older members of the movement, such a return to Jewish observance had overshadowed faith in Yeshua.

Another topic which divided Jewish believers was the ideology of Messianic Judaism. By 1974 Messianic congregations existed in Philadelphia, Washington, Cincinnati, Chicago and Los Angeles. The earliest congregation, Beth Messiah, was founded by Martin and Yohanna Chernoff in Cincinnati in 1970 after Chernoff was informed by the AAJE that he was not permitted to hold services under their auspices. The young people in his congregation, including his sons Joel and David who later became leaders of the movement, encouraged him to adopt a variety of Jewish practices such as lighting Sabbath candles, reciting *kiddush* and wearing *kippot* during services. Eventually the congregation celebrated the Jewish holidays, and Joel Chernoff wrote contemporary music which was sung by the congregation. Beth Messiah also sponsored an outreach programme at the University of Cincinnati, attracting both Jewish and Gentile students.

In Washington Manny Brotman organized the Beth Messiah Synagogue, referring to himself as rabbi. One of the founding members of the congregation, Sandra Sheskin, led the worship services which were held on Friday evening, Sunday, and on Jewish holidays. Like Chernoff's congregation, the services were revivalist in character, integrating various charismatic features. At the same time in Encino, California, the Beth Emanuel congregation was led by the Revd Ray Gannon of the Assemblies of God. Made up of Jews and Gentiles, the congregation originated through a programme of home Bible studies and outreach. Anxious to foster similar congregations, the associate pastor, Philip Goble, wrote a book, *Everything You Need to Know to Grow a Messianic Synagogue*, which was designed to help Jews create their own Messianic synagogues. In Chicago, the First Hebrew Christian Church was initially led by David and Esther Bronstein and their successors, Morris and Ida Kaminsky. Originally Presbyterian in character with a number of Jewish elements, the congregation became Messianic under the leadership of Lawrence Rich in the late 1960s. In 1975 its name was changed to Adat ha-Tikvah under the leadership of Dan Juster.

These Messianic congregations reflected the ideological changes that were taking place within the movement. As a result, a clear division emerged between those who wished to forge a new lifestyle and those who sought to pursue traditional Hebrew Christian goals. The advocates for change sought to persuade older members of the need to embrace Jewish values, yet they remained unconvinced and left the Alliance. Within the Christian community, there was similar opposition to the Messianic movement. In the view of a number of Protestant evangelicals, the change of name from Hebrew Christian Alliance to Messianic Jewish Alliance indicated a rejection of Christianity and a return to the Jewish faith. The Director of the Friends of Israel Gospel Ministry, the Revd Marvin Rosenthal, for example, argued that Messianic Judaism is neither Jewish nor Christian. Within the Christian Press, similar views were expressed. In an article in *Eternity* magazine Robert C. Coote criticized the Messiah 75 Conference for its over-emphasis on Jewishness, lack of humility, the use of the term 'rabbi' instead of 'pastor', the change of Jesus' name to Yeshua, and the movement's support for Israel.[9] In response the MJAA issued a booklet, 'If It Be of God',[10] which defended the movement from such charges, arguing that Gamaliel's words in Acts be applied to Messianic Judaism: 'And now I say to you, do not interfere with these men; for if this counsel or these works be of men, it will come to nothing. But if it be of God, you cannot overthrow it; and you may find yourself fighting against God' (Acts 5:38–39).

Reactions to the Messianic movement

The change of name of the movement to Messianic Judaism signalled a fundamental shift within the movement. Any return to Hebrew Christianity was ruled out, and a significant number of older members left the Alliance. As a result, the average age of members was significantly reduced. At the conference, Jewish believers bore witness to their loyalty to the tradition. Increasingly worship services became Jewish in orientation even though they included dance, music and extemporaneous prayer. During this period the quarterly magazine was renamed *The American Messianic Jew* with Rachmiel Frydland as editor.

From outside the movement hostile criticism of Messianic Judaism was voiced by such bodies as the Fellowship of Christian Testimonies to the Jews (FCTJ). At their annual conference from 16 to 19 October 1975 a resolution was passed condemning the movement:

> Whereas a segment of Messianic Judaism strives to be a denomination within Judaism alongside of Orthodox, Conservative, and Reform Judaism, thus confusing law and grace, we of the FCTJ affirm that the New Testament teaches that Christian faith is consistent with, but not a continuation of Biblical Judaism, and is distinct from rabbinical Judaism.

Whereas a segment of Messianic Judaism claims to be a synagogue, and not a church, we of the FCTJ affirm that the New Testament clearly distinguishes between the synagogue and the church; Bible believing Hebrew Christians should be aligned with the local church in fellowship with Gentile believers.

Whereas a segment of Messianic Judaism encourages Gentile Christians to undergo a conversion to Judaism, we of the FCTJ affirm that this violates the tenor of the New Testament in general and the Books of Galatians and Hebrews in particular for it involves converting to a religion that clearly denies the messiahship of Jesus.

Whereas a segment of Messianic Judaism adopts the practices of rabbinic Judaism, e.g. kosher laws, wearing skullcaps and prayer shawls, *et al.*, we of the FCTJ affirm that any practice of culture, Jewish or non-Jewish, must be brought into conformity with New Testament theology.

Whereas a segment of Messianic Judaism isolates itself from the local church rebuilding the 'middle wall of partition', thus establishing a pseudo-cultural pride, we of the FCTJ affirm the necessity of the Hebrew Christian expressing his culture and his spiritual gifts in the context of the local church thus edifying the Body of Christ as a whole, and not an isolated pseudo-culture.

Whereas a segment of Messianic Judaism opposes the usage of terms such as 'Jesus', 'Christ', 'Christian', 'cross', *et al.*, and insists on using the Hebrew term exclusively, we of the FCTJ affirm that though we endorse tactfulness in witness, we reject a presentation of the Gospel which is a subtle attempt to veil and camouflage the Person and work of our Lord Jesus Christ.

Whereas segments of Messianic Judaism, by portraying themselves to be synagogues with rabbis for the purpose of attracting unsuspecting Jews, employ methods which are unethical, we of the FCTJ affirm that Jewish missions must be honest and Biblical in their message and approach, and reject the concept that 'the end justifies the means'.[11]

In the following year an open letter responding to such criticism was written by Jerome and Ruth Fleischer which cautioned that Messianic Jews, while remaining loyal to the Jewish heritage, should embrace the cardinal beliefs about Yeshua. Several articles, they pointed out, had been written about the MJAA and Jewish revival among Messianic Jews. Yet, they stated:

We declare herewith that we do believe in the fundamentals of the faith, the virgin birth, trinity, deity of the Lord Yeshua, blood atonement, verbal and plenary inspiration of Scriptures, man's sinfulness . . . Some say that we hold Messianic Judaism to be the fourth branch of Judaism . . . In fact, we hold that real Christianity is the fulfilment of the Old Testament and the only true faith of Israel. We are accused of recreating a 'middle wall of partition'. Many who fellowship with us are Gentiles who have come to believe in the Jewish Messiah, the Lord Yeshua. Some of us practise certain cultural customs, not because we are bound to keep the Law, but as a means of cultural identification with our people. Others who did likewise . . . have won praise for their understanding, their love, and their great missionary spirit. In fact, some of the early church fathers wore the garb of philosophers in order to witness effectively. Should we be condemned for similar practice? Ultimately, we will be judged by the Lord himself who knows our works and thoughts. It is he who placed in our hearts the urge to seek the salvation of our people.[12]

Within the movement discontent was expressed by such figures as Marvin Rosenthal, who castigated the changes that were taking place within the Alliance. In *Israel My Glory Quarterly*, he maintained that

about five years ago, a lie got started, its authors called it Messianic Judaism, or a movement within Judaism for Messiah. From the rabbinical point of view, the movement is not Jewish . . . Though neither 'fish' nor 'fowl', it has enamoured and gathered to itself a growing company of followers. Its appeal lies in the fact that Jews are invited to remain Jews and simply accept the Messiah . . . They are encouraged to observe Jewish holidays and ritual – and in some instances to attend the Jewish Synagogue as a form of worship. That the leaders of Messianic Judaism no one denies – that most are zealous and sincere is not at issue – but that much of their theology and methodology distorts the teaching of the New Testament is patently clear.[13]

Responding to such criticism, Rachmiel Frydland argued that – contrary to the claim that Messianic Jews deny the teaching of the Lord by identifying with the Jewish nation – these individuals are entitled to such loyalty. Why, he asked, can an American remain an American and be a Christian, why can a Pole, a Russian, a Japanese retain his national identity, whereas only the Jew can no longer identify himself with his people?[14]

In reply to the charge that Messianic Jews are trying to build the wall of partition between themselves and others, Frydland admitted that a number attend synagogue. But he insisted that through such identification Messianic Jews associate themselves with the Jewish followers of Yeshua:

We join the host of the apostles who attended Temple worship (Acts 3:1), the Apostle Paul, who always attended synagogue in whatever town he came, and the Lord Yeshua himself who unashamedly worshipped in the Temple and the Synagogue. (Luke 4:16)

These individuals, Frydland pointed out, did not build a wall of partition, nor do Messianic Jews.[15]

Nor, Frydland remarked, do Messianic Jews blindly follow rabbinic injunctions. With regard to the observance of *Yom Kippur*, for example, he stated:

Most Messianic Jews fast on this day in order to identify themselves with the Jewish people . . . Messianic Jews do not keep *Yom Kippur* as the rabbis prescribed to keep it with five kinds of fasting; not to eat and drink, not to wash, not to use shoes, not to use perfumes or deodorants, not to use the bed, and to spend the day in the synagogue with hundreds of lighted candles. Some Messianic Jews . . . cannot eat food on this day and cry out with the Apostle Paul . . . in Romans 9:2–3, 10:1 . . . Let us rejoice even if some of us prefer his Hebrew name Yeshua which means salvation . . . and Messiah which means the 'Anointed One' of God . . . With the words of father Abram we plead, 'Let there be no strife, I pray thee, between me and thee'. (Genesis 13:9)[16]

7 Contemporary Messianic Judaism

Messianic congregational organizations

As we have seen, from the nineteenth century Jewish believers were anxious to form independent organizations. At the end of the nineteenth century Joseph Rabinowitz formed a congregation of Hebrew Christians in Kishinev. In North Aemrica Hebrew Christian congregations were founded in New York in 1895, Toronto in 1917, Philadelphia in 1922, Chicago in 1931, Los Angeles in the 1930s and later in 1955, Baltimore in the 1940s, Detroit in the 1950s. Before the Second World War the Hebrew Christian Alliance was deeply concerned with the plight of European Jewry, and it was felt that a Hebrew Christian congregational organizational structure was of vital importance.

At the 1934 IHCA Conference in England, a Special Commission reported to the conference about the creation of an international body, the Hebrew Christian Church. Commenting on this proposal, Sir Leon Levison, President of the IHCA, reflected on the state of the Christian faith. The Church, he wrote:

> has lost her vision, and of late has taken shortviews; hence her apathy toward Jewish missions . . . Through a Hebrew Christian Church that apathy could be removed . . . The church has never learned to accept the Jews as they were. The root of many of the frictions, ill-feelings, and misunderstandings is often their desire to conform them to their own kind of pattern . . . Only the Hebrew Christians could accept their own people as they were, could bear with what was irksome in them, and refuse to let the differences stand in the way of their love for them in order to lead them to Messiah.[1]

Anxious to establish a worldwide body of Jewish believers, Sir Leon pressed ahead with this plan, and a Constitution as well as Articles of Faith were composed. These consisted of eleven principles:

> *Article 1:* I believe in God, the source of all being, the Covenant God, the Holy One of Israel, our Heavenly Father.
> *Article 2:* I believe that God who spoke at sundry times and in diverse manners in time past to the fathers through the prophets promised to redeem the world

from sin and death in and through his Anointed, who would be a light to the Gentiles and the glory of his people Israel.

Article 3: I believe in the fullness of time God fulfilled his promise and sent his son, his eternal word, Yeshua the Messiah, who was born by the power of the Holy Spirit, of the virgin Miriam, who was of the family of David, so that in him the word was made flesh and dwelt among us full of grace and truth.

Article 4: I believe that Yeshua the Messiah is in very truth the *Shekinah*, the brightness of the Father's glory, the very impress of his person, that he was made unto us wisdom from God, and righteousness, and sanctification, and that by his life, death on the tree and glorious resurrection, he has accomplished our reconciliation with the Father.

Article 5: I believe that the Father sealed all that the Son was, did and taught, by raising him through the Holy Spirit from the dead, and that the risen and glorified Lord appeared to many and communed with them, and then ascended to be our Mediator with the Father and to reign with him one God.

Article 6: I believe that the Holy Spirit, the paraclete who proceeds from the Father and the Son, was sent to be with us, to give us assurance of the forgiveness of sin and to lead us unto the fullness of truth and the more abundant life.

Article 7: I believe that the Holy Spirit, who beareth witness within our spirits that we are the sons of God, will quicken us in the resurrection when we shall be clothed in the body which it shall please the Father to give us.

Article 8: I believe that the Church of Messiah is the family of God in heaven and on earth, the sanctuary of the redeemed in which God dwells and of which the Messiah Yeshua is the only head.

Article 9: I believe that the Old and New Testaments are the divinely inspired records of God's revelation to Israel and the world and are the only rule of life and faith.

Article 10: I believe that it is the will of God, who has graciously brought us into the New Covenant, that we should strive to be his witnesses, making the teaching and life of the Messiah our standard and example, till he comes again to reign in glory.

Article 11: I believe that the Church visible maintains unbroken continuity with the Church in heaven by partaking of the same blessed sacraments of immersion and of communion and by confessing the same Father, Son and Holy Spirit, One Godhead.[2]

Although this attempt to create a worldwide organization was not successful, Jewish believers continued to think that the establishment of such a congregational structure was an important goal. At the Messiah 1975 Conference, there were only eight functioning Messianic congregations along with several other groups. At a meeting which proposed that an official body of Messianic congregations be established, Martin Chernoff advised against such an undertaking even though he was in favour of the eventual establishment of a fellowship of Messianic congregations. In his view, it was too early for such a body to be formed and might increase the fears of those who were concerned that a new denomination was being established. Further, he believed that such a body might hinder the free-flowing character of spiritual revival within the movement.

In the light of such reservations, it was decided to postpone such a project. Yet a number of leaders of the movement disagreed with this decision, and in 1978 the Union of Messianic Jewish Congregations was founded. Commenting on the aims of such a body, Dan Juster, its first President and General Secretary, stated:

> The primary purpose of the UMJC is to strengthen and foster Messianic Jewish congregations. As part of that, leadership training, leadership encouragement and fellowship . . . raising the funds and spurring congregations to plant congregations . . . The Union serves as a resource to inspire that and to help congregations in how to do that. The coming together for conferences in different parts of the country, . . . as well as other things is a spur of vision so that the Christian community will support in heart what the Messianic Jewish communities are doing, as well as to gain an identity in the city where the Jewish community is, of the viability of the Messianic Jewish movement.[3]

Paralleling this development, the MJAA encouraged congregations informally, and in 1984 founded the National Conference of Messianic Leaders which was designed to help congregational leaders and those seeking to establish Messianic Jewish congregations. Following the creation of the National Conference of Messianic Leaders, it was decided that an International Alliance of Messianic Congregations and Synagogues should be formed. Reflecting on the formation of this body, David Chernoff, the first Chairman of the IAMCS Steering Committee, stated:

> For many years my father had a desire to see a fellowship of the leaders of Messianic congregations. Gradually, I too came to share this vision. The main purpose was to have a time where leaders could hear relevant teachings, pray together, and share burdens with one another. A fellowship would be useless unless it met the needs of the leaders.
>
> We had this type of interaction but it remained informal until 1984. I had to hear from God that it was time to move forward. I felt that an IAMCS that formed too early could miss a great blessing from God. We wanted an organization that could promote unity, not uniformity.
>
> Our first pastors' fellowship meeting took place in 1984. There were only fourteen congregations represented at the first meeting. It was a tremendous spiritual experience. As we started to pray together, we sensed the spirit of God upon us in an unusually strong way. This happened repeatedly during the weekend meeting. To me, it represented a confirmation from the Lord of this ministry, despite our small size.
>
> When I see Messianic rabbis and pastors opening up, sharing from their hearts in these meetings, I get a sense of the importance of this ministry. The

IAMCS has a resource of men who are experienced in congregational issues. Their insights and past experiences are a source of strength to the movement.

I view the IAMCS as a permanent ministry of the Alliance that God has established. If one thinks of the YMJA as the right hand of the Alliance, then the IAMCS is the left hand. Together, all three parts form a composite whose strength is greater than any of its separate parts. Our ultimate vision is not just to see the growth of Messianic congregations in the United States, but to see the movement of Messianic Judaism break forth world wide.[4]

As the pastoral wing of the MJAA, the IAMCS works together with Messianic congregations and pastors in the quest to promote unity among Messianic congregations. In addition, it seeks to strengthen and assist in the spiritual growth and welfare of Messianic congregations and pastors. Further, it promotes the formation of new Messianic congregations as well as the establishment of a worldwide prayer fellowship. By sponsoring regular leadership conferences and training seminars, it also encourages and supports Messianic rabbis and pastors. Finally, it provides materials and educational resources for Messianic congregations and their leadership as well as a programme for rabbinic ordination.

Modern Messianic Judaism

As we have seen, the Messianic movement emerged out of the insights of leading Hebrew Christians who sought to remain loyal to the Jewish tradition while embracing Yeshua into their lives. As early as 1917 Mark John Levy encouraged Jewish believers to keep Scriptural feasts and festivals, to circumcise their sons, and commemorate the rites and ceremonies of Israel. Although most Jewish believers were unable to accept this vision, there was a general recognition of the need for an independent identity for Jews who viewed Yeshua as Lord and Saviour. While Hebrew Christian churches were established for this purpose, these congregations did not provide a framework for Jewish living. Increasingly, Jewish believers recognized the necessity of creating a new organizational structure for Messianic Jews.

In contrast with early forms of Hebrew Christianity, Messianic Judaism affirms its links with the followers of Yeshua. By accepting Yeshua, Messianic Jews believe that they are fulfilled Jews. As Paul Liberman explains in *The Fig Tree Blossoms*:

A tenet of Messianic Judaism asserts that when a Jew accepts a Jewish Messiah, born in a Jewish land, who was foretold by Jewish prophets in the Jewish Scriptures, such a Jew does not become a Gentile . . . he becomes a completed Jew . . . This is because he not only has the promise of a Messiah, he actually knows him. Where ritual and tradition previously were obligatory, they now take on a higher meaning. They are seen as the foreshadowing of God's overall plan. Such traditions now give a Jew a sense of purpose and a link with his cultural past. Messianic Judaism is not a new cult, seeking to separate itself from the body of believers in the Messiah. It is a way of reconciling belief in the Messiah while continuing to be a Jew.[5]

Such leaders as Martin Chernoff fostered this conception of living as a fulfilled Jew by acknowledging Yeshua as Messiah. Both Manny Brotman and Joseph Finkelstein helped pioneer this new interpretation of the faith together with a number of early youth leaders, including Barry Leventhal and Arnold Fruchtenbaum, who encouraged Bible study and theological training.

Other figures in the movement, while sharing Messianic ideals, fostered a different conception of a Messianic lifestyle. Within the Union of Messianic Jewish Congregations, Dan Juster, John Fischer, Barry Budoff, Elliot Klayman and others encouraged a less charismatic and conservative approach. As previously noted, this organization was created following the Messiah 75 Conference. The charter meeting took place during the Messiah 79 Conference at the Holiday Inn in Mechanicsburg, Pennsylvania. Dan Juster was elected President; John Fischer of congregation B'nai Maccabim in Chicago as Vice-President; Leslie Jacobs of congregation Melech Yisrael in Toronto as Secretary; and Jeff Adler of Kehilat Mashiach congregation in Cincinnati as Treasurer.

The Constitution of the UMJC lists five major aims of this new body:

1. To provide whatever possible in the initiation, establishment, and growth of Messianic Jewish Congregations world-wide.
2. To be a voice for Messianic Jewish Congregations and Messianic Judaism world-wide.
3. To provide a forum for the discussion of issues relevant to Messianic Judaism and Messianic Jewish Congregations.
4. To aid in the causes of our Jewish people world-wide, especially in Israel.
5. To support the training of Messianic leaders.[6]

In order to fulfil these goals a number of committees were established to deal with theology, worship, music, education, communication, service and conferences. Nineteen congregations became charter members and by 1982 twenty-five congregations belonged to the movement. By 1991 the UMJC had sixty-five member congregations. Among the principles adopted by this organization was the belief that the Bible is the absolute authority on all matters of teaching and practice. Congregations are required to accept that salvation is by grace through faith in Yeshua's atonement and resurrection. Yeshua is viewed as Messiah and Lord, and belief in his divinity is a cardinal precept of the faith. In addition to these beliefs, dedication to the Jewish tradition is regarded as central. As the By-laws state:

As Jewish followers of Yeshua, we are called to maintain our Jewish Biblical heritage and remain a part of our people Israel and the universal body of believers. This is part of our identity and a witness to the faithfulness of God.[7]

Over the years the UMJC has become a vital force within the Messianic movement. It holds yearly national conferences at various cities which are attended by delegates from member congregations. In addition, it sponsors regional conferences, provides educational materials, trains Messianic leaders, and represents Messianic Judaism to both the Jewish and Christian communities.

Another Messianic congregational organization for Jewish believers is the FMC, founded in 1987. Unlike the majority of congregations in the UMJC and the IAMCS, this body is non-charismatic in style. Nonetheless, it actively promotes many of the same programmes as these other congregational organizations including education, leadership training, and fellowship. Describing the nature of this body, Arnold Fruchtenbaum stated:

> When the FMC first began, it was to provide a fellowship of Messianic congregations where rabbinics did not play as prominent a role as it did in the others. But since then, there has not been as much a discernible difference as it was in the past. From my observations now, the differences between FMC and the other two are mostly theological more than they are in philosophy of ministry.[8]

Beyond differences in leadership style of these three organizations, there are important theological distinctions. As Ruth Fleischer explained:

> Because of the influence of Dan Juster on the UMJC, covenantal theology (Calvinist or Reform) has been meshed with pre-millennial theology to form a synthesis which would be anathema to proponents of either. Juster believes that it is his role to bring these dissimilar perspectives together, thereby giving those of the covenant persuasion a view of 'Israel: (interpreted as "the church") which includes a Jewish spiritual revival'. FMC and MJAA leaders oppose this position, accepting only a literal view of Scripture and prophecy concerning the nation and people of Israel. They believe in a literal physical and spiritual restoration of the Jewish people to their land and God. The majority of MJAA/IAMCS members believe that the revival has begun and will be completed at the time of Messiah's return and 1,000-year earthly reign, while FMC members see the fulfilment of prophecy only in the return of Jesus.[9]

In addition to these bodies, other smaller groups have emerged in recent years within the Messianic Jewish community. The Association of Torah-Observant Messianics encourages Jewish observance, not out of loyalty to the tradition, but because *halakhah* is understood as divinely revealed. Most of the members belonging to this Association wear fringes and follow rabbinic regulations regarding *kashrut*. Even though Messianics affiliating with this body are frequently criticized by other Messianics because they do not rigorously follow Orthodox Jewish practice even though they claim to follow the law, they believe they are making an important contribution to Messianic Judaism. Another group, the International Federation of Messianic Jews, was created to promote *Torah* observance based on Sephardic rather than Ashkenazic practice. Both of these marginal bodies illustrate the diversity that exists within the movement.

Despite the differences in orientation between these various organizations, the lifestyle of Messianic Jews is generally similar. In Messianic families, boys are circumcised in fulfilment of the biblical precept. Subsequently boys and girls attend religious school at the synagogue, normally at the time of *Shabbat* (Sabbath) services. Within the Messianic movement, there is no confirmation service; however, many children become *Bar Mitzvah* or *Bat Mitzvah* at the age of 13. On such occasions it is common for public affirmations of faith to be made after the reading of the *Torah* and *Haftarah* portion. Within the home many Messianic families observe the kosher food laws which are contained in Scripture.

On the Sabbath, candles are lit, accompanied by the special Hebrew blessing which is recited by the woman of the house. At the beginning of the *Shabbat* meal, the *kiddush* prayer is said over wine and special blessings are recited over two loaves of bread by the man of the house. It is usual for the father to bless his children using the traditional blessing. At Passover the family holds a *seder* (Passover meal) during which the *Haggadah* (Passover prayer book) is read. The Messianic *Haggadah* differs from the traditional *Haggadah* in that special attention is paid to the middle *matzah* which is broken and hidden. Messianic Jews believe that this ceremony originated during the *seders* of Jewish believers in Yeshua.

During *Hanukkah* Messianic families celebrate this festival by lighting the *menorah* (candelabrum) during eight days. During this holiday it is mentioned that Yeshua referred to himself as the light of the world and that he himself celebrated *Hanukkah*. During *Sukkot* (Festival of Tabernacles) Messianic families participate in building a family *sukkah*; in some congregations it is usual for congregants to share their *sukkah* with others. At *Purim* it is common for plays to be performed, and families may host costume parties at which traditional *Purim* food is eaten.

In the Messianic community *Rosh Hashanah* (New Year), *Yom Kippur* (Day of Atonement) and *Shavuot* (Pentecost) are observed both at home and in the synagogue. Most congregations hold services for the High Holy Days. It is usual for Messianic congregations to advertise these services within the local community in an effort to encourage Jews who are not members of traditional congregations to attend. In addition to these services, Messianic Jews attend house-group fellowship, Bible study, and prayer groups. It is common as well for Messianic Jews to be involved in outreach programmes as well as dance or music worship ministry. Most Messianic Jews attend at least one Messianic conference; this is either a regional conference held by the MJAA, UMJC, FMC or other Messianic groups. At home Messianic Jews are encouraged to read the Bible daily and engage in prayer. In these various ways, Messianic Jews seek to fulfil their commitment to Yeshua while remaining loyal to the Jewish tradition.

Jewish and Christian reactions

The growth of Messianic Judaism has caused considerable consternation within both the Jewish and Christian communities. In some cases direct action has been taken against the Messianic community by Jewish activists. In February 1980, for example, two members of the Jewish Defense League stole the *Torah* scroll from a Messianic congregation, Ahazat Zion Synagogue in Los Angeles. The next month a group from the Jewish Defense League picketed the synagogue and hurled rocks through a window. According to Rabbi Kenneth Cohen of Young Israel congregation who accompanied this protest, Messianic Jews mislead Jews and engage in idol worship. In his view, the synagogue should be called a church.

In Philadelphia similar events took place and numerous articles were written opposing the local Messianic congregation. Attempts were made to prevent Messianic Jews from buying a congregational building in a Jewish neighbourhood. In addition, an advertisement was taken out by opponents of the Messianic Jews in the classified section of a local newspaper designed to foment contempt for the movement. Giving the names of several women belonging to the congregation as well as the address of the congregation's ministries, the advertisement read:

> THREE RAVISHING WOMEN – blonde, brunette and redhead. Blonde (Susan) for straight sex. Brunette (Linda) submissive to masterful men. Fiery Redhead (Debbie) for all S/M fantasies. All replies answered. A religious experience. Box 1024 Havertown, Pa. 19083.[10]

While deploring such tactics, officials within the Jewish community generally regard Messianic Judaism as a pernicious influence. In the view of many, it is simply impossible for Jews who believe in Jesus to remain members of the faith. As Rabbi Marc H. Tanenbaum, national inter-religious affairs director of the American Jewish Committee stated:

> Jewish tradition allows that Gentiles can believe in the Trinitarian concept, termed in Hebrew as *shittuf* (partnership). Belief in *shittuf*, Judaism affirms, does not constitute idolatry for non-Jews, but does so for Jews. Jews, born of a Jewish mother, who become so-called Messianic Jews, are bound by the Covenant of Sinai, which explicitly excludes the possibility of any belief that God shares his being in any partnership with any other being (Exodus 20:2–6; Deuteronomy 4:15–21). While humanely one might empathize with Messianic Jews who wish nostalgically to retain some cultural linkages with the Jewish people – whether

for guilt or other emotional reasons – in point of fact, re-enacting Jewish rituals of the Sabbath, the Passover, the *Bar Mitzvah*, without commitment to the convictions they symbolize soon make a mockery of their sacred meanings.[11]

According to Tanenbaum, when such Jewish observances are used to persuade Jews of the authenticity of Messianic Judaism, this is nothing less than deliberate deceit.

Leading figures within the American Jewish Committee have also emphasized the inherent dangers of Messianic Judaism. In an article by Rabbi A. James Rudin and his wife Marcia entitled 'Onward (Hebrew) Christian Soldiers: They're Out to Grab Your Kids', they explained that Hebrew Christianity or Messianic Judaism is not new; rather Hebrew Christian missions to the Jews operated in the nineteenth century. Initially these evangelical bodies attracted few Jewish converts, yet in recent years the movement has undergone a major transformation. According to the Rudins, 'The (Hebrew Christian/Messianic Jews) attempt to lull the Jew into belief that he is not actually changing his religion, when in fact the ultimate goal is to convert him to Christianity and have him join an established Christian church.'[12]

In another article in the *New York Times* the Rudins explained what should be done to counter the cults. Among various suggestions, they recommended that laws regulating proselytization should be tightened; in addition, they proposed that laws barring conversion of minors should be passed and that cults could be prosecuted for interfering with family relationships.[13]

Discussions between leaders of the Jewish community and Messianic Jews have also led to considerable misunderstanding and friction. After meeting with Dan Juster, Rabbi Arthur C. Blecher of Beth Tivah congregation in Rockville, Maryland, stated:

> As I have emphasized to you in person and on the phone, I object to your allowing individuals to believe that you are a rabbi. I object to your deceptive use of language to mask the Christian nature of your congregation. I have only with great difficulty succeeded in beginning a healing process with two of my own families that were torn apart by your proselytizing efforts. You could have told me on several occasions that you intend to convince Jews to accept the New Testament and to be baptized. You have admitted to me that you are aware that the Jewish community considers Jews who have accepted the New Testament and been baptized to be Christians. I am dismayed that you make it a policy to withhold these facts from the individuals you counsel.[14]

In reply Juster stated that Blecher's letter 'to me exhibits a type of dogmatism and an unwillingness to put oneself in the position of the other'. 'Please allow me', he continued, 'to respond to a few of your gross misconceptions reflected in your letter despite repeated attempts to correct these misconceptions as well as to prove the sincerity of our stance.' In defence, Juster stated that he neither sought nor encouraged his congregants to refer to him as rabbi; in addition, he pointed out that Jewish believers do not accept the traditional boundaries between Judaism and Christianity. In conclusion he stated that 'if a Jewish person reads the New Testament and comes to conviction of the truth of its teaching, it can cause disruption'.[15]

Continuing this exchange, Rabbi Blecher questioned why Juster could not understand the severity of the issues he raised. He then cited the case of a severely disturbed patient at a mental hospital whose illness included guilt about the death of a parent. This person accidentally called Beth Messiah, believing it was a traditional synagogue. Beth Messiah sent a car to bring her to the congregation, and the person suffered an extreme setback when she found herself in a Christian setting. Juster, however, professed total ignorance of this event.[16]

This was followed by an exchange between Rabbi Matthew H. Simon of congregation B'nai Israel. In correspondence with Juster, he wrote:

> What prompts this letter is a second case of deceit which I encountered this past weekend. An Iranian Jewish student in need of support, both legal and personal, has a friend who is a member of your congregation . . . The young man is not familiar with Christian missionary techniques and your evangelical outreach to Jews. He was brought to Beth Messiah a couple of times and explained that this was a 'form of American Jewish practice'. At no time was he told that he was participating in a Christian church, with Christian believers, where the ultimate goal was to bring him to Christianity. I am familiar with the many sophistries used in explaining that Beth Messiah is different, but it surely is not Jewish.[17]

Within the Christian community, Messianic Judaism has evoked similar hostility. Many evangelical Christians are opposed to Messianic Jews because they are regarded as too Jewish: they are viewed as rebuilding a wall of partition. A considerable number of mainstream Protestant movements are also opposed to the Jewishness of Messianic Jews, but are even more contemptuous of Hebrew Christian 'Jews for Jesus' evangelism. In 1980, for example, the Long Island Council of Churches condemned Jewish–Christian groups, including Messianic Judaism, declaring 'that certain groups are engaging in subterfuge and dishonesty in representing the claims of their faith groups'.[18] As Revd Lawrence McCoombe, chairman of the Episcopal Church's Diocese of the Long Island Commission on Christian–Jewish Relations stated with regard to Hebrew Christian – including Messianic Judaism – missionizing:

> It is upsetting to Jews because it impugns the integrity of Jewish belief. It is alarming to Christians because it misrepresents Christianity. It is disturbing to both Jews and Christians because it undermines the basis of mutual respect which it has taken so long for us to establish.[19]

Messianic congregations

In a study of Messianic congregations published in 1990, Michael Schiffman sought to determine the nature of congregational life.[20] Surveying a representative sample of various Messianic synagogues, he was able to provide a comprehensive analysis of participating groups. On the basis of his questionnaire, it appears that the majority of congregations were formed in the decade preceding his study, the majority between 1975 and 1984. In his view, this reflects the newness of the Messianic movement and the upsurge of Messianic Jewish expression. Comparing the ages of the congregations with the length the spiritual leader was in the congregation, the data indicate a low pastoral turnover rate. According to Schiffman, this may be due to the fact that leading a Messianic congregation is a specialized occupation; in addition, some of the congregations are led by men who founded them, thereby making their continuing presence more secure.

The age of most of the leaders of Messianic congregations ranges between 31 and 45, with the highest percentage between 36 and 40. This, Schiffman believed, may be due to the relative youth of the movement. Of the six largest congregations surveyed, the youngest leader is 35 and the oldest 52. This suggests that the age of the leader has little bearing on the size or growth of the congregation. Of the smallest congregations, the spiritual leaders range in age between 31 and 44, suggesting that the age of the congregational leader has little relevance to congregational size.

Turning to the educational background of the spiritual leader, 47 per cent of spiritual leaders have a Master of Divinity degree. Of the leaders in the six largest congregations, four have Master of Divinity degrees or the equivalent; two are Bible college graduates. Of the four smallest congregations, two have seminary education, and one no formal Bible training. Such a pattern suggests that some formal training may be helpful in establishing a healthy congregation, but possibly does not affect its size. Regarding the spiritual leader's upbringing, the survey illustrates that most Messianic leaders are from Jewish backgrounds of the more traditional type. The percentage of leaders from traditional backgrounds is inverted with the percentage of traditional households in the Jewish community. In the Jewish community at large, Reform or secular households are the most numerous compared with Orthodox. In Schiffman's view, 'it could be that the Orthodox/Conservative emphasis on God in their upbringing may have contributed to these leaders becoming believers'.[21]

Assessing the spiritual leader's theological position, Schiffman concluded that even though 77 per cent of those surveyed label themselves charismatic in orientation, only 17 per cent consider the exercise of spiritual gifts a major part of their ministry. Sixty per cent consider it of minor importance. This suggests that while the leaders seek to identify with

God's gifts, power, and blessing, their practice does not reflect this orientation. Among the six largest congregations, four are charismatic, and two of the four place major emphasis on the exercise of spiritual gifts. Of the four smallest congregations, three of the four have a charismatic orientation. Compared with the larger congregations, this suggests that charismatic expression is not a major factor in congregational growth.

Concerning primary preaching style, the survey reveals that most Messianic leaders preach expositionally; this emphasis may reflect that Jewish believers come to faith because of the testimony of Scripture. 'The Word of God,' Schiffman wrote, 'is primary in Messianic congregations because it, and not tradition or upbringing, is the basis of the Messianic faith in Yeshua.'[22] Schiffman's survey also illustrates that most congregations follow an eldership form of government comprised of an equal plurality of elders with the pastor as its head. None of the Messianic congregations have women in a pastoral role, although many allow women other leadership positions. Nonetheless, the role of women in Messianic congregations is in a state of flux.

Turning to the composition of the membership, Schiffman's survey reveals that most Messianic congregations have percentages of Jewish membership between 25 and 50 per cent. The larger congregations average between 50 and 75 per cent of their membership being Jewish. In the smaller congregations, three average between 50 and 75 per cent, and one between 75 and 100 per cent Jewish. As with membership, the majority of congregations are composed of between 25 and 75 per cent intermarried couples. Generally the smaller congregations have a lower rate overall of intermarriage than the larger congregations. As Schiffman observed, Messianic congregations appear to provide a welcoming environment for couples who have intermarried.

The size of the average Messianic congregation is between 26 and 100 people. The bulk of services in Messianic synagogues take place on Friday evenings or Saturday mornings. Most congregations have Friday/ Saturday or Friday/Sunday services. The majority of Messianic congregations celebrate the major Jewish holidays whereas the minor holidays are of less importance. Among Messianic congregations there is a reluctance to celebrate Christmas and Easter. However, some congregations celebrate Yeshua's birth and resurrection in conjunction with existing Jewish holidays. Among the elements of Jewish tradition used in Messianic congregations, the wearing of a *kippah* (head covering) and *kiddush* blessing over wine and bread are the most common, followed by the use of some traditional prayers and the wearing of a prayer shawl. One third of the congregations surveyed have a *Torah*. Among these congregations, there is a higher percentage of those wearing a *kippah* and prayer shawl.

According to the survey, the major emphases in Messianic worship are the proclamation of the word and music; of secondary emphasis are liturgy and the exercise of spiritual gifts. As Schiffman noted: 'This seems to indicate that the average Messianic congregation is a word proclaiming congregation with a strong emphasis on music. Spiritual gifts and liturgy are part of the service, but neither are of central emphasis or primary importance.'[23] The music ministry of most congregations is limited to singing and playing various instruments; some, however, have dance ministries.

Forty per cent of congregations meet in church buildings; the remainder conduct services elsewhere. Of the six largest congregations, two meet in schools; two meet in churches; one has its own building; and one leases a facility. Church buildings can often be leased at a lesser cost if the church is sympathetic to the movement. Most Messianic congregations are not affiliated with outside denominations. Those who are have either been planted by these groups or in some way are financially dependent on them. Three of the largest congregations are affiliated with outside bodies: one with the Assemblies of God, one with the Evangelical Free Church, and one with the Presbyterian Church. Almost all congregations belong to at least one of the three Messianic congregational organizations.

According to this survey, most Messianic congregations are located in part-Jewish areas rather than in the centre of the Jewish neighbourhood. In most cases the spiritual leaders of Messianic congregations view the Jewish reaction to Messianic Judaism as antagonistic or indifferent. Despite such hostility or lack of interest, most congregations average between five and twenty visitors each month; of these at least one and as many as ten are Jewish. Eighty per cent of the congregations have one to four visitors return. Twenty per cent have as many as ten. In a number of cases Messianic congregations are effective in reaching relatives who are unbelievers. Other outreach activities include door-to-door evangelism, coffee houses, campus outreach, dance ministry, nursing home ministry, and homeless outreach. Of these activities, friendship evangelism and holiday celebrations are the most effective. Most congregations reported growth over the last few years, with the exception of one which altered its worship day and another that divided into two congregations.

Other factors contributing to the growth of congregations include evangelism, publicity, worship style, a move to larger facilities, and the proclamation of the word. Only one congregation indicated a decline in attendance due to moving the worship service from Sunday to Saturday. Amongst the largest congregations, special activities have proved to be the most successful approach to outreach, along with friendship evangelism and holiday celebrations. Of the smaller congregations, friendship evangelism was common.

In the survey congregational leaders listed the following reasons to account for those who left their congregations: moving out of the area; disagreement with the Messianic vision; charismatic emphasis; distance to travel; backsliding; death. Despite such departures, most congregations are perceived as growing, expressing optimism about the movement and what God is doing in bringing the Jewish people to embrace Yeshua. Reflecting on this survey, Schiffman emphasized the need to train leaders in the future. Further, he stressed the importance of developing music ministries, educational programmes, and outreach to the unaffiliated and intermarried.

PART II

Messianic Jewish observance

Throughout the history of the Church, there has been considerable misunderstanding between Gentile believers and the Jewish people. Both Jews and Christians have concluded that there is little connection between the two faiths. With the absorption of Christianity into the Roman Empire during the reign of Constantine, Judaism and the Jewish people have been continually vilified. Yet even the most cursory study of the New Testament reveals the inherent Jewish character of the Christian tradition. Yeshua and his followers lived according to Jewish law; worshipping in the synagogue, they saw themselves as part of the Jewish community, embracing the same traditions as their fellow Jews.

Standing within this tradition, Messianic Jews see themselves as the true heirs of these early disciples of the risen Lord. Anxious to identify with the Jewish nation, Messianic Jews have sought to observe the central biblical festivals. In their view, the Sabbath as well as the various festivals prescribed in Scripture are as valid today as they were in ancient times. Similarly, the multifarious customs regulating the lifecycle and lifestyle of Jews in biblical times are binding on members of the Messianic community. Messianic believers are thus united in their loyalty to the Jewish heritage as enshrined in Scripture.

Nonetheless, Messianic Jews are not legalistic in their approach to Judaism. Traditional Jewish observance is tempered with the desire to allow the Holy Spirit to permeate the Messianic community and animate believers in their quest to serve the Lord. For this reason, there is considerable freedom among Messianic Jews in the ways in which they incorporate the Jewish tradition into their daily lives. In seeking to understand the nature of contemporary Messianic practice, it must be emphasized that there is considerable variation among communities. Congregations do not rigidly follow the patterns recommended in the various prayer books produced by the movement; instead, they modify their observance in accordance with their own spiritual needs. Visitors to Messianic congregations will thus be struck by the considerable variation that exists within Messianic Judaism. What follows is a description of Messianic Jewish practice, though it must be emphasized that there is enormous variation among Messianic synagogues. There are many congregations within the movement which have eliminated some of the traditional features of the liturgy, embracing instead a much more charismatic approach to worship.

8 Sabbath

The Sabbath and Messianic Judaism

For Messianic Jews *Shabbat* is of paramount importance. Following Yeshua's teaching in Mark 2:27: 'The Sabbath was made for man and not man for the Sabbath', Messianic Jews believe that the Sabbath is not meant to be understood as a day of legalistic conformity. Rather, it should be a day of rest, worship and renewal. This should be so for all peoples, but for Israel the seventh day has particular significance: it is a sign of the covenant between God and his chosen people. For this reason, the *Shabbat kiddush* prayer emphasizes the connection between creation and revelation:

> Blessed are you O Lord our God, King of the Universe, who has sanctified us with his commandments and has taken delight in us. With love and favour he gave us the holy *Shabbat* as a heritage, a remembrance of the works of creation. For it is the beginning of our sacred convocations, a memorial of the Exodus from Egypt. For you have chosen us, and you have sanctified us from all the nations. And you gave us your holy *Shabbat*, with love and favour as a heritage, blessed are you O Lord, who sanctifies the *Shabbat*.

Unlike the other branches of the Jewish faith, Messianic Judaism looks to Yeshua who referred to himself as 'Lord of the Sabbath' in Mark 2:28 to gain a sense of direction for Sabbath observance. For Messianic Jews refreshment of the soul is of central importance. Through rest and renewal, Messianic Jews acknowledge that human beings should not be subject to the tyranny of work. A person of faith testifies to his trust that the Lord will ultimately provide for those who accept Yeshua into their lives.

Turning to the Scriptural understanding of the Sabbath which Messianic Jews regard as fundamental, Exodus 20:8–11 depicts the Sabbath as a testimony to God's Lordship over creation. For Messianic Jews, this Scriptural witness counters all forms of atheism, agnosticism, evolutionary naturalism and pantheism. As Genesis proclaims: 'In the beginning God created the heavens and the earth' (Genesis 1:1). In the book of Deuteronomy, the Sabbath is described as a memorial of the Exodus. For Messianic Jews, the liberation from bondage symbolizes God's continual concern with his faithful people.

In the prophetic books, the Sabbath is regarded as of central importance in the life of the nation. As Isaiah declared: 'Blessed is . . . the man . . . who keeps the Sabbath without desecrating it, and keeps his hand from doing any evil' (Isaiah 56:2). The passage continues with an account of the blessings which shall be given to those who keep God's covenant and express their dedication through Sabbath observance. Continuing this theme, Isaiah cautioned:

> If you keep your feet from breaking the Sabbath and from doing as you please on my holy day, if you call the Sabbath a delight, and the Lord's holy day honourable; and if you honour it by not going your own way, and not doing as you please or speaking idle words, then you will find your joy in the Lord, and I will cause you to ride on the heights of the land and to feast on the inheritance of your father Jacob. The mouth of the Lord has spoken. (Isaiah 58:13–14)

Such teaching continues in the New Testament. Nowhere does Yeshua advocate breaking the Sabbath law; rather, he criticizes Jewish legalists who make the Sabbath a burden rather than a delight. The Pharisees, for example, condemned Yeshua's disciples for plucking grain on the Sabbath. Although their teaching was in accord with rabbinic principles, Yeshua viewed such legalism as a violation of God's intention. In his view, the multiplication of restrictions simply prevented Jews from gaining a true understanding of the meaning of the Sabbath. As Lord of the Sabbath, he offered a new interpretation of God's decree.

Following New Testament teaching, Messianic Jews remain loyal to Yeshua's message. Seeking to avoid any form of Jewish legalism, they remain committed to making the Sabbath a day of freedom from work. The Sabbath, they believe, must be marked off from other days through a special Friday evening meal, the lighting of candles and prayer. Through special prayers Messianic Jews emphasize that Yeshua is the light of the world. In synagogue worship this theme is woven into the fabric of the liturgy. At the end of the Sabbath, the *Havdalah* service symbolically separates the Sabbath from the rest of the week: a special candle is lit and extinguished in wine. Spices are used as a reminder of the special sweetness of the Sabbath. For Messianic Jews, what is of primary importance is that activity on the Sabbath constitutes a renewal of life and faith in the redeeming power of the Messiah Yeshua.

Shabbat evening

Preparation for the Sabbath begins in the early afternoon. It is common for festive linens as well as silverware to be placed on the dinner table. Two candlesticks are placed on the table, symbolizing the twofold commandments in Scripture. These candles are lit by the woman of the house before sunset with the following blessing:

Blessed are you, O Lord our God, Ruler of the universe who sanctified us by your commandments and commanded us to be a light for the nations and gave us Yeshua our Messiah, the light of the world.[1]

As this ceremony takes place, the woman closes her eyes, and her hands circle the candles three times, symbolically spreading the light and joy of the Sabbath throughout the home. Because the Sabbath is perceived as a portent of the reign of the Messiah, the home illuminated by candles is understood as a vision of the Messianic age. The lights point to Yeshua the Messiah as the light of the world, the one who will bring in the eternal Sabbath and become the centre of that time of blessing.

Before the Sabbath meal, the family says the traditional eve of *Shabbat* sanctification prayer and the blessing over the wine:

Blessed are you O Lord our God, king of the universe, who creates the fruit of the vine.[2]

Following this *kiddush* prayer, a blessing is recited over two loaves of twisted egg-bread (*challah*) which symbolize the double portion of manna given by God to the children of Israel in the wilderness:

Blessed are you O Lord our God, king of the universe, who brings forth bread from the earth.[3]

This is followed by the singing of verses of Scripture (Proverbs 31:10–11) to honour the wife. A final blessing is usually recited over the children by either the father or both parents. They place their hands on the shoulders or heads of the children, or a large prayer shawl (*tallit*) is held up over a large group of youngsters. Over boys the following blessing is recited:

May God make you as Ephraim and Manasseh.[4]

whereas over girls the blessing is:

May God make you as Sarah, Rebecca, Rachel and Leah.[5]

If a large group of children is assembled, the Aaronic Blessing is used:

The Lord bless you and keep you;
The Lord make his face shine upon you and be gracious to you;
The Lord lift up his countenance upon you and give you peace.[6]

In some congregations this ceremony takes place in the synagogue itself. The synagogue services commence with the traditional *Baruchu* prayer:

Bless the Lord who is blessed
Blessed be the Lord who is blessed for ever and ever.[7]

This is followed by the *Lekah Dodi* prayer, welcoming the Sabbath:

Come my beloved to welcome the bride, the presence of *Shabbat* we receive.

'Observe and Remember' in one divine utterance, we heard from the one and
only God, the Lord is one and his name one, for renown, for splendour, and for
praise. Come my beloved . . . Shake off the dust, arise! Dress in garments of glory,
my people, through the son of Jesse, the Bethlehemite, redemption draws near to
my soul. Come my beloved . . . Wake up, wake up! For your light has come,
awaken, awaken, sing a song, for the glory of the Lord is revealed to you! Come
my beloved . . .[8]

The major theme of this prayer is the anticipation of the coming of the
Messiah and Israel's redemption. As the congregation joins in singing this
hymn, they anticipate the coming of the Messiah the King and the great day
of continual rest inaugurated by his arrival.

The service continues with the blessing of the Messiah, thanking God for
providing the way of salvation through Yeshua:

Blessed are you O Lord our God, king of the universe,
Who has given us the way of salvation in Messiah Yeshua. Amen.[9]

The service then proceeds with the *Shema* prayer coupled with the commandment in Leviticus: you shall love your neighbour as yourself. In these
prayers the congregation joins together in proclaiming the two great commandments taught by Yeshua: to love God with all one's heart, soul and
strength, and to love one's neighbour as oneself:

Hear O Israel, the Lord is our God, the Lord is One. Blessed is the name of his
glorious kingdom for all eternity. And you shall love the Lord your God with all
your heart, with all your soul and with all your might. And these words which I
command you this day, be upon your heart. And you shall teach them diligently
to your children, and speak of them when you sit in your house, when you walk
by the way, when you retire, and when you arise. And you shall bind them for a
sign upon your hand and let them be frontlets between your eyes. And you shall
write them on the doorposts of your house and upon your gates. And you shall
love your neighbour as yourself.[10]

In some congregations other paragraphs of the traditional *Shema* prayer are
recited as well which emphasize the importance of the divine commandments and promise reward for those who are faithful to the Lord.

A traditional Sabbath hymn is sung which sums up the seven blessings
with the attributes of God found in the *Amidah* prayer; this is followed by

Psalm 23. In some congregations a modification of the *Amidah* prayer is recited which emphasizes God's faithfulness, his promise to bring a redeemer, and the resurrection of the dead. In other congregations the entire *Amidah* is recited. Traditionally the *Amidah* consists of three basic sections: praises, petitions and thanksgiving. The three opening blessings exalt God's love, power and holiness. They also affirm his covenant with the patriarchs, redemption through the Messiah, and the resurrection of the dead. Of the middle section, six blessings petition God for personal well-being, six for national well-being and one for him to answer prayer. For Messianic Jews these nineteen benedictions are reminders of God's love, including the Messiah's mission.

The service concludes with the *Kaddish* prayer for the dead. Although this prayer emphasizes praise of God, it also anticipates the arrival of the Messiah's Kingdom and its promise of resurrection and peace. For Messianic Jews it functions as a hymn of praise to God and as a joyous anticipation of the Messiah's Second Coming. At the end of the service the *Alenu* prayer is sung, expressing gratitude and praise of God for choosing the Jews as his people and granting them the *Torah*. This hymn also proclaims God as the ruler of the universe. In addition, it focuses attention on the Messianic age when all the promises of Scripture will be fulfilled and Yeshua will reign over creation. This is followed by various Sabbath hymns.

Sabbath morning service

The service begins with Isaiah 12:3 which rouses the congregation to draw forth living water from the fountains of salvation – Yeshua, the Lord:

> And with joy you shall draw forth water from the fountains of salvation.[11]

A collection of praise verses traditionally chanted on assembling in the synagogue is then sung. This is followed by the *Baruchu* prayer. The congregation then joins in responsive reading of a collection of Scriptural verses from the book of Exodus concerning the Sabbath. This is followed by a New Covenant blessing thanking God for providing the way of salvation through the Messiah, Yeshua:

> Blessed are you O Lord our God, king of the universe,
> Who has given us the way of salvation in Messiah Yeshua. Amen.[12]

As in the Sabbath evening service, the *Shema* prayer proclaims the two great commandments taught by Yeshua: to love God with all one's heart and to love one's neighbour as oneself. This prayer is then followed by the *Magen Avot* prayer:

A shield to our fathers is his word, giving life to the dead in his utterance. The holy king, that there is none like unto him, gives rest to his people on his holy *Shabbat*, for he was pleased with them to grant them rest. Before him we shall serve with reverence and fear, and we will give thanks to his name every day continually, with due blessings upon him. God of grateful praise, master of peace, who sanctifies the *Shabbat* and blesses the seventh day, and who gives rest in holiness to a people full of delight, in commemoration of the work of creation.[13]

Psalm 23 is then recited responsively:

The Lord is my shepherd, I shall not want.
He makes me lie down in green pastures, he leads me beside the still waters.
He restores my soul, he leads me in the paths of righteousness for his name's sake.
Even though I walk through the valley of the shadow of death, I will fear no evil, for you are with me; your rod and your staff they comfort me.
You prepare a table before me in the presence of my enemies; you anoint my head with oil; my cup overflows.
Surely goodness and grace will follow me all the days of my life; and I will dwell in the house of the Lord for ever.[14]

Several other prayers are then recited prior to the *Amidah* prayer which recalls the patriarchs, Abraham, Isaac and Jacob, God's might, salvation, and the resurrection of the dead.

The *Kedushah* prayer which was instituted by the Men of the Great Assembly during the period of the Second Temple speaks of God's holiness and contains several verses from the books of the prophets:

We will sanctify Your name in this world even as it is sanctified in the heavens above, as it is written by Your prophet, and they call to each other saying:
Holy, holy, holy is the Lord of Hosts; the whole earth is full of his glory.
Blessed is the glory of the Lord from his place.
From your heavenly abode you will appear O our king, and reign over us for we wait for you. When will you reign over Zion? Soon, even in our days, may you dwell there for ever and ever. May you be exalted and sanctified with Jerusalem your city, from generation to generation and for all eternity. May our eyes see your kingdom, as it is expressed in the songs of your might, by the hand of David, your righteous anointed:
The Lord shall reign for ever, your God O Zion from generation to generation. Hallelujah![15]

Some Messianic congregations include prayers dealing with the Messiah Yeshua before the reading of the *Torah*:

Blessed are you, O Lord, who has given us the way of salvation in Messiah Yeshua.

He walked among us filled with your Spirit, the only one who ever fulfilled your *Torah*.

He healed the sick and raised the dead. The multitudes of our people sought his touch.

He taught as no man taught. With authority, he brought forth the treasures of the *Torah*.

How the children sought him. The lepers he touched and made clean!

How the despised and outcast found love and release from their sin!

How the hypocrites feared him whose words uncovered their sin!

Despised and rejected, acquainted with grief, he bore the sins of Israel.

All we like sheep have gone astray, turned every one to his own way.

Our iniquities were laid upon the King, the sins of the world, his burden to bear.

He rose from the dead and opened the way to life everlasting, praise his name.

We are in him, his Spirit empowers; new life is ours with joy and peace.

Blessed are you, O Lord, our God, who has given us Messiah Yeshua our King.[16]

This is followed by the disciples' prayer:

Our Father in heaven, may your name be hallowed. May your kingdom come, your will be done on earth, as it is in heaven. Give us today our daily bread. And forgive us our debts, as we have forgiven our debtors. And lead us not into trials but deliver us from evil; for the kingdom, and the power, and the glory is yours for ever. Amen.[17]

The reading of the *Torah* commences with the opening of the ark. The congregation stands and recites a prayer acknowledging God's sovereignty:

There is none like you among the gods, O Lord, and there is nothing like your works. Your kingdom is an everlasting kingdom, and your dominion is throughout all generations. The Lord reigns, the Lord has reigned, the Lord will reign for ever and ever. The Lord will give strength unto his people; the Lord will bless his people with peace.[18]

This is followed by a process during which the *Torah* scroll is carried around the synagogue. In the processional, homage is paid to the *Torah*, the word of God, which represents the living word, Yeshua. As the *Torah* passes by, it is traditional to kiss it by placing a corner of the prayer shawl, a prayer book, the Bible or one's hand on the cover of the *Torah*, and then kissing that which was used to touch the *Torah*. During the procession the following prayer is recited:

When the ark would travel, Moses would say, 'Arise O Lord, and let your enemies be scattered, and let them that hate you flee from you.' For from Zion will go forth the *Torah,* and the word of the Lord from Jerusalem. Blessed be he, who in his holiness, gave the *Torah* to his people Israel.[19]

Before the reading of the *Torah,* the traditional blessing is recited:

Bless the Lord the blessed one.
Blessed is the Lord, the blessed one, for all eternity.
Blessed are you O Lord our God, king of the universe, who has chosen us from all peoples and given us his *Torah,* blessed are you O Lord, giver of the *Torah.*[20]

The *Torah* portion is then chanted, and the traditional blessing is said following the *Torah* reading:

Blessed are you O Lord our God, king of the universe, who has given us a *Torah* of truth, and has planted eternal life in our midst, blessed are you O Lord, giver of the *Torah.*[21]

The *Torah* is then lifted up and the congregation rises. The person who lifted the *Torah* then sits down. The *Haftarah* blessing is then recited:

Blessed are you O Lord our God, king of the universe, who selected good prophets, and was pleased with their words which were spoken truthfully. Blessed are you O Lord, who chooses the *Torah,* your servant Moses, your people Israel, and prophets of truth and righteousness.[22]

This is followed by a reading from the prophetic books and a further *Haftarah* blessing:

Blessed are you O Lord our God, king of the universe, rock of all eternities, faithful in all generations, the trustworthy God, who says and does, who speaks and makes it come to pass, all of whose words are true and righteous. Faithful are you O Lord our God, and faithful are your words, for not one word of yours is turned back unfulfilled. For you are a faithful and compassionate God and king, blessed are you O Lord, the God who is faithful in all his words.[23]

If a section of the New Testament (*Brit Chadasha*) is read, the following blessing is recited:

Blessed are you O Lord our God, king of the universe, who has given us Messiah Yeshua and the commandments of the New Covenant, blessed are you O Lord, giver of the New Covenant.[24]

Following this reading, another blessing is recited:

Blessed are you O Lord our God, king of the universe, who has given us the word of truth and has planted everlasting life in our midst, blessed are you O Lord, giver of the New Covenant.[25]

The *Torah* is then returned to the ark with the appropriate blessings. In some congregations the following prayer is recited after the *Torah* is returned:

When the ark rested, Moses would say: 'Return, O Lord to the myriads of Israel's families.' Arise, O Lord to your resting place, you and your mighty ark. Clothe your priests with righteousness. May those who have experienced your faithful love shout for joy. For the sake of your servant David, don't delay the return of your Messiah.[26]

The service then continues with the *Kaddish* prayer, which expresses praise of God and hope in the Messiah:

Magnified and sanctified be his great name in the world which he has created according to his will. May he establish his kingdom during your life and during your days, and during the life of the whole house of Israel, even swiftly and soon, and say amen.
Let his great name be blessed for ever and to all eternity. Blessed, praised, and glorified, exalted, extolled and honoured, magnified and lauded be the name of the Holy One, blessed is he, though he be high above all the blessings and songs, praises, and consolations which are uttered in the world, and say amen.
May he who makes peace in his high places make peace upon us and upon all Israel, and say amen.[27]

This is followed by a hymn of praise and worship to the living God:

There is none like our God, there is none like our Lord, there is none like our king, there is none like our deliverer.
Who is like our God? Who is like our Lord? Who is like our king? Who is like our deliverer?
Let us give thanks to our God, let us give thanks to our Lord, let us give thanks to our king, let us give thanks to our deliverer.
Blessed be our God, blessed be our Lord, blessed be our king, blessed be our deliverer.
You are our God, you are our Lord, you are our king, you are our deliverer.
You are he to whom our fathers offered before you the fragrant incense.[28]

The service continues with the *Alenu* prayer, the latter part of which focuses attention on Messianic redemption:

It is incumbent upon us to praise the Master of all, to exalt the creator of the world, for he has made us distinct from the nations and unique among the families of the earth. Our destiny is not like theirs, our calling is our task.

We bow down and acknowledge before the king of kings that there is none like him. For he stretched forth the heavens like a tent and established the earth. Truly there is none like our Lord and king.

As the *Torah* says, 'You shall know this day and reflect in your heart that it is the Lord who is God in the heavens above and on the earth beneath, there is none else.'

We hope, O Lord our God, to soon behold your majestic glory when all abominations shall be removed and all false gods shall be at an end.

Then shall the world be perfected under the rule of the Lord Almighty and all mankind shall call upon your name. For to you every knee must bow and every tongue declare that you are God.

Reign over us soon and for ever. May the kingdom of David's greater son be established for ever.

For then shall the words be fulfilled, 'The Lord shall be king for ever', and 'The Lord shall be king over all the earth; on that day the Lord shall be one, and his name one.'[29]

This is followed by the *Yigdal*, which extols God and glorifies the Messianic age:

Exalt the living God and praise him.
He exists without time, God's existence is eternal.
He is unique, and no oneness is like his oneness.
He has no semblance of body, nor any body.
Nothing compares to his holiness.
He was before all things which were created.
He was first, without beginning.
He is the Lord eternal, and all creatures
Declare his greatness and kingship.
Abundant prophecy he gave
To the men of his choice and his glory.
There never arose in Israel one as Moses,
A prophet and beholder of his image.
The *Torah* of truth he gave to his people.
God gave it through his prophet, his faithful servant.
God will not replace, nor change
His law for ever for any other.
He inspects and knows our secrets,
He perceives the end of things at their birth.
He rewards the righteous man for his deeds.
He gives to the evil, evil for his deeds.
At the end of days he will send our Messiah,

To save those who wait for his final help.
The dead, God will revive in great mercy.
Blessed for ever and ever be his name and his glory.[30]

The *Shabbat Kiddush* is then recited, followed by the chanting of *Adon Olam*:

Lord of the world, the king supreme
Before all creation came to be
When by his will all things were wrought
The name of our king was first made known.

And when this age shall cease to be
He still shall reign in majesty
He was, he is and he will be
All glorious eternally.

Incomparable, the Lord is one
No other can his nature share
Without beginning, without end
Unto him all strength and majesty.

He is my living God who saves
My rock when grief or sorrows fall
My banner and my refuge strong
My cup of life whenever I call.

And in his hand I place my life
Both when I sleep and when I wake
And with my soul and body too
God is with me, there is no fear.[31]

The service concludes with the Aaronic Blessing:

The Lord bless you and keep you.
The Lord make his face shine upon you and be gracious to you,
The Lord lift up his countenance upon you and give you peace.[32]

Havdalah

The *Havdalah* service takes place at the end of the Sabbath. The braided *Havdalah* candle symbolizes the joining together of believers with the Messiah who is the light of the world. The spice box reminds the faithful of the sweetness of *Shabbat*. The service begins with the lighting of the candle, and the following prayer is recited over a cup of wine:

Behold God is my salvation, I will trust and not be afraid; for the Lord my God is my strength and my song, and he also has become my salvation. And with joy you shall draw forth water from the springs of salvation. Salvation is the Lord's; upon your people be your blessing, Selah. The Lord of hosts is with us, a stronghold for us is the God of Jacob, Selah. Lord of hosts, praised is the man who trusts in you. Lord save, and may the king answer us on the day when we call. The Jews had light and gladness, joy and honour, so may it be for us. I will lift up the cup of salvation and will call on the name of the Lord our God, king of the universe, who creates the fruit of the vine.[34]

The cup is then set down, and the spice box is held up as the following prayer is chanted:

Blessed are you O Lord our God, king of the universe, who creates species of spices.[34]

The spice box is passed to all worshippers. Then it is set aside and the following blessing is chanted:

Blessed are you O Lord our God, king of the universe, who creates the lights of fire.[35]

The cup is lifted, and the following prayer is chanted:

Blessed are you O Lord our God, king of the universe, who makes a distinction between the holy and the secular, light and darkness, Israel and the nations, the seventh day and the six days of labour. Blessed are you O Lord, who makes a distinction between holy and secular.[36]

The wine is drunk and the light extinguished. The service concludes with the singing of the song *Eliahu ha-Navi*, extolling the coming of the Messiah:

Elijah the prophet, Elijah the Teesh-bite, Elijah from Giladi. Quickly in our day come to us, with the Messiah, son of David.[37]

9 Pilgrim festivals

Passover

According to the book of Deuteronomy, Jews are to celebrate three pilgrim festivals each year: 'Three times each year shall all your males appear before the Lord your God at the place which he will choose, at the feast of unleavened bread, at the feast of weeks, and at the feast of booths' (Deuteronomy 16:16). On the basis of this commandment large numbers of pilgrims went to Jerusalem during the First and Second Temple periods from throughout the Holy Land and Babylonia. There they assembled in the Temple area to offer sacrifice and pray to God.

The first of these festivals is Passover, which is celebrated for eight days from 15 to 22 of *Nisan*. In preparation for Passover, Jewish law stipulates that all leaven must be removed from the house. Some Messianic Jews who seek to participate fully in the celebration of the holy day begin by cleansing all leaven from the house. Floors are swept and vacuumed; cupboards are cleared of all products containing leaven; pots and dishes are washed to remove any possible fragments of leaven. Such actions are understood symbolically as a process of spiritual cleansing.

The first night of Passover is celebrated in a home ceremony referred to as the *seder*. This is done to fulfil the biblical commandment to relate the story of the Exodus to one's son: 'And you shall tell thy son on the day, saying: "It is because of what the Lord did for me when I came out of Egypt"' (Exodus 13:8). The order of the service dates back to Temple times. The symbols placed on the *seder* table serve to remind those present of Egyptian bondage, God's redemption, and the celebration in Temple times. They consist of:

1. Three *matzot*: these three pieces of unleavened bread are placed on top of one another, usually in a special cover. The upper and lower *matzot* symbolize the double portion of manna provided for the Israelites in the wilderness. The middle *matzah* represents the 'bread of affliction'. The smaller part is eaten to comply with the commandment to eat *matzah*. The larger part is set aside for the *afikomen*, which recalls Temple times when the meal was completed with the eating of the *paschal* lamb.
2. Four cups of wine: according to tradition, each Jew must drink four cups of wine at the *seder*.

3. The cup of Elijah: this cup symbolizes the hospitality awaiting the passer-by and wayfarer.
4. Bitter herbs: these symbolize the bitterness of Egyptian slavery.
5. Parsley: this is dipped in salt water and eaten after the *Kiddush*.
6. *Haroset*: this is a mixture of apples, nuts, cinnamon and wine. It is a reminder of the bricks and mortar that Jews were forced to use in Egypt.
7. Roasted shankbone: this symbolizes the *paschal* offering.
8. Roasted egg: this commemorates the festival sacrifice in the Temple.
9. Salt water: this symbolizes the salt that was offered with all sacrifices. It also symbolizes the salt water of the tears of the ancient Israelites.

At the *seder*, the *Haggadah* (Passover prayer-book) details the order of service, which begins with the lighting of the candles, and is followed by a prayer about redemption:

> Blessed are you O Lord our God, ruler of the universe, who has set us apart by his word, and in whose name we light the festival lights.
> As light for the festival of redemption is kindled by the hand of a woman, we remember that our redeemer, the light of the world, came into the world as the promised seed of a woman.[1]

The *Kiddush* for Passover is then recited; this recalls Yeshua's final act among his disciples:

> As the Lord spoke these words of encouragement to Moses, he revealed to his servant the plan by which he would redeem the children of Israel.
> 'I will bring you out from under the yoke of the Egyptians . . .
> I will free you from being slaves . . .
> I will redeem you with an outstretched arm . . .
> I will take you as my own people, and I will be your God . . .'
> At Passover, we celebrate these promises of redemption and relationship by drinking from our cups four times. With each cup, let us remember the union that God desires.
> Let us lift up our first cup together and bless the name of the Lord!
> Blessed are you O Lord our God, ruler of the universe, who creates the fruit of the vine.
> As he began his final Passover *seder*, Yeshua the Messiah shared a cup with his disciples and said to them, 'Take this and divide it among you. For I tell you I will not drink again of the fruit of the vine until the kingdom of God comes.'[2]

This is followed by the washing of hands, which recalls Yeshua's compassion:

Let us now offer the bowl of water to one another and share in this hand-washing ceremony.

Let us also reflect upon the gesture of humility and the lesson of commitment made by Messiah Yeshua, when, on that night, he laid aside his garments and girded himself with a towel. After that, he poured water into a basin and began to wash his disciples' feet, drying them with the towel that was wrapped around him. 'Do you understand what I have done for you?' he asked them. 'You call me "teacher" and "Lord", and rightly so, for that is what I am. Now that I, your Lord and teacher, have washed your feet, you should also wash one another's feet.'[3]

The blessing over parsley is then recited, followed by the traditional four questions about the meaning of the Passover *seder* which are asked by the youngest person present. These questions are answered with reference to Yeshua's Messiahship:

This is the bread of affliction, the poor bread which our fathers ate in the land of Egypt. Let all who are hungry come and eat. Let all who are in need share in the hope of Passover.

Three *matzot* are wrapped together for Passover. There are various explanations for this ceremony. The rabbis call these three a 'unity'. Some consider it a unity of the patriarchs – Abraham, Isaac, and Jacob. Other explain it as a unity of worship – the priests, the Levites, and the people of Israel. We who know Messiah can see in this the unique tri-unity of God – Father, Son and Spirit. Three in one. In the *matzah* we can see a picture of the Messiah.[4]

When the leader removes and breaks the middle *matzah*, he states:

Just as the middle piece of the bread of affliction is broken, Messiah, too, was afflicted and broken. One half is now called the *afikomen* – 'the coming one'. It is wrapped in a white cloth just as the Messiah's body was wrapped for burial . . . But just as the *afikomen* will return to complete our Passover *seder*, so the sinless Messiah rose from the dead to ascend into heaven.[5]

A blessing is then recited over the *maror* (bitter herbs); in the prayers which follow, reference is made to Yeshua's presence at the Passover feast:

While they were reclining at the table eating, Yeshua said, 'I tell you the truth, one of you will betray me – one who is eating with me.' They were saddened and one by one they said to him, 'Surely, not I?' 'It is one of the twelve', he replied, 'one who dips (unleavened) bread into the bowl with me.'[6]

The *Haggadah* continues with a discussion of reclining at the *seder* meal and is followed by a story of the Passover. This is followed by a recitation about the plagues and an account of the Passover Lamb which is associated with Yeshua:

We who have trusted Yeshua the Messiah believe he is the lamb of God, our Passover. Like the ancient Israelites, we know that it was God himself, and not an angel, God himself, and not a seraph, God himself, and not a messenger, who achieved final redemption from sin and death. God himself, through Yeshua, who takes away the sin of the world.[7]

The *Dayenu* prayer is then recited which includes a reference to Yeshua:

Blessed are you, O God, for you have, in mercy, supplied all our needs. You have given us Messiah, forgiveness for sin, life abundant and life everlasting. Hallelujah.[8]

Once the meal is eaten, the *seder* continues with a section dealing with the *afikomen*:

It is time for us to share the *afikomen*, the dessert, the final food eaten at Passover. It is shared as the Passover lamb was shared from the time of the exodus until the destruction of the Temple. It is said that the taste of the *afikomen* should linger in our mouths. Messiah broke the *matzah* and gave thanks to the Lord.[9]

The leader then says:

It was then that Messiah added the words,
   'This is my body given for you; do this in remembrance of me.'
Let us now eat the *matzah*, meditating on the broken body of the Lamb of God who takes away the sin of the world. Let us allow the taste to linger in our mouths.[10]

Blessings are then made over the Cup of Redemption:

Let us fill our cups for the third time this evening. This is the cup of redemption, symbolizing the blood of the Passover lamb. It was the cup 'after the supper', with which Messiah identified himself . . .
The prophet Isaiah reminds us,
   'Surely the arm of the Lord is not too short to save . . . '
It is our own righteousness that falls short.
Though the Lord searched, He could find no one to intercede.
   ' . . . so his own arm worked salvation for him,
   and his own righteousness sustained him.'
Yeshua the Messiah lifted the cup saying,
   'This cup is the new covenant in my blood,
   which is poured out for you.'
Just as the blood of the lamb brought salvation in Egypt, so Messiah's atoning death can bring salvation to all who believe.[11]

The service continues with the welcoming of the prophet Elijah. Here reference is made to Elijah's announcement of the coming of the Messiah:

> Elijah did not see death, but was swept up to heaven by a great whirlwind, in a chariot of fire. It has been our hope that Elijah would come at Passover, to announce the Messiah, Son of David.
> Before the birth of John the Baptizer, an angel of the Lord said,
> 'And he will go on before the Lord, in the spirit and power of Elijah ... to make ready a people prepared for the Lord.'
> Later Yeshua spoke of John,
> 'And if you are willing to accept it, he is the Elijah who was to come.'
> It was this same John who saw Yeshua and declared,
> 'Look, the lamb of God, who takes away the sin of the world!'[12]

The service concludes with the *Hallel* and the blessing over the fourth cup and the traditional proclamation: 'Next Year in Jerusalem!'

Counting of the *omer*

Following the Passover festival, the Israelites were commanded to count 49 days from the second day of Passover (when the *omer* was brought to the Temple). The fiftieth day was celebrated as the wheat harvest. As Leviticus states, this first of the barley harvest was to be brought as an offering to the priest in the Temple:

> The Lord said to Moses, 'Say to the people of Israel, when you come into the land which I give you and reap its harvest, you shall bring the sheaf of the first fruits of your harvest to the priest, and he shall wave the sheaf before the Lord, that you may find acceptance; on the morrow after the Sabbath, the priest shall wave it. And on the day when you wave the sheaf, you shall offer a male lamb a year old without blemish as a burnt offering to the Lord. (Leviticus 23:9–12)

Jewish observance of this festival varied through the centuries. In ancient times, it was an elaborate ceremony involving the offering of a thanksgiving tithe. According to rabbinic tradition, a priest would meet a group of Jewish worshippers on the edge of the city and lead them to the Temple mount. As they progressed, the priest would hold a praise service accompanied by music, psalms and dance. Once they arrived at the Temple, the priest would take the sheaves and wave them in every direction. In time, however, there was considerable disagreement about when this counting of the *omer* was to begin, a dispute which was resolved once the Temple was destroyed in 70 CE.

In traditional synagogues, the counting of the *omer* begins on the second night of Passover at the second *seder* with the recitation of the blessing:

Blessed art thou, O Lord our God, king of the universe, who has set us apart by your commandments and has commanded us concerning the counting of the sheaf.[13]

This blessing continues to be recited every evening for the next 49 days with an adjustment for the days that have elapsed. This period is conceived as a time of mourning since a number of tragedies occurred during this season including the plague which struck the disciples of Rabbi Akiva during the revolt against Rome in 135 CE. The thirty-third day of the *omer*, however, is an exception; according to tradition, on this day the plague was lifted from Akiva's armies. Traditional Jews do not shave, cut their hair, or celebrate weddings during this period.

Among a number of Messianic Jews, this minor festival has considerable importance since it is associated with Yeshua's resurrection. In their view, 1 Corinthians 15:20–23 links the counting of the *omer* to Yeshua's ministry. In this passage Paul teaches about the doctrine of the resurrection:

But in fact Christ has been raised from the dead, the first fruits of those who have fallen asleep. For as by a man came death, by a man has come also the resurrection of the dead. For as in Adam all die, so also in Christ . . . the first fruits, then at his coming those who belong to Christ. (1 Corinthians 15:20–23)

Here in this discussion it appears that Paul visualizes Yeshua's resurrection as the fulfilment of the feast of the first fruits. This is in line with Yeshua's parable which was spoken to his disciples as they had come to celebrate the Passover, just before the counting of the *omer*:

And Jesus answered them, 'The hour has come for the Son of man to be glorified. Truly, truly, I say to you, unless a grain of wheat falls into the earth and dies, it remains alone; but if it dies, it bears much fruit . . . And I, when I am lifted up from the earth, will draw all men to myself'. (John 12:23–24, 32)

The connection between Yeshua's resurrection and the festival of the counting of the *omer* is also highlighted by the gospel narrative concerning Jesus' burial and resurrection. According to tradition, Yeshua celebrated his last *seder* with the disciples on the evening of 14 *Nisan*, was arrested that night and was brought before the Roman authorities. The next morning he was crucified and died that afternoon just before the weekly Sabbath. His body was buried, left in the tomb through the next day until the women came to the tomb to find it open. On this account, Yeshua was in the tomb for approximately three days: part of Friday until sundown, sundown Friday to sundown Saturday, and the next day starting at sundown. Although his empty tomb was discovered on Sunday, Yeshua could have been raised from the dead any time from sundown on Saturday. Thus Yeshua died on Passover and was risen from the dead on the festival of first fruits.

Given the significance of this ancient festival a number of Messianic Jews celebrate this festival by saying the traditional blessings while lifting up sheaves of barley or a cup of grain, and subsequently chanting the appropriate blessings during the period of counting of the *omer*. In the service for this festival, the following prayer is recited:

> Sovereign of the universe, as we begin to count the days of the *omer*, we recall the time when our people lived in the Land of Israel and the first fruits were presented to you. May this observance serve as another reminder of the need to reclaim the Holy Land so that it may again flow with milk and honey. May our love for Israel's land quicken our love for the *Torah*, Israel's heritage. As in the past, may *Eretz Yisrael* become the centre of our spiritual life, and may your word go forth from Zion, O Lord, revealing your will to all men.
>
> Let us see the days of our Messiah when these things shall take place. Speedily cause the offspring of David, your servant, to flourish and lift up his glory by your divine help because we wait for your deliverance all the day. Deserving of praise are you, O Lord, who causes the strength of our salvation to flourish.[14]

Shavuot

The festival of *Shavuot* (Feast of Weeks) is celebrated for two days. The word '*shavuot*' means weeks – seven weeks are counted from the bringing of the *omer* on the second day of Passover. The festival is also referred to as Pentecost, a Greek word meaning 'fiftieth' since it was celebrated on the fiftieth day. Symbolically the day commemorates the culmination of the process of emancipation which began with the Exodus at Passover. It is concluded with the proclamation of the Law on Mount Sinai.

During the Temple period farmers set out for Jerusalem to offer a selection of first ripe fruits as a thank-offering. In post-Temple times, the emphasis shifted to the festival's identification as the anniversary of the giving of the Law on Mount Sinai. In some traditional Jewish communities it is a practice to remain awake during *Shavuot* nights. Today, in those communities where this custom is observed, a passage of the *Talmud* or other rabbinic literature is recited. Some congregations in the diaspora read a book of psalms on the second night. Synagogues themselves are decorated with flowers or plants, and dairy food is consumed during the festival. The liturgical readings for the festival include the Ten Commandments. The book of Ruth and the book of Ezekiel are also recited. In a number of Jewish communities this festival marks the graduation of young people from formal synagogue education.

An important discussion of *Shavuot* is found in the book of Acts:

> When the day of Pentecost had come, they were all together in one place. And suddenly a sound came from heaven like the rush of a mighty wind, and it filled

all the house where they were sitting. And there appeared to them tongues as of fire, distributed and resting on each one of them. And they were all filled with the Holy Spirit and began to speak in other tongues, as the Spirit gave them utterance. Now there were dwelling in Jerusalem Jews, devout men from every nation under heaven . . . And all were amazed and perplexed, saying to one another, 'What does this mean?' (Acts 2:1–12)

Here the focus is on the religious significance of this festival. After having heard the traditional reading of the book of Ezekiel for *Shavuot* in which the prophet describes the vision of the divine chariot, the followers of Yeshua experienced an overpowering experience of the Spirit. These events were the first fruits of the spiritual harvest of the Messianic era.

Among Messianic Jews many of the traditional observances for this festival are followed. On the day before the start of *Shavuot*, a number of preparations are customarily made: the dinner table is set with best linens and dishes, and in some families the house is decorated with fresh flowers. At sunset, the family gathers around the dinner table. The candles are lit and the following blessings are recited:

Blessed art thou, O Lord our God, king of the universe, who has sanctified us by thy commandments and commanded us to be a light unto the nations and has given us Yeshua, our Messiah, the Light of the world.[15]

On the first night, the following words are added:

Blessed are thou, O Lord our God, king of the universe, who has given us life, sanctified us and brought us to this season.[16]

The blessings over the wine and the bread are then chanted, and the festival dinner is served, which includes various dairy dishes.

In many Messianic congregations the evening service for *Shavuot* contains the *Ha-Elohim* prayer:

In the past God spoke to our fathers through the prophets, at many times in various ways; but now in the end of days he has spoken to us by the Messiah, his Son, whom he appointed the heir of all things and through whom he made the universe. The Son is the full radiance of God's glory and the flawless manifestation of his reality. He sustains all things by his powerful word. After he made atonement for sins, he sat down in the place of authority beside the Majesty in heaven.[17]

In some Messianic congregations, believers gather together after the evening service to ponder the blessings of the Holy Spirit which are commemorated by this festival.

Sukkot

The festival *Sukkot* is also prescribed in the Bible: 'On the fifteenth day of this seventh month and for seven days is the feast of tabernacles to the Lord' (Leviticus 23:34). This festival commemorates God's protection of the Israelites during their sojourn in the desert. The book of Leviticus commands that Jews are to construct booths during this period as a reminder that the people of Israel dwelt in booths when they fled from Egypt (Leviticus 23:42–43).

During *Sukkot* a booth (*sukkah*) is constructed and its roof covered with branches of trees and plants. During the festival, meals are to be eaten inside the *sukkah*. Leviticus also declares that various agricultural species should play a part in the observance of this festival:

> And you shall take on the first day the fruit of goodly trees, branches of palm trees, and boughs of leafy trees, and willows of the brook; and you shall rejoice before the Lord your God seven days. (Leviticus 23:40)

In compliance with this injunction the four species are used in the traditional Jewish liturgy – palm, myrtle, willow and citron. On each day of the festival the *lulav* (palm branch) is waved in every direction before and during the *Hallel* prayer – this symbolizes God's presence throughout the world. Holding the four species, Jews make one circuit around the *Torah* which is carried on the *bimah* (platform) on each of the first six days. During this circuit, *hoshanah* prayers are recited. On the seventh day of *Sukkot*, *Hoshanah Rabbah*, seven circuits are made around the *Torah* while reciting *hoshanah* prayers.

In conformity with Leviticus 23:36, 'On the eighth day you shall hold a holy convocation . . . it is a solemn assembly', *Shemini Atseret* is celebrated, and a prayer for rain is recited. The next day is *Simhat Torah*; on this joyous occasion the reading of the *Torah* is completed. The *Torah* scrolls are taken out of the ark and members of the congregation carry them in a procession around the synagogue.

In the New Testament, Yeshua appears on the seventh day of the *Sukkot* festival declaring that the Spirit would be poured out upon those who trust in the Lord:

> On the last day of the feast, the great day, Jesus stood up and proclaimed: 'If any one thirst, let him come to me and drink. He who believes in me, as the scripture has said, "Out of his heart shall flow rivers of living water"'. Now this he said about the Spirit, which those who believed in him were to receive; for as yet the Spirit had not been given, because Jesus was not yet glorified. (John 7:37–39)

This passage emphasizes that the days of Messianic redemption have come, when the waters of the Holy Spirit will be poured out on all Israel.

During this time God will dwell among his people under the rule of the Messiah.

In the book of Revelation such a vision of God's presence as symbolized by *Sukkot* is described in detail:

> Then I saw a new heaven and a new earth; for the first heaven and the first earth had passed away, and the sea was no more. And I saw the holy city, new Jerusalem, coming down out of heaven from God, prepared as a bride adorned for her husband; and I heard a loud voice from the throne saying, 'Behold, the dwelling of God is with men. He will dwell with them, and they shall be his people, and God himself will be with them.' (Revelation 21:1–3)

Given that the major element of this festival is the *sukkah*, many Messianic Jews build a *sukkah* on the side of their homes as free-standing structures. The outer frame is normally assembled from various materials which is fortified by leaves or traditional palm branches. In many cases Messianic Jews begin constructing the *sukkah* immediately after *Yom Kippur*, inviting believers to a *sukkah* decorating party.

As the festival approaches, a holiday dinner is prepared, the table set, and the meal served. As on other festive occasions, a blessing is recited over wine and bread. The first day of the festival is greeted with a blessing thanking God for bringing his people to this joyous celebration. Distinctive prayers are also chanted for this holy day, including the blessing:

> Blessed art thou, O Lord our God, king of the universe, who has set us apart by thy commandments and commanded us to dwell in the *sukkah*.[18]

In some congregations the following prayer is said prior to waving the *lulav*:

> Praise be to the Lord, the God of Israel, because he has come and redeemed his people. He has raised up a horn of salvation for us in the house of his servant David (as he said through his holy prophets of long ago), salvation from our enemies and from the hand of all who hate us – to show mercy to our fathers and to remember his holy covenant, the oath he swore to our father Abraham: to rescue us from the hand of our enemies, and to enable us to serve him without fear in holiness and righteousness before him all our days.[19]

As the *lulav* (palm branches) and *etrog* (citron) are held up, the following prayer is recited:

> Blessed art thou, O Lord our God, king of the universe, who has set us apart by thy commandments and commanded us to take up the *lulav*.[20]

In many congregations synagogue services are held on the first two days of the festival. For many Messianic Jews, the seventh day, *Hoshanah Rabbah*, and the eighth day, *Shemini Atseret*, also have special significance and services are held, commemorating God's abiding presence with his chosen people. Although *Simhat Torah*, which takes place on the day following *Sukkot,* is not mentioned in Scripture, Messianic Jews celebrate this holy day, affirming the theme of this festival that God's revelation of the *Torah* is to be celebrated with joy and thanksgiving.

10 New Year and Day of Atonement

New Year

In ancient times the Jewish New Year (*Rosh Hashanah*) took place on one day; it is presently observed for two days, marking the beginning of the Ten Days of Penitence which end on the Day of Atonement. According to the *Mishnah*, all human beings will pass before God on the New Year; the *Talmud* expands this idea by stressing the need for self-examination. In rabbinic literature each person stands before the throne of God, and judgement on every person is entered on the New Year and sealed on the Day of Atonement. The tractate *Rosh Hashanah* in the *Talmud* declares that there are three ledgers opened in Heaven: one for the completely righteous who are immediately inscribed and sealed in the Book of Life; another is for the thoroughly wicked who are recorded in the Book of Death; the third is for the ordinary type of person whose fate hangs in the balance and is suspended until the Day of Atonement.

On *Rosh Hashanah* in traditional synagogues the ark curtain, reading desk and *Torah* scroll mantles are decked in white, and the rabbi, cantor and person who blows the *shofar* (ram's horn) all wear a white *kittle* (robe). In the synagogue service the *Amidah* of the *musaf* service contains three sections relating to God's sovereignty, providence and revelation: *Malkhuyyot* deals with God's rule; *Zikhronot* portrays God's remembrance of the ancestors of the Jewish people when he judges each generation; *Shofarot* contains verses relating to the *shofar* and deals with the revelation on Mount Sinai and the Messianic age.

On both days of *Rosh Hashanah* the *shofar* is blown at four points during the service: 30 times after the reading of the Law, 30 times during *musaf*, 30 times after *musaf*, and 10 before *Alenu*. In the liturgy there are three variants of the blowing of the *shofar*: *tekiah* (a long note); *shevarim* (three notes), and *teruot* (nine short notes). According to Maimonides the *shofar* is blown to call sinners to repent. In the Ashkenazi rite the *U-Netanneh Tokef* prayer concludes the service on a hopeful note as congregants declare that repentance, prayer and charity can avert the evil decree.

Traditionally it was the custom to go to the seaside or the banks of a river on the afternoon of the first day. There the ceremony of *Tashlikh* symbolizes the casting of one's sins into a body of water. The prayers for *Tashlikh* and three verses from the book of Micah express confidence in divine forgiveness. In the home after *kiddush* a piece of bread is dipped in honey followed by a piece of apple, and a prayer is recited that the year ahead may be good and sweet.

Among Messianic Jews, the New Year is linked to the future regathering of the believers in Yeshua Messiah. In this connection, Paul appears to link this holy day with this event:

> For the Lord himself will come down from heaven with a rousing cry, with a call from one of the ruling angels, and with God's *shofar*, those who died united with the Messiah will be the first to rise; then we who are left still alive will be caught up with them in the clouds to meet the Lord in the air, and thus we will always be with the Lord. (1 Thessalonians 4:16–18)

In this vision of a future age those who believe in Yeshua will be gathered to meet him in the clouds: those already dead will rise first and be followed by the faithful. This event will be ushered in by the sounding of the *shofar*. Given this interpretation of the Jewish New Year, those who believe in Messiah Yeshua find in this festival the promise of spiritual regeneration and hope for deliverance. Each year they are reminded of God's promise to restore his chosen people at the end of days. Messianic Jews thus celebrate *Rosh Hashanah* as a day of rest, stressing the preparation needed for the return of the Messiah and the resurrection of the dead.

In Messianic congregations preparation starts during the preceding month of *Elul* by sounding the *shofar* on *Shabbat*; in addition, special prayers are recited to cultivate a spirit of repentance. Some Messianic Jews sound *shofars* throughout the month every morning to instil an attitude of penitence. For *Rosh Hashanah* itself extensive preparations are made: the table is set with the best dishes, tablecloth, and two candlesticks. Traditionally the festival candles are lit with the appropriate blessing:

> Deserving of praise are you, O Lord our God, ruler of the universe who has hallowed us by your commandments and has instructed us to kindle the lights for the festival.
> Deserving of praise are you, O Lord our God, ruler of the universe who has kept us alive, sustained us, and privileged us to reach this season.[1]

After the candles are lit, blessings are said over the wine and a special raisin *challah* bread – both the wine and the bread are reminders of the sweetness of the holiday season. This theme is reflected in some of the foods eaten on *Rosh Hashanah*, such as the traditional *tzimmes* made with carrots and honey as well as the honey cake for dessert. During the meal it is customary to dip apples in honey to savour the sweetness that comes from God. After dinner many Messianic Jews worship in the synagogue. The evening service begins with the *Baruchu* followed by the *Shema* and the *Amidah*. The Ark is then opened and the following prayer is recited:

> The Lord is king!
> The Lord was king!
> For ever shall the Lord be king!
>
> Ere space exists, or earth, or sky,
> The Lord is king!
> Ere sun or star shone forth on high,
> The Lord was king!
> When earth shall be a robe outworn,
> And sky shall fade like mists of morn,
> Still shall the Lord for e'er be king!
>
> The Lord is king!
> The Lord was king!
> For ever shall the Lord be king!
>
> When earth he flings mid star-filled space,
> The Lord is king!
> When living creatures there found place,
> The Lord was king,
> When homeward from earth's corners four,
> He calls the scattered folk once more,
> Then shall the Lord for e'er be king!
>
> The Lord is king!
> The Lord was king!
> For ever shall the Lord be king![2]

The *Alenu* and the *Kaddish* are recited; this is followed by the *shofarot* (trumpet verses) followed by the *shofar* blessing:

> Deserving of praise are you, O Lord our God, ruler of the universe, who has set us apart by your commandments and commanded us to hear the sound of the *shofar*.
> Deserving of praise are you, O Lord our God, ruler of the universe, who has kept us alive, sustained us and privileged us to reach this season.[3]

The *shofar* is then sounded and the following blessing recited:

> Just as lightning comes from the east and flashes to the west, so shall the coming of the Son of Man be. The Lord himself will descend from heaven with a shout, with the voice of the archangel, and with the *shofar* of God; and the dead in Messiah shall rise first. Then we who remain alive shall be caught up together with them in the clouds to meet the Lord in the air, and so we shall always be with the Lord.
> May it be your will that the sounding of the *shofar* which we have done will be embroidered in the veil by the appointed angel, as you accepted it, by Elijah of

blessed memory and by Yeshua the Prince of the Face and the one who sits on God's throne. May you be filled with compassion on us. Deserving of praise are you, Lord of compassion.

This day the world was called into being; this day all the creatures of the universe stand in judgement before you as children or as servants. If as children, have pity upon us as a father pities his children; and if as servants, we call upon you to be gracious to us and merciful in judgement of us, O revered and holy God. In Yeshua our Messiah we examine ourselves for the next ten days, and through him, we trust you, our God, to pronounce us righteous.[4]

The service concludes with *Adon Olam* and the Aaronic Blessing.

The *Rosh Hashanah* morning service begins with the *Baruchu* and the *Shema*. This is followed by the *Avinu Malkenu* prayer:

Our father, our king, we have sinned before you.
Our father, our king, we have no king except you.
Our father, our king, deal with us kindly for the sake of your name.
Our father, our king, renew a year of good for us.
Our father, our king, annul every evil decree against us.
Our father our king, exalt the majesty of your Messiah.

Our father, our king, be gracious unto us and answer us, for we are unworthy; deal with us in compassion and faithful love and deliver us.

Our father, our king, forgive and pardon our sins.
Our father, our king, blot out our transgressions, and remove our sins from your sight.

Our father, our king, may we return to you in perfect repentance.
Our father, our king, bring glory to Israel, your people.
Our father, our king, provide us with your abundant blessings.
Our father, our king, grant our prayers for your sake, if not for ours.

Our father, our king, be gracious to us and answer us, for we are unworthy: deal with us in compassion and faithful love and deliver us.[5]

This is followed by the *Torah* service, in which Genesis 22:1–8 is read followed by the *Haftarah* consisting of Jeremiah 31:1–20, 31–40. This is followed by a series of blessings including a prayer for the Messianic era:

Make us joyful, O Lord our God with the prophet Elijah your servant, and with the kingdom of the house of David your anointed. May Elijah come soon and bring joy to our hearts. Allow no stranger to sit on David's throne or inherit his glory. For by your holy name you swore to him that his light would not be quenched for ever. You grant blessings, O Lord, the shield of David.[6]

As an alternative to the traditional *Haftarah* reading, a passage from Hebrews is read, preceded by the *Brit Chadasha* Blessing:

> You grant blessings, O Lord our God, ruler of the universe who has given us Messiah Yeshua and the words of the renewed covenant. You grant blessings, O Lord, giver of the renewed covenant.[7]

This is followed by Hebrews 11:17–19; 9:15, 28:

> By faith Abraham, when he was tested, offered up Isaac, and he who had received the promises was ready to offer up his only son, of whom it was said, 'Through Isaac shall your descendants be named.' He considered that God was able to raise men even from the dead; hence, figuratively speaking, he did receive him back ... Therefore he is the mediator of a new covenant, so that those who are called may receive the promised eternal inheritance, since a death has occurred which redeems them from the transgressions under the first covenant ... So Christ, having been offered once to bear the sins of many, will appear a second time, not to deal with sin but to save those who are eagerly waiting for him.

The *Torah* scroll is then returned to the ark and the following prayer is said:

> When the ark rested, Moses would say: 'Return, O Lord, to the myriads of Israel's families.' Arise, O Lord, to your resting place, you and your mighty ark. Clothe your priests with righteousness. May those who have experienced your faithful love shout for joy. For the sake of your servant David, don't delay the return of your Messiah.[8]

As the ark is closed the following is said:

> You grant blessings, O Lord our God, ruler of the universe who gives us the living word in the Messiah, Yeshua.[9]

The *shofar* is then sounded with the accompanying blessings:

> May it be your will that the sounding of the *shofar*, which we have done will be embroidered in the veil by the appointed angel, as you accepted it by Elijah of blessed memory and by Yeshua, the prince of the face and the one who sits on God's throne. May you be filled with compassion to us. Deserving of praise are you, Lord of compassion.
> This day is the day we commemorate the birth of the world, it is a day when we as children and servants look to the mercy of God for life and forgiveness. In Yeshua our Messiah we examine ourselves for the next ten days and through him we trust God to pronounce us righteous.[10]

The service proceeds with the *Kaddish* and concludes with the 'Lord is King' prayer, the *Adon Olam* and the Aaronic Blessing.

Day of Atonement

The Ten Days of Penitence begin with the New Year and last until the Day of Atonement (*Yom Kippur*). This is considered the most solemn time of the year when all are judged and their fate determined for the coming year. During the Ten Days a number of additions are made to the liturgy in traditional synagogues. The holiest day of the Jewish calendar is the Day of Atonement. Like other major festivals its observance is prescribed in Scripture:

> On the tenth day of this seventh month is the Day of Atonement; . . . and you shall afflict yourselves . . . It shall be to you a sabbath of solemn rest, and you shall afflict yourselves; on the ninth day of the month beginning at evening, from evening to evening. (Leviticus 23:27, 32)

According to the sages, afflicting one's soul involves abstaining from food and drink. Thus every male over the age of 13 and every female over 12 is obliged to fast from sunset until nightfall the next evening. Sick people, however, may take medicine and small amounts of food and drink; similarly, those who are ill may be forbidden to fast.

During the day normal Sabbath prohibitions apply, but worshippers are to abstain from food and drink, marital relations, wearing leather shoes, using cosmetics and lotions, and washing the body except for fingers and eyes. The rabbis stress that the Day of Atonement enables human beings to atone for sins against God; however, regarding transgressions committed against others, pardon cannot be obtained unless forgiveness has been sought from the persons injured: as a consequence, it is customary for Jews to seek reconciliation with anyone they might have offended during the year. Previously lashes were administered in the synagogue to impart a feeling of repentance, but this custom has disappeared.

The *kapparot* ritual still takes place before the Day of Atonement among Sephardi and Eastern communities as well as among some Ashkenazim. During this ceremony a fowl is slaughtered and either eaten before the fast or sold for money which is given to charity – its death symbolizes the transfer of guilt from the person to the bird that has been killed. In many congregations Jews substitute coins for the fowl, and charity boxes are available at the morning and afternoon services before *Yom Kippur*.

Customarily Jews were able to absolve vows on the eve of *Yom Kippur*. Some pious Jews immerse themselves in a *mikveh* (ritual bath) in order to undergo purification before the fast. In the home a final meal is eaten, and prior to lighting the festival candles, a memorial candle is kindled to burn throughout the day. The prayer shawl is worn throughout all the services, and a white curtain adorns the synagogue ark and the scrolls of the Law. The reader's desk and other furnishings are also covered in white. Among Ashkenazim rabbis, cantors and other officiants also wear a white robe.

Among Messianic Jews *Yom Kippur* has important spiritual significance. In Romans Paul explained the meaning of atonement in the context of this holiday:

> Since all have sinned and fall short of the glory of God, they are justified by his grace as a gift through the redemption which is in Christ Jesus, whom God put forward as an expiation by his blood, to be received by faith. This was to show God's righteousness, because in his divine forbearance he had passed over former sins; it was to prove at the present time that he himself is righteous and that he justifies him who has faith in Jesus. (Romans 3:23–26)

Yom Kippur is thus understood as foreshadowing a time when all Israel will accept the atoning sacrifice provided by Yeshua Messiah. This will be an occasion, not simply for the atonement of God's chosen people, but for all peoples. As the Messianic community waits for this day, Messianic Jews celebrate *Yom Kippur* by thanking God for the atonement made possible through Yeshua and by praying that all nations will acknowledge that he is Lord and Saviour.

Given this understanding of *Yom Kippur*, believers in Yeshua follow many of the customs observed by traditional Jews. As with the traditional Jewish community, the Days of Repentance are perceived as having particular spiritual meaning. On the evening of *Yom Kippur* special arrangements are made. Because it is referred to as *Shabbat*, the usual customs for the Sabbath are followed. The table is set with white linen and silver. *Kiddush* is recited over the wine and the bread. Dinner is served which contains sweet dishes symbolizing the sweet new year of forgiveness. As the sun sets, the fast commences. The evening *Yom Kippur* service celebrates atonement in Yeshua Messiah. On *Yom Kippur* the faithful pray for forgiveness and rejoice in God's salvation through his Anointed. During the late afternoon worshippers gather together for the final service.

In Messianic synagogues the service for *Yom Kippur* begins with the lighting of the candles:

> Deserving of praise are you, O Lord our God, ruler of the universe, who has hallowed us by your word, and instructed us to kindle the light of the Day of Atonement.
> Deserving of praise are you, O Lord our God, ruler of the universe, who kept us alive, and sustained us, and privileged us to reach this season.[11]

This is followed by the *Kol Nidre* prayer:

All vows, oaths, and pledges which we may be forced to take between this *Yom Kippur* and the next, of these we repent and these we renounce. Let them all be nullified and voided, and let us be absolved and released. Let such personal vows, pledges, and oaths be considered neither vows, nor pledges, nor oaths.[12]

This is followed by the prayer 'Our God and God of our fathers':

Yes, it is true, our evil tendency influences us;
Clear us, merciful one, so answer us:
I forgive.

Silence the accuser, let an advocate take his place;
O Lord, give our advocate your support and say:
I forgive.

Confer on the merit of our Messiah.
Remove all sin and loudly proclaim from heaven,
I forgive.

Good and forgiving one, pardon and forgive sinners.
O God give heed, and also reply from the heights,
I forgive.

Heal my wound, hide deeply my iniquity;
For your name, on my behalf say the word:
I forgive.

Blot out evil from among your people;
Show your faithful love and your glory and say,
I forgive.

Cleanse every evil quickly as mist vanishes,
Blot out the guilt of a people delivered and say:
I forgive.

Remember the atonement of our Messiah Yeshua,
'Father forgive' was on his lips, so say to us,
'I forgive.'[13]

The service continues with the *Baruchu*, *Shema*, *Amidah* and the *Kedushah* prayer. This is followed by the prayer 'We are guilty':

We are guilty of . . .
Arrogance, blasphemy, corruption, and dereliction; evil counsel, frivolity, guile, hypocrisy, and insolence; jealousy, levity, mendacity, nefariousness, obstinacy, profanity, querulousness, rebelliousness, slander, and transgression; unrighteousness, villany, wrongdoing, and zealotry.
We have turned aside from your commandments and your good instructions,

and it has not profited us. But you are just concerning all that is come upon us; for you have done truly, but we have dealt wickedly.[14]

The *Al Het* prayer is then recited:

May it be your will, Lord our God and God of our fathers, to forgive all our sins, to pardon all our iniquities, and to cleanse us from all our sins.

For the sin we have committed in your sight forcibly or willingly,
And for the sin we have committed against you with hard heartedness.
For the sin we committed in your sight without intention,
And for the sin we committed against you by idle talk.
For the sin we committed in your sight by lustful actions,
And for the sin we committed against you by offensive speech.
For the sin we committed in your sight by oppressing others,
And for the sin we committed by contempt for parents or teachers.
For the sin we committed in your sight by lewd association,
And for the sin we committed against you by insincere confession.
For the sin we committed against you by violence,
And for the sin we committed against you by defaming your name.

Forgive us all sins, O God of forgiveness, and cleanse us.

For the sin we committed in your sight by fraud and deception,
And for the sin we committed against you by bribery.
For the sin we committed in your sight by mocking,
And for the sin we committed against you by slander.
For the sin we committed in your sight by usury and interest,
And for the sin we committed against you by pride.
For the sin we committed in your sight by our manner of speech,
And for the sin we committed against you by wanton glances.
For the sin we committed in your sight by arrogance,
And for the sin we committed against you by scornful defiance.

Forgive us all sins, O God of forgiveness, and cleanse us.

For the sin we committed in your sight by shirking responsibility,
And for the sin we committed against you in passing judgement.
For the sin we committed in your sight by plotting against others,
And for the sin we committed against you by gross selfishness.
For the sin we committed in your sight by foolishness,
And for the sin we committed against you by being stubborn.
For the sin we committed against you by running to do evil,
And for the sin we committed against you by tale-bearing.
For the sin we committed in your sight by swearing falsely,
And for the sin we committed by groundless hatred.
For the sin we committed in your sight by breach of trust,
And for the sin we committed against you by a confused heart.

Forgive us all sins, O God of forgivenesss, and cleanse us.

For the sins requiring a burnt-offering,
And for the sins requiring a sin-offering.
For the sins requiring varying offerings,
And for the sins requiring guilt offerings.
For the sins requiring corporal punishment,
And for the sins requiring forty lashes.
For the sins requiring premature death,
And for the sins requiring excommunication and childlessness.

Forgive us for all these sins, for we read of our Messiah,
He was wounded for our transgressions, he was bruised for our iniquities, the
chastisement of our sins was on him, and with his stripes we are healed.[15]

A section of Leviticus is then read which deals with sacrifice; this is
followed by a passage from Hebrews with the following introduction:
'Now, he provides the atonement through Yeshua our Messiah, as he
explains to us':

For if the sprinkling of defiled persons with the blood of goats and bulls and with
the ashes of a heifer sanctifies for the purification of the flesh, how much more
shall the blood of Christ, who through the eternal Spirit offered himself without
blemish to God, purify your conscience from dead works to serve the living God
... But when Christ had offered for all time a single sacrifice for sins, he sat down
at the right hand of God, then to wait until his enemies should be made a stool
for his feet. For by a single offering he has perfected for all time those who are
sanctified. (Hebrews 9:13–14; 10:12–14)

This is followed by a sermon and the *Avinu Malkenu*:

Our father, our king, we have no king but you.
Our father, our king, deal with us kindly for the sake of your name.
Our father, our king, renew for us a good year.
Our father, our king, we have sinned before you.
Our father, our king, annul all evil decrees against us.
Our father, our king, thwart the plans of our enemies.
Our father, our king, frustrate the counsel of our foes.
Our father, our king, rid us of every oppressor and adversary.
Our father, our king, close the mouths of our adversaries and attackers.
Our father, our king, remove disease, sword, famine, captivity, destruction,
iniquity and persecution from your people of the covenant.
Our father, our king, forgive and pardon all our sins.
Our father, our king, remove our transgressions and sins from your sight.
Our father, our king, bring us back in real repentance to you.
Our father, our king, heal the sick among your people.

Our father, our king, raise the strength of your Messiah.
Our father, our king, send us not empty-handed from your presence.
Our father, our king, remember that we are but dust.
Our father, our king, have compassion on us, on our children, and our infants.
Our father, our king, act for the sake of those who were killed for your holy name.
Our father, our king, do it for your sake, if not for ours.
Our father, our king, do it for the sake of your abundant mercy.
Our father, our king, be gracious to us and answer us, though we have no merits;
deal graciously and kindly with us and deliver us.
Our father, our king, do it for the sake of our Messiah Yeshua and in his name.[16]

The service continues with the *Oz M'Lifnai B'reshit* prayer:

Our righteous Anointed is departed from us; horror has seized us and we have
none to justify us. He has borne the yoke of our iniquities and our transgressions,
and is wounded because of our transgression. He bears our sins on his shoulder
that we may find pardon for our iniquities. We shall be healed by his wounds, at
the time that the Eternal will bring him anew. Hasten the day when he will
assemble us a second time by the hand of the one who shall endure for ever.[17]

This is followed by the 'Answer Us' prayer, the *Alenu, Adon Olam*, and the
Aaronic Benediction.

The morning service for *Yom Kippur* begins with a series of prayers
followed by the *Baruchu*, the *Shema* and the *Amidah*. This is followed by
several prayers including the *U-Netanneh Tokef* prayer:

And thus let the words by which we revere you come before you for you, our
God, are king.
Let us proclaim the mighty holiness of this day, for it is solemn and awesome.
On this day is your rule exalted, your throne established in compassion, and you
judge in truth.
It is true that you judge and rebuke, you discern and witness, you record and
seal, you recount and measure, you remember things forgotten.
You open the book of remembrance, and it speaks for itself, for every man's seal
is found in it.
The great *shofar* is sounded, and a quiet soft voice is heard. The angelic hosts,
seized with fear and awe, declare: 'Behold, it is the Day of Judgement, when the
hosts of heaven are to stand in judgement, for even they are not blameless before
you.'
You make all who are born into this world pass before you in judgement, as a
flock of sheep.
As a shepherd gathers his sheep, making them pass under his staff, so you cause
every living thing to pass before you.
You appoint the length of every creature's life and mandate its end.[18]

This is followed by the *Torah* service followed by a sermon. Then the *Oz M'Lifnai B'reshit* prayer is recited. The service concludes with the *Yizkor* memorial service, the *Alenu* and the Aaronic Benediction.

The *Neilah* service for *Yom Kippur* begins with a series of prayers, followed by the *Kaddish*, the *Amidah* and the *Kedushah*. This is followed by a *Haftarah* reading followed by a statement from Acts: 'Therefore let all be assured of this: God has made this Yeshua, whom you crucified, both Lord and Messiah.'

The service continues with the 'Act for the Sake of' prayer which concludes:

> But God commended his love toward us in that while we were yet sinners, Messiah died for us. Herein is love, not that we loved God, but that he loved us and sent his Son to be the expiation for our sins. We trust you our God; act for the sake of Messiah Yeshua. Amen.[19]

This is followed by 'Our God and God of Our Fathers':

> Our God and God of our fathers, remember our father Abraham and the binding of his son Isaac, Jerusalem your holy city, Messiah the son of David, and all your people; and grant deliverance and happiness, grace and kindness, mercy and life, and peace on this *Yom Kippur*.
> The Lord, the Lord is a merciful and gracious God, slow to anger and overflowing in kindness and truth. He shows his mercy to thousands of generations, forgiving iniquity and transgression and sin, and clearing those who repent.
> The Lord said, 'I pardon as you have asked.'
> For God loved the world so much that he gave his one and only Son that whoever trusts him should have everlasting life. God did not send his Son into the world to condemn the world but to save the world through him. To as many as received him, to those who trusted in his name, he gave the right to become the children of God.[20]

A passage from Hebrews is then read:

> But this man, after he had offered one sacrifice for sins for ever sat down on the right hand of God;
> From henceforth expecting till his enemies be made his footstool.
> For by one offering he hath perfected for ever them that are sanctified.
> Whereof the Holy Ghost also is a witness to us: for after that he had said before.
> This is the covenant that I will make with them after those days, saith the Lord, I will put my laws into their hearts, and in their minds will I write them.
> And their sins and iniquities will I remember no more. (Hebrews 10:12–17)

This is followed by the *Shema*, and the 'The Lord He Is God' prayer:

This specific phrase was first used when Eliahu Ha-Navi called Ahab and the people of Israel to Mount Carmel, where they saw . . .

Adonai hu Ha-Elohim.
The Lord he is God.

Even earlier Avraham *Avinu* realized . . .

Adonai hu Ha-Elohim.
The Lord he is God.

Israel during the Exodus and at Sinai understood . . .

Adonai hu Ha-Elohim
The Lord he is God.

The powerful Babylonian King Nebuchadnezzar finally concluded . . .

Adonai hu Ha-Elohim.
The Lord he is God.

Yeshua *Ha-Meshiach*'s resurrection demonstrated . . .

Adonai hu Ha-Elohim.
The Lord he is God.

At Messiah's return all will proclaim . . .

Adonai hu Ha-Elohim.
The Lord he is God.

Together we affirm today . . .

Adonai hu Ha-Elohim. The Lord he is God!'[21]

At the end of the service the *shofar* is sounded and the Aaronic Benediction (Blessing) is recited.

11 Festivals of joy

Simhat Torah

Traditionally this joyful festivity is observed on the day after *Shemini Atseret*, thereby making the festival of *Sukkot* a nine-day celebration. In the synagogue the festivities are all connected with the reading of the *Torah*. In the evening service, all the scrolls are taken out of the ark and carried around the *bimah* and the synagogue in a sevenfold procession. This is accompanied by the chant: 'O Lord, save, we beseech you!' and a doxology. Each procession is separated from the next by an interlude of singing and dancing. The *Torah* scrolls are joined by members of the congregation in a spirit of religious enthusiasm. In some synagogues children participate in the processions carrying *Simhat Torah* flags or small scrolls. These processions are normally followed by the reading of part of the next-to-last chapter of the Five Books of Moses.

In the morning service, there is an elaborate Bible reading: the final chapters of the Pentateuch are chanted. It is customary for all men to be called to the reading of the Law. In some congregations, several *Torah* readings occur simultaneously. Most of the two chapters are repeated so that all worshippers are included in the service. In Conservative congregations women accompany men to the platform. A special reading is also reserved for youngsters below *Bar Mitzvah* age; in some congregations a large prayer shawl is held over the children while they recite *Torah* blessings and when their prescribed section is recited. At the conclusion, a special benediction is pronounced over the children. In Reform synagogues both men and women participate equally in the service. The last section of the reading of the book of Deuteronomy is reserved for the specially honoured congregant. Once this takes place, a second scroll is taken and the cycle of yearly readings begins with the first chapter of the book of Genesis.

In Messianic synagogues, the evening service begins with the *Baruchu* and the *Shema*. This is followed by the *Amidah*. The service continues with the *Kaddish* and a reading of the *Torah*. Deuteronomy 34:5–12 is read first, followed by Genesis 1:1–5. The *Haftarah* is then recited from the books of Jeremiah and Isaiah. This is followed by the *Brit Chadasha* blessing:

You grant blessings, O Lord our God, ruler of the universe who has given us Messiah Yeshua and the words of the renewed covenant. You grant blessings, O Lord, giver of the renewed covenant.[1]

This is followed by a reading from James:

But be doers of the word, and not hearers only, deceiving yourselves. For if any one is a hearer of the word and not a doer, he is like a man who observes his natural face in a mirror; for he observes himself and goes away and at once forgets what he was like. But he who looks into the perfect law, the law of liberty, and perseveres, being no hearer that forgets but a doer that acts, he shall be blessed in his doing. (James 1:22–25)

The service continues with a sermon and the prayer:

The *Torah* of the Lord is perfect, restoring the soul;
the teaching of the Lord is sure, making wise the simple.
The precepts of the Lord are right, rejoicing the heart;
the commandment of the Lord is pure, enlightening the eyes.
Happy is the man that walks not in the counsel of the wicked,
nor stands in the way of sinners,
nor sits in the seat of the scornful.
But his delight is in the *Torah* of the Lord;
and in his *Torah* he meditates day and night.
He shall be like a tree planted by streams of waters,
that brings forth its fruit in its season,
and whose leaf does not wither;
and in whatever he does he shall prosper:
behold, the days come, says the Lord,
when the house of Israel will come to know me.
I will put my commandments within you and write them in your hearts,
and I will be your God and you shall be my people.
And I will betroth you to me for ever;
yes, I will betroth you to me in righteousness, in justice, and in love.
And I will betroth you to me in faithfulness,
and you shall know the Lord.
A new heart also will I give you,
and a new spirit will put within you;
I will take away the heart of stone
and I will give you a heart of flesh.
I will put my spirit within you,
and cause you to walk in my statutes,
and you shall keep my ordinances and do them.
For my ordinances which command you
are not too difficult for you, neither are they far off.

My laws are not high in the heavens that you should say,
'Who shall go up and bring them down?'
Neither are they beyond the sea that you should say,
'Who shall go over the sea for us, and bring them to us,
that we may hear them and do them?'
Behold my ordinances are near you,
in your heart that you may do them.
Anyone who sets aside one of the least of these commandments
and teaches others to do the same
will be called the least in the kingdom of heaven.
But anyone who does and teaches what they say,
will be called great in the kingdom of heaven.
It is easier for heaven and earth to disappear
than for one part of a letter of *Torah* to fail.
Do we make void *Torah* through faith?
Not at all! We establish *Torah*.
So then the *Torah* is holy,
And the commandment is holy, just and good.
That the righteous requirements of *Torah* might be fully met in us,
we do not live according to our evil inclinations,
but according to the *Ruach Ha-Shem*.
The day will come when my *Torah* will flow from Zion,
and the word of the Lord from Jerusalem.
And all people shall know me,
from the least of them unto the greatest of them,
and all shall be my people,
and I will be their God.
Deserving of praise are you, O Lord our God, ruler of the universe who gives
us the living word in the Messiah, Yeshua.[2]

This is followed by the *Alenu* and the *Kiddush*; the service concludes with singing and dancing with the *Torah*.

Hanukkah

The festival of *Hanukkah* is celebrated for eight days; it commemorates the victory of the Maccabees over the Seleucids in the second century BCE. At this time the Maccabees engaged in a military struggle with the Seleucids who had desecrated the Temple of Jerusalem. After a three-year struggle (165–163 BCE), the Maccabees under Judah Maccabee conquered Jerusalem and rebuilt the altar. According to Talmudic legend, one day's worth of oil miraculously kept the *menorah* burning in the Temple for eight days. *Hanukkah* commemorates this miracle.

The central observance of this festival is the kindling of the festive lamp on each of the eight nights. This gave this holiday the name 'The Festival of

Lights'. In ancient times this lamp was placed in the doorway or in the street outside; subsequently the lamp was placed inside the house. The lighting occurs after dark. The procedure for lighting the *Hanukkah* candles is to light one candle on the first night, and an additional candle each night until the last night when all eight candles are lit. The kindling should go from left to right. An alternative tradition prescribes that the eight candles are lit on the first night, seven on the second night, and so forth. These candles are lit by an additional candle called the *shammash*. In addition to this home ceremony, candles are lit in the synagogue.

In the traditional synagogue service this festival is commemorated by the recitation of the *Al Ha-Nissim* prayer in the *Amidah*, and Grace after Meals. In the morning service the *Hallel* is recited, and a special reading of the Law takes place on each day of the holiday. In both the home and the synagogue the hymn *Maoz Tsur* is sung in Ashkenazi communities; the Sephardim read Psalm 30 instead. During *Hanukkah* it is customary to hold parties which include games and singing. The most well-known game involves a *dreydel* (spinning top). During *Hanukkah* it is customary to eat potato latkes and doughnuts. In modern Israel, the festival is associated with national heroism, and a torch is carried from the traditional burial site of the Maccabees to various parts of the country.

Messianic Jews are anxious to point out that Yeshua himself observed this festival. As the Gospel of John relates:

> It was the feast of the Dedication at Jerusalem; it was winter, and Jesus was walking in the temple in the portico of Solomon. So the Jews gathered round him and said to him, 'How long will you keep us in suspense? If you are the Christ, tell us plainly.' Jesus answered them, 'I told you, and you do not believe. The works that I do in my Father's name, they bear witness to me; but you do not believe because you do not belong to my sheep . . .' The Jews took up stones again to stone him. Jesus answered them, 'I have shown you many good works from the Father; for which of these do you stone me?' The Jews answered him, 'It is not for a good work that we stone you but for blasphemy; because you being a man, make yourself God.' Jesus answered them, 'Is it not written in your law, "I said, you are gods"? If he called them gods to whom the word of God came (and scripture cannot be broken), do you say of him whom the Father consecrated and sent into the world, "You are blaspheming" because I said "I am the Son of God"? If I am not doing the works of my Father, then do not believe me; but if I do them, even though you do not believe me, believe the works, that you may know and understand that the Father is in me and I am in the Father.' Again they tried to arrest him, but he escaped from their hands. (John 10:22–29)

Given this background, Messianic Jews find in this festival the spiritual lesson of faith in the Lord. *Hanukkah* celebrates a time when the true worship of the God of Abraham, Isaac and Jacob was restored in the Promised Land. In addition, *Hanukkah* symbolizes that the heart of each believer in Yeshua dwells in the Temple of the Lord. For Messianic Jews this festival further symbolizes the victory of God's faithful people over their enemies. Just as those who remained loyal to the tradition in ancient times were able to overcome their oppressors, so Jews in the modern world will emerge triumphant in the face of opposition and hostility. Such divine protection will in time culminate in the victory of the Great Shepherd Yeshua.

The evening service for *Hanukkah* begins with the lighting of the festival lights:

> Deserving of praise are you, O Lord our God, ruler over the universe, who hallowed us by your commandments and allowed us to light the *Hanukkah* lights.
>
> Deserving of praise are you, O Lord our God, ruler over the universe, who worked miracles for our fathers in days of old, during this season.
>
> Deserving of praise are you, O Lord our God, ruler over the universe, who kept us alive, sustained us and privileged us to reach this season.[3]

This is followed by a prayer concerning God's miraculous actions:

> We light these candles because of the miracles, deliverance and wonders you performed for our fathers by means of your holy priests. During the eight days of *Hanukkah* these lights are sacred. We look at them in order to remember to thank you for your miracles, deliverance and wonders.[4]

This is followed by *Maoz Tsur*, the *Baruchu*, the *Shema*, and the *Amidah*, including a reference to the events related to this festival:

> In the days of the Hasmonean, Mattiteyahu ben Yohanan, the great priest, and his sons, when a wicked Hellenistic government rose up against Israel, your people, to make them forget your *Torah* and to break the laws you gave, you with great mercy stood by them in the time of their distress. You championed their cause, defended their rights and avenged their wrong. You delivered the strong into the hands of the pure, the ungodly into the hands of the godly and the arrogant into the hands of the students of *Torah*. You made a great and holy name for yourself in the world, and for your people Israel you performed a great deliverance. Whereupon your children entered your sanctuary, cleansed the Temple, purified your house, kindled lights in your holy courts and instituted these eight days of *Hanukkah* for thanksgiving and praise to your great name.[5]

The service continues with readings from the *Torah* and the *Haftarah* reading from the Gospel of John. This is followed by a sermon, the *Kaddish*, and various readings connected with *Hanukkah* concerning Judah the Maccabee and Hannah and her sons. The service concludes with the *Hallel* and the Aaronic Blessing.

Purim

The festival of *Purim* celebrates the deliverance of Persian Jewry from the plans of Haman, the chief minister of King Ahasuerus. The nature of this holiday is derived from the Akkadian word '*pur*', which refers to Haman's casting of lots to determine a date to destroy the Jewish people (Esther 3:7–14). In remembrance of this date the Fast of Esther is observed on the day that Queen Esther proclaimed a fast before she interceded with the king. *Purim* is celebrated as the Feast of Lots which Mordecai, Esther's cousin, inaugurated to remember the deliverance of the Jewish people (Esther 9:20ff). The next day is *Shushan Purim* since the conflict between the Jews and Haman's supporters did not cease until the previous day. Ahasuerus allowed the Jews an extra day to overcome their foes. This means that the deliverance could only be celebrated a day later (Esther 9:13–18).

The laws regarding the observance of *Purim* are specified in the tractate *Megillah* in the *Talmud*. In the evening and morning services the Esther scroll is chanted to a traditional melody. In most traditional congregations *Purim* resembles a carnival – children frequently attend the reading from the scroll in fancy dress, and whenever Haman's name is mentioned, worshippers stamp their feet and whirl noisemakers (*greggers*). In the *Amidah* and Grace after Meals a prayer of thanksgiving is included; however, the *Hallel* psalms are excluded. During the afternoon a special festival meal takes place including such traditional dishes as *Hamentashen*, triangular buns or pastries filled with poppyseed, prunes, dates, etc. It is usual for parents and relatives to give children money. On *Purim* it is customary to stage plays as well, and in *yeshivot* students mimic their teachers. In modern Israel parades take place with revellers dressed in *Purim* costumes.

Even though the festival of *Purim* is not mentioned in the New Testament, Messianic Jews believe that the lessons of this feast are of considerable spiritual significance. As in traditional synagogues, the usual decorum of the service is replaced by an atmosphere of joy and celebration. The evening service begins with the *Baruchu* and the *Shema*, followed by the *Amidah*. This is followed by the reading of the book of Esther. The congregation is encouraged to wear costumes related to the biblical story, as well as other sorts of dress. During the reading of the scroll of Esther, members of the congregation make noise using *greggers* or home-made noisemakers. In some synagogues, original *Purim* plays are enacted. In all cases Messianic Jews view this festival as symbolizing the triumph of God's people over their adversaries. The lesson of *Purim* is that God will be faithful to his promises; whenever the nation is threatened, God will intervene on behalf of his chosen people.

New Moon

New Moon (*Rosh Hodesh*) is a festival of joy which occurs with the new moon each month. Since the Jewish calendar is lunar, each month lasts a little more than 29 days. Because it was not possible to arrange the calendar with months of alternative length, the Sanhedrin declared whether a month had 29 or 30 days. If the outgoing month had 29 days, the next day was *Rosh Hodesh*. In early rabbinic times, the Sanhedrin was responsible for determining the day of the new moon on the basis of eye witnesses who had claimed to see the new moon. Only in the fourth century was a permanent calendar fixed by Hillel II.

During the period of the First Temple, *Rosh Hodesh* was observed with the offering of special sacrifices, the blowing of *shofars*, feasting and a rest from work. By the end of the sixth century BCE *Rosh Hodesh* became a semi-holiday. Eventually even this status disappeared, and *Rosh Hodesh* became a normal working day except for various liturgical changes. The liturgy for *Rosh Hodesh* includes the *Yaaleh-Ve-Yavo* prayer, read in the *Amidah* and in the Grace after Meals, which asks God to remember his people for good, for blessing and for life. In the morning service the *Hallel* psalms of praise are recited. The Bible reading is from Numbers 28 which describes the Temple service for the new moon. An additional service is also included corresponding to the additional sacrifice which was offered on the new moon.

Among Messianic Jews *Rosh Hodesh* is viewed as symbolic of God's renewal of Israel. The new month is perceived as a sign of the redemption and restoration of the chosen people. Hence, this festival is perceived as pointing to the restoration of David's kingdom under Yeshua Messiah. The new-month blessing looks forward to the time of Israel's redemption when God's Anointed will arrive to redeem humankind. Another aspect of this holiday is indicated by a section of the *Amidah*: 'You assigned the beginning of months for your people as a season of atonement.' Initially *Rosh Hodesh* was viewed as a mini *Yom Kippur*. Not only does the holiday anticipate the coming of the Messiah; it is also a reminder of divine atonement and forgiveness. Hence, when Yeshua celebrated the Passover during the *seder*, he instructed his followers to remember the atonement he effected until he returns again to rule over the Messianic kingdom.

The service for *Rosh Hodesh* begins with a prayer offering thanksgiving for God's redemptive actions:

> He who performed miracles for our fathers, and liberated them from slavery to freedom, may he quickly liberate us, and gather our exiles from the four corners of the earth, even all of Israel; and let us say Amen.
>
> The new moon (name of the month) will be on (name of the day). May it prove to be good for all Israel.[6]

This is followed by the *Baruchu*, *Shema* and *Amidah*. This is followed by the

Hallel. The service then continues with a reading from the *Torah*, and a second reading from the book of Revelation:

> Then I saw a new heaven and a new earth; for the first heaven and the first earth had passed away, and the sea was no more. And I saw the holy city, new Jerusalem, coming down out of heaven from God, prepared as a bride adorned for her husband; and I heard a loud voice from the throne saying, 'Behold, the dwelling of God is with men. He will dwell with them, and they shall be his people, and God himself will be with them; he will wipe away every tear from their eyes, and death shall be no more, neither shall there be mourning nor crying nor pain any more, for the former things have passed away.' And he who sat upon the throne said, 'Behold, I make all things new.' Also he said, 'Write this, for these words are trustworthy and true.' And he said to me, 'It is done! I am the Alpha and the Omega, the beginning and the end. To the thirsty I will give from the fountain of the water of life without payment. He who conquers shall have this heritage, and I will be his God and he shall be my son. But as for the cowardly, the faithless, the polluted, as for murderers, fornicators, sorcerers, idolaters, and all liars, their lot shall be in the lake that burns with fire and sulphur, which is the second death.' Then came one of the seven angels who had the seven bowls full of the seven last plagues, and spoke to me, saying, 'Come, I will show you the Bride, the wife of the Lamb.' And in the Spirit he carried me away to a great, high mountain, and showed me the holy city Jerusalem coming down out of heaven from God, having the glory of God, its radiance like a most rare jewel, like a jasper, clear as crystal. It had a great, high wall, with twelve gates, and at the gates twelve angels, and on the gates the names of the twelve tribes of the sons of Israel were inscribed; on the east three gates, on the north three gates, on the south three gates, and on the west three gates. And the wall of the city had twelve foundations, and on them the twelve names of the twelve apostles and of the Lamb. (Revelation 21:1–14)

This is followed by a sermon, the Reader's *Kaddish* and the prayer *Ashrey Yoshevey Veysecho*:

> Happy are they that dwell in your house: they will forever praise you. (*Selah.*) Happy is the people thus favoured: happy is the people whose God is the Lord. And a redeemer shall come to Zion and to those that turn from transgression in Jacob, says the Lord. And as for me, this is my covenant with them, says the Lord: my spirit that is on you, and my words which I have put in your mouth, shall not depart from you, nor from your children, nor from your children's children, says the Lord, from henceforth and for ever.[7]

The service continues with Romans 11:26–27; 33–36:

> And so all Israel will be saved; as it is written, 'The Deliverer will come from Zion, he will banish ungodliness from Jacob; and this will be my covenant with

them when I take away their sins' . . . O the depth of the riches and wisdom and knowledge of God! How unsearchable are his judgments and how inscrutable his ways! 'For who has known the mind of the Lord, or who has been his counsellor?' 'Or who has given a gift to him that he might be repaid?' For from him and through him and to him are all things. To him be glory for ever. Amen.[8]

This is followed by Revelation 7:10; 5:12; 7:12:

And crying out with a loud voice, 'Salvation belongs to our God who sits upon the throne, and to the Lamb!' . . . Saying with a loud voice, 'Worthy is the Lamb who was slain, to receive power and wealth and wisdom and might and honour and glory and blessing!' . . . saying, 'Amen! Blessing and glory and wisdom and thanksgiving and honour and power and might be to our God for ever and ever and ever! Amen.'[9]

This is followed by the *Alenu* and the prayer preceding the sounding of the *shofar*:

Deserving of praise are you, O Lord our God, ruler of the universe, who hallowed us by your commandments and instructed us to hear the sounding of the *shofar*.
Deserving of praise are you O Lord our God, ruler of the universe, who has kept us alive and sustained us, and enabled us to enjoy this season.[10]

The service then concludes with a prayer of thanksgiving:

Happy is the people that know the sound of the *shofar*, in the light of your countenance, O Lord, shall they walk.[11]

Advent

Advent is traditionally the beginning of the Christian year which, in the West, is now celebrated as the Sunday nearest 30 November. It is used both as a time of preparation for Christmas (the first Advent of Jesus), and for Christ's Second Coming when he will judge the world and bring this era to an end. No formal season of Advent is celebrated in the Eastern Church.

Among Messianic Jews, Advent is referred to as *Rishon*. It serves as a time of preparation and reflection about the first coming of Yeshua. The scriptural readings during this season focus on the events leading up to Yeshua's birth. The mood of this festival is one of longing for deliverance combined with the anticipation of Messianic redemption. Some Messianic Jews celebrate this festival with a *Rishon* wreath containing a ring of four candles, each standing for one week in the advent season. Usually there are three purple candles and one pink candle. The purple symbolizes repentance; the pink candle stands for joy. In the centre a white candle represents the purity of the Messiah. On each week a new candle is lit as well as those which have previously been lit. The first candles to be lit are the purple. The first purple candle is the candle of sorrow, symbolizing the sorrow of human beings due to sin; the second purple candle is the candle of selection, representing the separation of the chosen people; the third purple candle is the candle of the Scriptures, representing the *Torah*; the pink candle is the candle of joy which signifies joy for Israel. The fifth candle, which is lit on the eve of *Yom Ha-Mashiach*, represents the Messiah Yeshua.

The evening service for Advent begins with the *Baruchu* and the *Amidah*. This is followed by the *Kaddish* and the *Alenu* and a series of readings from Scripture:

'The days of coming', declares the Lord, 'when I will raise up for David a righteous Branch, a king who will reign wisely and do what is just and right in the land. In his days Judah will be saved and Israel will live in safety. This is the name by which he will be called: The Lord our Righteousness. (Jeremiah 23:5–6)

A record of the genealogy of Yeshua the Messiah, the son of David, the son of Abraham. (Matthew 1:1)

Praise be to the Lord, the God of Israel, because he has come and has redeemed his people. He has raised up a horn of salvation for us in the house of his servant David. (Luke 1:68–69)

But you, Bethlehem Ephrathah, though you are small among the clans of Judah, out of you will come for me one who will be ruler over Israel, whose origins are from of old, from ancient times. Therefore Israel will be abandoned until the time when she who is in labour gives birth and the rest of his brothers return to join the Israelites. He will stand and shepherd his flock in the strength of the Lord, in the majesty of the name of the Lord his God. And they will live securely, for then his greatness will reach to the ends of the earth. (Micah 5:2–4)

So Joseph also went up from the town of Nazareth in Galilee to Judea, to Bethlehem the town of David, because he belonged to the house and line of David. He went there to register with Miriam, who was pledged to be married to him and was expecting a child. While they were there, the time came for the baby to be born, and she gave birth to her firstborn, a son. (Luke 2:4–7)

Therefore the Lord himself will give you a sign: The virgin will be with child and will give birth to a son, and will call him Immanuel. (Isaiah 7:14)

This is how the birth of Yeshua the Messiah came about. His mother Miriam was pledged to be married to Joseph, but before they came together, she was found to be with child through the Holy Spirit. Because Joseph her husband was a righteous man and did not want to expose her to public disgrace, he had in mind to divorce her quietly. But after he had considered this, an angel of the Lord appeared to him in a dream and said, 'Joseph son of David, do not be afraid to take Miriam home as your wife, because what is conceived in her is from the Holy Spirit. She will give birth to a son, and you are to give him the name Yeshua, because he will save his people from their sins.' All this took place to fulfil what the Lord had said through the prophet: 'The virgin will be with child and will give birth to a son, and they will call him Immanuel' – which means, 'God with us.' (Matthew 1:18–23)

The kings of the earth take their stand and the rulers gather together against the Lord and against his Anointed One . . . The Lord said, 'I have installed my king on Zion, my holy hill.' I will proclaim the decree of the Lord: he said to me, 'You are my son; today I have become your father. Ask of me, and I will make the nations your inheritance, the ends of the earth your possession.' (Psalm 2:2, 6–8)

In the sixth month, God sent the angel Gabriel to Nazareth, a town in Galilee, to a virgin pledged to be married to a man named Joseph, a descendant of David. The virgin's name was Miriam. The angel went to her and said, 'Greetings, you who are highly favoured! The Lord is with you.' Miriam was greatly troubled at his words and wondered what kind of greeting this might be. But the angel said to her, 'Do not be afraid, Miriam, you have found favour with God. You will be with child and give birth to a son, and you are to give him the name Yeshua. He will be great and will be called the Son of the Most High. The Lord God will give him the throne of his father David, and he will reign over the house of Jacob for ever; his kingdom will never end.' 'How will this be', Miriam asked the angel, 'since I am a virgin?' The angel answered, 'The Holy Spirit will come upon you and the power of the Most High will overshadow you. So the holy one to be born will be called the Son of God.' (Luke 1:26–35)

We all, like sheep, have gone astray, each of us has turned to his own way; and the Lord has laid on him the iniquity of us all . . . By oppression and judgment, he was taken away. And who can speak of his descendants? For he was cut off from the land of the living; for the transgression of my people he was stricken . . . Therefore I will give him a portion among the great, and he will divide the spoils with the strong, because he poured out his life unto death, and was numbered with the transgressors. For he bore the sin of many, and made intercession for the transgressors. (Isaiah 53:6, 8, 12)

You see, at just the right time, when we were still powerless, Yeshua died for the ungodly. Very rarely will anyone die for a righteous man, though for a good man someone might possibly dare to die. But God demonstrates his own love for us in this: While we were still sinners, Messiah died for us. Since we have now been justified by his blood, how much more shall we be saved from God's wrath through him! For if, when we were God's enemies, we were reconciled to him through the death of his Son, how much more having been reconciled shall we be saved through his life! (Romans 5:6–10)

But he was pierced for our transgressions, he was crushed for our iniquities; the punishment that brought us peace was upon him, and by his wounds we are healed. (Isaiah 53:5)

Instead, one of the soldiers pierced Yeshua's side with a spear, bringing a sudden flow of blood and water. (John 19:34)

Yet it was the Lord's good plan to bruise him and fill him with grief. But when his soul has been made an offering for sin, then he shall have a multitude of children, many heirs. He shall live again and God's programme will prosper in his hands. (Isaiah 53:10)

God has raised this Yeshua to life, and we are all witnesses of the fact. (Acts 2:32)

On that day the Lord will shield those who live in Jerusalem, so that the feeblest among them will be like David, and the house of David will be like God, like the Angel of the Lord going before them. On that day I will set out to destroy all the nations that attack Jerusalem. And I will pour out on the house of David and the inhabitants of Jerusalem the spirit of grace and supplication. They will look on him, the one they have pierced. (Zechariah 12:8–10)

They were looking intently up into the sky as he was going, when suddenly two men dressed in white stood beside them. 'Men of Galilee', they said, 'why do you stand here looking into the sky? This same Yeshua, who has been taken from you into heaven, will come back in the same way you have seen him go into heaven. (Acts 1:10–11)

Following the sermon, a series of prayers is said:

Deserving of praise are you, O Lord, who has given us the way of salvation in Messiah Yeshua.

He walked among us filled with your spirit, the only one who ever fully fulfilled your *Torah*.

He healed the sick and raised the dead. The multitudes of our people sought his touch.
He taught as no man taught. With authority, he brought forth the treasures of the *Torah*.
How the children sought him, the lepers he touched and made clean!

How the despised and outcast found love and release from their sin.
How the hypocrites feared him whose words uncovered their sin!

Despised and rejected, acquainted with grief, he bore the sins of Israel.

All we like sheep have gone astray, turned every one to his own way.

Our iniquities were laid upon the king, the sins of the world, his burden to bear.

He rose from the dead and opened the way to life everlasting, praise his name.
We are in him, his spirit empowers; new life is ours with joy and peace.

Deserving of praise, are you, O Lord, our God, who has given us Messiah our king.[12]

This is followed by several prayers, and the service concludes with The Miracle of *Yom Ha-Mashiach* which is preceded by several passages from Scripture:

All that has been prepared
and announced.
Ageless power
would be split for a span
to redeem created
and glorify creator.

Triune pleasure
said it was time.
The Life spark was planted.
Neither gloom or hate
rattled its fury from below
while myriads of angels
sang adoration.

On earth, we heard a baby's cry.[13]

This is followed by songs and praise and the Aaronic Blessing.

Independence Day

Another festival is Independence Day. This is Israel's national day, which commemorates the proclamation of its independence in 1948. The Chief Rabbinate of Israel declared it a religious holiday, and established a special order of service for the evening and morning worship. This service includes the *Hallel* and a reading from Isaiah. The rabbinate also suspended any fast which occurs on the day, the recital of the *Tahanun* prayer, and mourning restrictions of the *omer* period. In Israel the preceding day is set aside as a day of remembrance for soldiers who died in battle. *Yizkor* prayers are recited then, and next-of-kin visit the military cemeteries. At home memorial candles are lit, and Psalm 9 is recited in many synagogues.

The Messianic service for this festival begins with readings from Isaiah; this is followed by prayers for the State of Israel:

> The sounding of the *shofar* reminds us that God has brought us back home to Israel just as he promised. But the *shofar* blasts also remind us that God has even greater things in store for our people.
> 'Sound the great *shofar* to announce our freedom; raise the great banner to gather our exiles and to assemble us together from the four corners of the earth.'
> You are to be praised, O Lord who gathers the dispersed of your people Israel.

This is followed by a sounding of the *shofar*.

The lighting of the *menorah* begins with a reading from Isaiah. This is followed by a prayer dealing with the origins of the *menorah*:

> The *menorah* is the most ancient symbol of our people and our nation. As we light its candles, we remember how God has rekindled our nation just when others had thought they had extinguished our people, but the lights also teach us other lessons.
> Light reminds us of God; 'The Lord is my light and salvation.'

The first candle is then lit and the following prayer recited:

> Light reminds us of his image within us; 'The human spirit is the light of the Lord.'

Once the second candle is lit, the congregation says the prayer:

> Light reminds us of God's covenant with us; 'For the *mitzvah* is a lamp and the Torah is a light.'

After the third candle, another prayer is said:

> Light reminds us of *Shabbat* – when we kindle lights – because it is the sign of God's covenant with us; 'It is a sign between me and the children of Israel for ever.'

After the fourth candle:

> Light reminds us of Israel's calling; 'I have made you a covenant people, a light to the nations.'

After the fifth candle:

> Light reminds us of the world to come; 'In that day they will need no light for the Lord God will give them light.'

After the sixth candle:

> Light reminds us of the Messiah; he said: 'I am the light of the world.'

Finally, after the seventh candle:

> The *menorah* reminds us how God has rekindled our hopes, redeemed our people, restored our nation, and returned us to our land. It also reminds us that Yeshua our Messiah will soon reign over us.

After the reading of Psalm 98, the following prayer is said:

> May it be your will, that as you have considered us worthy to see the beginning of our people's redemption, so also may we be considered worthy to hear the *shofar* announce our Messiah, very soon, in our time.
> We praise you, O Lord redeemer of Israel.
> We praise you, O Lord our God, ruler of the universe, who has kept us alive, sustained us, and privileged us to reach this season.[14]

12 Life cycle events

Naming ceremony

In traditional Jewish families the naming of a newborn child takes place on one of two occasions: a baby boy is named at the circumcision ceremony; a baby girl is named in the synagogue on the first time the *Torah* is read after her birth. The Hebrew form of the name consists of the individual's name followed by '*ben*' (son) or '*bat*' (daughter) of the father. This form is used in all Hebrew documents as well as for the call to the reading of the *Torah*.

In the life of Messianic Jews, the naming of a child is of considerable significance; this ceremony recalls the covenant between God and his people, and the promise of Messianic redemption. The service begins with a blessing of thanks recited by the mother:

> What can I render to the Lord for all his benefits towards me? I will offer the sacrifice of thanksgiving and will call on the name of the Lord. I will pay my vows to the Lord in the presence of all his people in the courts of the Lord's house, and someday in the midst of you, O Jerusalem. Hallelujah.
> Deserving of praise are you, O Lord our God, ruler of the universe, who does good to the undeserving, and who has dealt kindly with me.[1]

This is followed by a series of prayers concerning the ceremony:

> God spoke to Abraham further, 'As for me, this is my covenant with you: you will be the father of many nations. No longer will you be called Abram, your name will be Abraham . . . As for Sarai you wife . . . her name will be Sarah . . . she will be the mother of nations.'
> As with Abraham and Sarah, the receiving of new names is associated with entry into the covenant relationship.[2]

Following a reading from Deuteronomy, other prayers are recited concerning the covenant:

> As this Scripture indicates, all the generations, even those unborn, were at Sinai and participated in that covenant making. Today our child formally becomes a part of the covenant of Israel.

Shabbat has been the seal of the covenant for generations. It is written in Exodus 31:16: 'The Israelites are to observe *Shabbat*, celebrating it for the generations to come as a covenant for all time. It will be a sign between me and the Israelites for ever.'[3]

The parents then state:

So on this *Shabbat* we bring our daughter/son into the covenant of Israel. May she/he be led to a life of *Torah*, service to God, and devotion to Yeshua our Messiah.[4]

The naming of the child then follows:

Sustain this child along with her/his mother and father. Her/his name shall be called in Israel:_____ [5]

After several psalms are recited, the parents consecrate their child:

Deserving of praise are you, O Lord our God, ruler over the universe who has set us apart through your commandments and commanded us to bring our daughter/son into the covenant of the people of Israel.[6]

The parents then light the candles:

The lighting of the candles is one of the traditional pictures of setting something apart as special for God. It expresses a distinction between that which is specifically God's and that which is not. Tonight conveys the idea that _____ is consecrated to God and his service as a light to the world.
Deserving of praise are you O God, ruler over the universe, who daily continues your creation. You create life anew with each generation. Deserving of praise are you, O God, who brings forth life from the womb.

The parents then state:

We consecrate this child to you, O Holy One, who sets apart your servants for your service, the service of your Anointed, Yeshua. Deserving of praise are you, O God, who sanctifies the children of your servants.
Meiri, one of our sages, in commenting in the *Talmud* said that when Abraham was circumcised and thus entered the covenant, Sarah went through the *mikvah* to enter the covenant.
The *mikvah* has traditionally been an important sign on entering the covenant of the people of Israel. As a parallel or addition to circumcision, tonight it is the sign of _____ entering the covenant.

> Deserving of praise are you O Lord our God, king of the universe who hallowed us with his commandments and commanded us concerning this immersion.

Water is then poured on the child and the parents state:

> Help us to lead our child in the footsteps of the great leaders of Israel, whose deeds continue to shine across the ages of our people. May she/he be like Devorah/Moshe of old, by whose hand you delivered our people. We praise you, O God, whose *Torah* links the generations one to another.

The godparents then state:

> We pledge our full support in teaching this daughter/son of Israel to love the Lord her/his God with all her/his heart, strength and life. We will encourage her/him to make God's commandments an integral part of her/his life. We will seek to stimulate her/him to experience a personal relationship with God through Yeshua, his Anointed and the Deliverer of Israel. We will impress these things on her/him and will relate these truths to all of her/his life, talking about them when we sit at home with her/him and when we walk along the road, when we lie down and when we get up. And if ever her/his parents are unable to fulfil their responsibilities in bringing her/him up before God, we promise to raise her/him in their place. We pledge this in dependence upon God, the gracious enabler of his people.

The congregation then states:

> We promise to support the parents, godparents and others in bringing up this child. We will pray for her/him and will seek to provide the community and environment necessary for her/his growth in relationship with God through Yeshua our Messiah.
> Deserving of praise are you, O Lord our God, ruler over the universe, who has kept us alive and sustained us and enabled us to enjoy this season.
> Bless us, O God, all of us together, with the light of your presence.[7]

The service concludes with a blessing over wine followed by the Aaronic Blessing.

Circumcision

According to Jewish law, all male children are to undergo circumcision, in accordance with God's decree, and as a sign of the covenant between God and Abraham's offspring. As Genesis 17 relates:

> God said to Abraham . . . 'This is my covenant which you shall keep between me and you and your descendants after you: every male among you shall be

circumcised. You shall be circumcised in the flesh of your foreskins, and it shall be a sign of the covenant between me and you.' (Genesis 17:9–11)

Jewish ritual circumcision involves the removal of the entire foreskin. It is to be performed on the eighth day after the birth of the child by a person who is properly qualified (*mohel*). Jewish law specifies that this ceremony can be performed even on the Sabbath, festivals, or the Day of Atonement; however, postponement is allowed if there is any danger to the child's health.

The laws regulating this procedure are derived from biblical sources as well as rabbinical enactments. Traditionally the ceremony takes place in the presence of a quorum of ten adult Jewish men (*minyan*). On the morning of the eighth day, the infant is taken from the mother by the godmother who hands him to the *sandak* (godfather). The *sandak* then carries the child into the room where the circumcision is to take place and hands him to the individual who places the child on a chair called the Chair of Elijah. Another person then takes him from the Chair of Elijah and passes him to the child's father who puts him on the lap of the godfather who holds the boy during the ceremony. The circumcision is performed by a *mohel*; formerly blood was drawn orally by the *mohel* but today an instrument is used. The infant is then handed to the person who will hold him during the ceremony of naming, and the ceremony concludes with a special blessing over a cup of wine, followed by the naming of the child.

In New Testament times circumcision was a universal practice among Jewry. In the gospel of Luke, reference is made to Yeshua's circumcision:

On the eighth day when it was time for his *brit-milah*, he was given the name Yeshua, which is what the angel had called him before his conception. (Luke 2:21)

In the epistle to the Colossians, Paul emphasized the spiritual significance of this ceremony in relation to Messianic redemption:

For in him (Messiah), bodily, lives the fullness of all that God is. And it is in union with him that you have been made full – he is the head of every rule and authority. Also it was in union with him that you were circumcised with a circumcision not done by human hands, but accomplished by stripping away the old nature's control over the body. (Colossians 2:9–11)

Among the circle of Yeshua's followers, the practice of circumcision was rigorously followed. For this reason, Acts 16:1–3 portrays Timothy's circumcision. Born Jewish, Timothy was not raised in the faith – however, because Paul sought to take Timothy with him on his journeys, he insisted that he be circumcised. Yet on another occasion, he refused to be pressured to circumcise Titus who was not born a Jew (Galatians 2:3). Hence it appears that Paul viewed the act of circumcision as necessary for Jews, whereas non-Jews were not under the same obligation.

Following this distinction, Messianic Jews see themselves as under the covenantal responsibility of circumcision. Adapting certain features of the traditional ceremony, they seek to bind themselves into the Abrahamic covenant, as did first-century believers in Yeshua.

In a typical Messianic circumcision ceremony, the mother is seated in a chair outside the door where the guests and family are assembled holding the child. She then passes the child to the godmother who brings the baby to the entrance of the room as the leader declares:

> Blessed is he who comes in the name of the Lord.[8]

The leader then continues, saying:

> The rite of circumcision has been enjoined upon us as a sign of our covenant with God, as it is written: 'And God said unto Abraham, Thou shalt keep my covenant therefore, thou, and thy seed after thee in their generations. This is my covenant, which ye shall keep, between me and you and thy seed after thee; Every man child among you shall be circumcised. And ye shall circumcise the flesh of your foreskin; and it shall be a token of the covenant betwixt me and you. And he that is eight days old shall be circumcised among you, every man child in your generations, he that is born in the house, or bought with money of any stranger, which is not of thy seed. He that is born in thy house, and he that is bought with thy money, must needs be circumcised: and my covenant shall be in your flesh for an everlasting covenant. And the uncircumcised man child whose flesh of his foreskin is not circumcised, that soul shall be cut off from his people; he hath broken my covenant. (Genesis 17:9–14)

The leader then continues:

> As Messianic Jews, we follow the example of Messiah Yeshua and the first-century believers.[9]

After reading Luke 2:21: 'And when eight days were accomplished for the circumcising of the child, his name was called Jesus, which was so named of the angel before he was conceived in the womb', the leader gives a short address regarding the meaning of the circumcision ceremony for Messianic Jews.

The godfather then takes the child from the godmother and gives the boy to the person who watches over the Chair of Elijah. This person briefly puts the baby on the chair; he is then taken by another person who hands the child to the father who then says:

In conformity with sacred Jewish observance, I present my son for the covenant of circumcision.

Blessed art Thou, O Lord our God, king of the universe who has sanctified us by his commandments and commanded us to bring our sons into the covenant of Abraham our father.[10]

The father then gives his son to the *sandak* who is seated in a chair with a pillow on his lap. This person holds the child while the circumcision takes place. Prior to the circumcision, the leader recites the following blessing:

Blessed art Thou, O Lord our God, king of the universe, who has sanctified us by his commandments and commanded us concerning the rite of circumcision.[11]

After the circumcision, the leader recites a blessing over the wine cup:

Blessed art Thou, O Lord our God, king of the universe who creates the fruit of the vine.[12]

The parents then drink the wine, and the leader states:

Our God and God of our fathers, sustain this child in life and health and let him be known in the household of Israel by the name _____ ben _____. Cause the parents to rejoice in this child whom Thou has entrusted to their care. As he has been brought into the covenant of Abraham, so may he be led to the study of thy *Torah*, enter into a marriage worthy of thy blessing, and live a life enriched with good deeds.[13]

A personal prayer should then be recited, affirming that the child will be brought up to know the Messiah Yeshua from an early age.

Redemption of the First Born

The custom of redeeming first-born male children is based on the biblical prescription that first-born sons should be consecrated to the Temple. Just as first fruits and first-born animals had to be given to the priests, so first-born male children were dedicated to God. The obligation to redeem first-born sons from this service is referred to in Numbers 3:44–51: redemption is to take place by payment of five shekels to a priest. Detailed laws concerning the Redemption of the First-Born (*Pidyon Ha-Ben*) are presented in the *Mishnah* tractate *Bekhorot*, and expanded in the talmudic commentary on the passage.

According to this legislation, the sons of priests and Levites are exempt from redemption, as are first-born sons whose mother is the daughter of either a priest or a Levite. In the geonic period (*c.* 600–1300), a ceremony was instituted in which the father of the child declares to the priest on the thirty-first day after its birth that the infant is the first-born son of his mother and father and that, as a father, he is obliged to redeem him. The priest then asks the father if he prefers to give his son to the priest or redeem him for five shekels. The father replies that he wants to redeem his son, and hands the priest the required amount. The father then recites a blessing concerning the fulfilment of the precept of redeeming the child, and another expressing gratitude to God. This procedure has served as the basis for the ceremony since the Middle Ages.

In the New Testament, the redemption of Jesus as the first-born is depicted in Luke 2:22–24:

> And when the time came for their purification according to the law of Moses, they brought him up to Jerusalem to present him to the Lord (as it is written in the law of the Lord, 'Every male that opens the womb shall be called holy to the Lord') and to offer a sacrifice according to what is said in the law of the Lord, 'a pair of turtledoves, or two young pigeons'.

The ceremony is described in detail later in the chapter:

> Now there was a man in Jerusalem whose name was Simeon, and this man was righteous and devout, looking for the consolation of Israel, and the Holy Spirit was upon him. And it had been revealed to him by the Holy Spirit that he should not see death before he had seen the Lord's Christ. And inspired by the Spirit he came into the temple; and when the parents brought in the child Jesus, to do for him according to the custom of the law, he took him up in his arms and blessed God and said, 'Lord, now lettest thou thy servant depart in peace, according to thy word; for mine eyes have seen thy salvation which thou hast prepared in the presence of all peoples, a light for revelation to the Gentiles, and for glory to thy people Israel' . . . And his father and his mother marvelled at what was said about him. (Luke 2:25–33)

For the followers of Yeshua, this ceremony has particular significance. Redemption of the First-Born points to the eventual redemption of the Messiah, as 1 Peter explains:

> You know that you were ransomed from the futile ways inherited from your fathers, not with perishable things such as silver or gold, but with the precious blood of Christ, like that of a lamb without blemish or spot. (1 Peter 1:18–19)

In the light of this teaching, Messianic Jews celebrate this festival along traditional lines. It is normally desirable that a *cohen* be present in order to provide some background to this ceremony. At the beginning of the service the father gives his son to a designated *cohen* and states:

This is the firstborn son of his mother, and God has directed us to redeem him, as it is written in the *Torah*.[14]

The father then reads Exodus 13:11–15:

And when the Lord brings you into the land of the Canaanites, as he swore to you and your fathers, and shall give it to you, you shall set apart to the Lord all that first opens the womb. All the firstlings of your cattle that are males shall be the Lord's. Every firstling of an ass you shall redeem with a lamb, or if you will not redeem it you shall break its neck. Every first-born of man among your sons you shall redeem. And when in time to come your son asks you, 'What does this mean?' you shall say to him, 'By strength of hand the Lord brought us out of Egypt, from the house of bondage. For when Pharaoh stubbornly refused to let us go, the Lord slew all the first-born in the land of Egypt, both the first-born of man and the first-born of cattle. Therefore I sacrifice to the Lord all the males that first open the womb; but all the first-born of my sons I redeem.'

The father then places five silver coins in his hand. The *cohen* then says:

Which do you prefer, to give me your son or redeem him?[15]

The father then says:

I wish to redeem him with the equivalent of five shekels and thus fulfil my obligation in the *Torah*.[16]

The father then reads Numbers 18:15–16:

Everything that opens the womb of all flesh, whether man or beast, which they offer to the Lord, shall be yours; nevertheless the first-born of man you shall redeem, and the firstling of unclean beasts you shall redeem. And their redemption price (at a month old you shall redeem them) you shall fix at five shekels in silver, according to the shekel of the sanctuary, which is twenty gerahs.

The *cohen* accepts the payment and returns the son to the father as the father says:

Blessed art thou, O Lord our God, king of the universe who has sanctified us by his commandments and commanded us concerning the redemption of the firstborn. Amen.[17]

The father and mother then thank God for the gift of a newborn child:

Blessed art thou, O Lord our God, king of the universe who has kept us in life, sustained us and brought us to this time. Amen.[18]

As he holds the coins, the *cohen* states:

> I accept the five shekels and hereby declare your son redeemed. May he be granted a full and blessed life, living in devotion to our God. May this redemption ceremony remind us of our need for the spiritual redemption found in the Messiah, Yeshua, as it is written in the New Covenant.[19]

The *cohen* then reads 1 Peter 1:17–21 and then blesses the child:

> May God make you like Ephraim and Manasseh. The Lord bless you and keep you. The Lord make his face to shine upon you and be gracious to you. The Lord turn his face toward you and give you peace. Amen.[20]

Bar Mitzvah and Bat Mitzvah

Recently in both Ashkenazi and Sephardi communities the *Bar Mitzvah* ceremony included a discourse by the *Bar Mitzvah* boy which demonstrated his knowledge of rabbinic sources. In time other practices became part of the *Bar Mitzvah* ceremony; some boys chanted the entire weekly reading; others were trained as prayer leaders; some conducted the Sabbath eve service on Friday night as well as the Sabbath morning service. In some Western communities the *Bar Mitzvah* boy reads a special prayer, standing before the rabbi or the ark. In modern times it is usual for the rabbi to address the *Bar Mitzvah* boy after the reading of the Law.

Initially a *Bar Mitzvah* meal for family and friends was held after the weekday morning service, or a third meal was consumed after the Sabbath afternoon service. Subsequently this was expanded into a *kiddush* at the Sabbath morning service, followed by a family meal. Today there is frequently a *Bar Mitzvah* reception on a more lavish scale. Among Oriental Jews other variations of such festivities take place. In many Eastern Sephardi communities, Hebrew poems are composed for this occasion. In the nineteenth century, Reform Judaism substituted a confirmation ceremony for both boys and girls in place of *Bar Mitzvah*. However, as time passed, most Reform congregations have instituted *Bar Mitzvah* as well. Since 1967 both Orthodox and non-Orthodox *Bar Mitzvah*s have taken place at the Western Wall in Jerusalem.

Unlike *Bar Mitzvah* there is no legal requirement for a girl to take part in a religious ceremony to mark her religious majority. Nonetheless, a ceremonial equivalent of *Bar Mitzvah* has been designated for girls. This was originally a nineteenth-century Orthodox innovation. In the early twentieth century the Conservative scholar Mordecai Kaplan pioneered the *Bat Mitzvah* ceremony in the USA as part of the synagogue service, and since then this has become widely accepted by many American communities. In non-Orthodox congregations, a 12-year-old girl celebrates her coming of age on a Friday night or during the Sabbath morning service where she conducts prayers, chants the *Haftarah*, and in some cases reads from the *Torah* and delivers an address. In Orthodox synagogues, however, the *Bat Mitzvah* ceremony is much more limited.

Outside the USA the *Bat Mitzvah* ceremony takes various forms. In Reform congregations it is in line with the American pattern. Orthodox girls, however, do not participate in the synagogue service; rather a *Bat Mitzvah*'s father is called to the *Torah* on the appropriate Sabbath morning. His daughter then recites the *Sheheheyanu* prayer, and the rabbi addresses her in the synagogue or at a *kiddush* reception afterwards. Alternatively, the ceremony takes place at home or in the synagogue hall on a weekday. In Britain and South Africa the procedure is different. *Bat Mitzvah* girls must pass a special examination enabling them to participate in a collective ceremony.

According to Messianic Judaism, the New Testament appears to record an event in Yeshua's life which resembles this *rite de passage*:

> Every year Yeshua's parents went to Jerusalem for the festival of Passover. When he was twelve years old, they went up for the festival, as custom required. But after the festival was over, when his parents returned, Yeshua remained in Jerusalem. They did not realize this; supposing that he was somewhere in the caravan, they spent a whole day on the road before they began searching for him among their relatives and friends. Failing to find him, they returned to Jerusalem to look for him. On the third day they found him – he was sitting in the Temple court among the rabbis, not only listening to them but questioning what they said; and everyone who heard him was astonished at his insight and his responses. (Luke 2:41–47)

In the light of the centrality of this ceremony in the Jewish tradition, Messianic Jews observe *Bar* and *Bat Mitzvah* as a symbol of a young person's commitment to Yeshua. A typical service begins with introductory psalms followed by the *Baruchu* and the *Shema*. This is followed by a Messianic reading or a portion from the New Testament. The young person is then called to the ark for the *Torah* service. Before reading the *Torah* blessing, the young person recites a prayer of dedication:

> My God and God of my fathers! On this solemn and sacred day, which marks my passage from childhood to adulthood, I humbly raise my voice to you in fervent prayer that I always walk uprightly before you.
> As an infant I was brought within your sacred covenant with Israel; and today I again enter your chosen community as an active member, bearing the full responsibility for all I do, and under the sacred obligation to sanctify your holy name before all the world. O heavenly father, hear my prayer, and shower me with your gracious blessings, so that I may be sustained and enriched by your great mercies. Shape my will to yours and enable me to obey your guidelines and faithfully carry out your instructions. Direct my heart to love and fear your holy

name, and grant me your support and the strength necessary to overcome the trials which clutter the path lying before me. Deliver me through temptation, so that I may observe your holy *Torah* and its precepts, on which human happiness and life depend. Thus, throughout the days of my journey on earth, I will trustfully and gladly proclaim: 'Hear O Israel, the Lord is our God, the Lord alone!'[21]

After the appropriate prayers, the *Bar* or *Bat Mitzvah* leads the *Torah* processional through the synagogue. The blessing is then recited over the *Torah*; this is followed by a prayer by the father of the *Bar* or *Bat Mitzvah*:

> Praised be he who has allowed me to raise this child to assume responsibility for him (her) self. May he who blessed our fathers, Abraham, Isaac, and Jacob, bless this child on his/her *Bar* (*Bat*) *Mitzvah*, who was called to the *Torah* (and offered _____ for charity). May the Holy One preserve and deliver him/her through sorrow and distress; and may he plant in his/her heart the love and respect for God to do his will and serve him completely all his/her days; and let us say, Amen.[22]

The *Torah* portion is then chanted; this is followed by the *Haftarah* portion. After the *Haftarah* section, the *Bar* or *Bat Mitzvah* delivers a short speech in which the young person gives testimony of faith in Messiah Yeshua.

Marriage

According to tradition, marriage is God's plan for humanity, as illustrated by the story of Adam and Eve in the book of Genesis. In the Jewish faith it is viewed as a sacred bond as well as a means to personal fulfilment. It is more than a legal contract, rather an institution with cosmic significance, legitimized through divine authority. The purpose of marriage is to build a home, create a family and thereby perpetuate society. Initially Jews were allowed to have more than one wife, but this was banned in Ashkenazi countries with the decree of Rabbenu Gershom in 1000. In modern society, all Jewish communities – Sephardic and Ashkenazic – follow this ruling.

In the Bible, marriages were arranged by fathers: Abraham, for example, sent his servant to find a wife for Isaac (Genesis 24:10–53), and Judah arranged the marriage of his first-born son (Genesis 38:6). When the proposal of marriage was accepted by the girl's father (or elder brother in his absence), the nature and amount of the *mohar* (payment by the groom) was agreed. By Second Temple times, there was a degree of choice in the selection of a bride – on 15th of *Av* and the Day of Atonement, young men could select their brides from among the girls dancing in the vineyards.

According to tradition a period of engagement preceded marriage itself. The ceremony was a seven-day occasion for celebration during which love songs were sung in praise of the bride. In the Talmudic period a major development occurred concerning the *mohar* – since it could be used by the father of the bride, a wife could become penniless if her husband divorced or predeceased her. As a result the *mohar* evolved into the formulation of a marriage document (*ketubbah*), which gave protection to the bride. In addition, the act of marriage changed from being a personal civil procedure to a public religious ceremony which required the presence of a *minyan* (quorum) and the recitation of prayers. In biblical and Talmudic times marriage occurred in two stages: betrothal and *nissuin*.

From the Middle Ages, it became customary for Ashkenazic Jewish communities to postpone the betrothal ceremony until immediately prior to the *nissuin* wedding ceremony. This also became customary among Sephardi Jews. In Hasidic communities, however, the traditional *tenaim* ceremony is still usually observed. In modern times the Orthodox wedding ceremony normally follows a uniform pattern based on traditional law. Within Conservative and Reform Judaism the wedding service follows this traditional pattern with varying alterations.

Within Messianic Judaism, the essential elements of the Jewish wedding service have been maintained. Unlike the traditional branches of Judaism, it is not mandatory that both the groom and the bride are Jewish. What is crucial is that the non-Jewish spouse has a Jewish heart and is dedicated to rearing children within the Messianic community. A typical ceremony begins with the signing of the marriage contract (*ketubbah*). This document should be signed by both the bride and groom before the start of the service, as well as by the Messianic leader and two witnesses. It is common for a small group of family and friends to watch this part of the procedure.

The service itself begins with a music prelude consisting of any appropriate instrumental or vocal music. The Messianic leader should take his place under the back part of the marriage canopy (*huppah*), followed by the groomsmen and bridal party. The men should stand on the left side of the *huppah*; the women on the right. When the groom processes to the *huppah*, the Messianic leader states:

Blessed is he who comes in the name of the Lord.[23]

The groom is escorted by his parents to the front of the *huppah*; they are then seated while the groom remains standing at the *huppah*. Before the bride begins her procession to the *huppah*, the Messianic leader states:

Blessed is she who comes in the name of the Lord.[24]

The bride is led by her parents until she is in front of the *huppah*; the bride may then circle the groom three times as the Messianic leader reads Hosea 2:19:

And I will betroth you to me for ever; I will betroth you to me in righteousness and in justice, in steadfast love, and in mercy.

The bride then joins arms with the groom and they stand under the *huppah*. The Messianic leader then says:

He who is supremely mighty; he who is supremely praised; he who is supremely great – may he bless this bridegroom and bride.[25]

The Messianic leader then gives an address to the bride and groom. The best man then fills the first cup of wine and the Messianic leader says:

Blessed art thou, O Lord our God, king of the universe who creates the fruit of the vine. Amen.[26]

The best man then gives the first cup of wine to the groom, who drinks from it and gives it to his bride. The Messianic leader then says:

_____will now exchange the traditional wedding vows. By so doing, they will be openly committing themselves to each other; to share the same joys, the same sorrows, and whatever God may bring in their lives together.[27]

The Messianic leader then asks the groom first and then the bride:

_____do you of your own free will and consent take this woman (man) _____to be your wedded wife (husband) from this day forward, for better, for worse, for richer, for poorer, in sickness and in health, to live together after God's holy commandment? Will you love her (him), comfort her (him), honour her (him), cherish her (him), and keep her (him), forsaking all others, cleave only to her (him), as long as you both shall live?[28]

The Messianic leader then asks: 'What symbols do you have of these vows?' The ring-bearer gives the rings to the Messianic leader, who says:

From earliest times the ring has been a symbol of wedded love. It is made of pure gold to symbolize pure love. Being one unbroken circle, it symbolizes unending love. As often as either of you sees these golden circles, may you be reminded of this important moment and the unending love you promise.[29]

The Messianic leader then leads the groom in, saying the Hebrew blessing as the groom places the ring on the bride's finger:

With this ring you are wed to me in accordance with the Law of Moses and of Israel.[30]

If desired, the following phrase may be added: 'In the name of the Father, Yeshua the Messiah and the Holy Spirit'.[31]

The leader then states:

> Since you have promised your love to each other before God and these witnesses, and exchanged these symbols of genuine love, I hereby announce, by virtue of the authority vested in me, that you are now husband and wife, so to live together until death do you part. What therefore God has joined together, let no man separate.[32]

The Messianic leader then reads the *ketubbah*. This is followed by the seven blessings which are recited by the Messianic leader:

> Blessed art thou, O Lord our God, king of the universe, who has created all things for thy glory. Amen.
> Blessed art thou, O Lord our God, king of the universe, creator of man. Amen.
> Blessed art thou, O Lord our God, king of the universe, who has made man in thine image, after thy likeness, and has prepared for him, out of his very self, an eternal soul. Blessed art thou, O Lord creator of man. Amen.
> May Zion who was barren be exceedingly glad and exult, when her children are gathered within her in joy. Blessed art thou, O Lord, who makes Zion joyful through her children. Amen.
> O make these loved companions greatly to rejoice, even as of old thou didst gladden thy creatures in the Garden of Eden. Blessed art thou, O Lord, who makes bridegroom and bride to rejoice. Amen.
> Blessed art thou, O Lord our God, king of the universe, who has created joy and gladness, bridegroom and bride, mirth and exultation, pleasure and delight, love, brotherhood, peace and fellowship. Soon may there be heard in the cities of Judah, and in the streets of Jerusalem, the voice of joy and gladness, the voice of the bridegroom and the voice of the bride, the jubilant voice of bridegrooms from their canopies, and of youths from their feasts of song. Blessed art thou, O Lord, who makes the bridegroom to rejoice with the bride. Amen.
> Blessed art thou, O Lord our God, king of the universe, who creates the fruit of the vine. Amen.[33]

The best man then gives the groom and the bride the wine cup. At the end of the service, the groom steps on a wine cup, and the Messianic leader says a prayer over the couple.

Death and mourning

Concerning death, the Bible declares that human beings will return to the dust of the earth (Genesis 3:19). According to Scripture, burial – especially in a family tomb – was the normal procedure for dealing with the deceased. In a number of biblical passages, human beings are depicted as descending to a nether world (*sheol*) where they live a shadowy existence; only in the later books of the Bible is there any allusion to resurrection.

Once death has been determined, the eyes and mouth are closed, and if necessary the mouth is tied shut. The body is then put on the floor, covered with a sheet, and a lighted candle is placed close to the head. Mirrors are covered in the home of the deceased, and any standing water is poured out. A dead body is not to be left unattended, and it is considered a *mitzvah* (good deed) to sit and recite psalms to the person who has died.

The burial of the body should take place as soon as possible. After the members of the burial society have taken care of the body, they prepare it for burial; it is washed and dressed in a white linen shroud. The corpse is then placed in a coffin or on a bier before the funeral service. Traditional Jews only permit the use of a plain wooden coffin. The deceased is then borne to the grave face upward; adult males are buried wearing their prayer shawl. Among non-Orthodox Jews burial practice differs from that of the Orthodox. In the Reform community embalming and cremation are usually permitted. Burial may be delayed for several days, and the person who has died is usually buried in normal clothing.

The Jewish tradition provides a specific framework for mourning which applies to males over the age of 13 and females over the age of 12 who have lost a father or mother, husband or wife, son or daughter, brother or sister. From the moment that death takes place until the burial, the mourners are exempt from positive commandments. In addition, a mourner is not allowed to participate in festival meals or engage in pleasurable activities. Instead he must rend a garment. Once the burial has taken place, mourners are to return to the home of the deceased or where the mourning period will be observed.

The mourning period known as *shivah* lasts for seven days beginning with the day of burial. During this time mourners sit on the floor or on low cushions or benches and are forbidden to shave, bathe, go to work, study the *Torah*, engage in sexual relations, or wear laundered clothing. Through these seven days it is the practice to bring prepared foods. Those comforting mourners are not to greet them but rather offer words of consolation. *Shivah* concludes on the evening of the seventh day and is followed by mourning of a lesser intensity for 30 days known as *sheloshim*.

Although Messianic Jews do not follow the elaborate pattern of mourning outlined in rabbinic sources, they nonetheless seek to incorporate biblical customs into the pattern of mourning. A typical example of the funeral service begins with opening music, followed by scriptural readings. After introducing the service, the Messianic leader reads a selection of psalms. This is followed by a scriptural reading from Job 19, John 11, 1 Corinthians 15, or 1 Thessalonians 4. The Messianic leader then gives an address which is accompanied by a eulogy or testimonies from family or friends. Special music is then played and the *kaddish* recited. A closing prayer is then said by the Messianic leader.

Some Messianic Jews observe the traditional period of mourning for the dead. After the funeral, friends of the family provide food and hospitality for the immediate family as well as for those who have come from out of town. During the *shivah* period, mourners receive callers at home. In the view of Messianic Jews the *kaddish* prayer, which is traditionally said for the relative who has died, should not be perceived as a prayer for the dead. Rather, it should be understood as a prayer of praise of God and longing for the Kingdom:

> Glorified and sanctified be the great name of God in the world which he has created according to his will. May he establish his kingdom during your days and during the days of the whole house of Israel at a near time speedily and soon and say Amen.
>
> May his great name be praised for ever, glorified and exalted, and honoured, and praised and magnified be the name of the Holy One, blessed be he, whose glory transcends, yea is beyond all blessing and praise and consolation which is uttered in the world, and say Amen.
>
> May there be great peace from the heavens upon us and upon all Israel, and say Amen.
>
> May he who makes peace from the heavens, grant peace upon us and upon all Israel, and say Amen.[34]

Although it is customary for the *kaddish* prayer to be recited by the closest relative for an eleven-month period, there is no limit to its use in a Messianic context. (Alternatively, some Messianic Jews prefer to use the Lord's Prayer as more appropriate.) After the *shivah* period, mourners enter back into their daily lives; however, it is common for friends to visit to comfort them. During the following eleven months mourners are encouraged to praise God; subsequently the period of mourning ceases. These mourning practices, rooted in traditional Judaism, are of important spiritual and psychological significance for Messianic Jews – they allow believers to come to terms with their loss and remind the faithful of God's providential care.

13 Personal lifestyle

Mezuzah

Symbols of the Jewish faith characterize the Jewish home, beginning with the *mezuzah* on each doorpost. In Scripture it is written that 'these words' shall be written on the doorposts (*mezuzot*) of the house (Deuteronomy 6:4–9; 11:13–21). This prescription has been understood literally: these two passages must be copied by hand on a piece of parchment, put into a case, and affixed to the doorpost of every room in the house.

The first of these passages from Deuteronomy contains the *Shema* as well as the commandments to love God, study the *Torah*, express the unity of God, wear *tefillin*, and affix a *mezuzah*. The second passage connects prosperity with the observance of God's commandments. The *mezuzah* itself must be written by a scribe on parchment – the scroll is rolled and put into a case with a small opening through which the word *Shaddai* (Almighty) is visible. The *mezuzah* is placed on the upper part of the doorpost at the entrance in a slanting position. The following conditions should traditionally be met in placing the *mezuzah* on every right-hand entrance:

1. The room into which the doorway leads should be at least four by four cubits.
2. The doorway should have doorposts on both sides.
3. The doorway should serve as an entrance into a room with a ceiling.
4. The door should have a lintel.
5. The doorway should have doors that open as well as close.
6. The doorway should be at least 40 inches high and sixteen inches wide.
7. The room must be for ordinary residence.
8. The room should be for human dwelling.
9. The room should be used as a dignified dwelling.
10. The room should be for continued habitation.

When the *mezuzah* is placed on the doorpost a benediction is recited. Traditional Jews touch the *mezuzah* with their hand when entering or leaving the home.

Following this traditional practice, it is common for Messianic Jews to affix *mezuzahs* on the front doorway of their houses as well as on other doorways. Prior to attaching the *mezuzah*, the following blessing is recited:

> Blessed art thou, O Lord our God, king of the universe, who has sanctified us by his commandments and commanded us to affix the *mezuzah*.[1]

Once the *mezuzah* is nailed or glued to the doorpost, it is appropriate to read passages from the New Testament related to the meaning of the *mezuzah*. This should be followed by personal prayer.

Dietary laws

According to Jewish tradition, food must be ritually fit (*kosher*) if it is to be eaten. The Bible declares that the laws of *kashrut* (dietary laws) were given by God to Moses on Mount Sinai. Thus Jews are obliged to follow this legislation because of its divine origin. Nonetheless, various reasons have been adduced for observing these prescriptions. Allegedly forbidden foods are unhealthy; that is why they are forbidden. Another justification is that those who refrain from eating particular kinds of food serve God even while eating, and thereby attain an elevated spiritual state.

The laws concerning which animals, birds and fish may be eaten are contained in Leviticus 11 and Deuteronomy 14:3–21. According to Scripture, only those animals which both chew the cud and have split hooves may be eaten. Such animals include domestic animals like cows and sheep. No similar formula is stated concerning which birds may be consumed; rather a list is given of forbidden birds. Although no reasons are given to explain these choices, it has been suggested that forbidden birds are in fact birds of prey; by not eating them, human beings are able to express their abhorrence of cruelty as well as the exploitation of the weak over the strong. Regarding fish, the law states that only fish which have both fins and scales are allowed. Again, no reason is given to support this distinction; however, various explanations have been proposed, such as the argument that fish that do not have fins and scales frequently live in the depths of the sea, which was regarded as the abode of the gods of chaos.

A further category of *kashrut* deals with the method of killing animals for food (*shehitah*). Although the *Torah* does not offer details of this procedure, the *Talmud* states that this method has divine authority because it was explained by God to Moses on Mount Sinai. According to tradition, the act of slaughter must be done with a sharpened knife without a single notch, since that might tear the animal's foodpipe or windpipe. Numerous other laws govern this procedure, and a person must be trained in the law if he is to be a slaughterer. According to the sages, the central idea underlying the laws of ritual slaughter is to give the animal as painless a death as possible.

Another restriction concerning ritual food is the prohibition against eating milk and meat together. This stipulation is based on Exodus 23:19:

'Thou shalt not boil a kid in its mother's milk.' According to the rabbis, this rule refers not only to the act of boiling a kid in its mother's milk, but to any combination of meat and milk. Tradition stipulates that it is forbidden to cook meat and milk together. Later, this prohibition was expanded to eating milk and meat products at the same time. Eventually the law was introduced that dairy dishes should not be eaten after meat until a stipulated period of time had passed.

Turning to the place of *kashrut* in Messianic Judaism, Messianic Jews point out that in the New Testament, Jewish ritual law was an area of considerable discussion. In the gospel of Mark, Yeshua appears to dismiss the significance of the laws of *kashrut* in comparison with the moral life:

> 'Listen to me, all of you, and understand this! There is nothing outside a person which, by going into him, can make him unclean. Rather, it is the things that come out of a person which make a person unclean!' When he had left the people and entered the house, his followers asked him about the parable. He replied to them, 'So you too are without understanding? Don't you see that nothing going into a person from outside can make him unclean? For it doesn't go into his heart but into his stomach, and it passes out into the latrine.' 'It is what comes out of a person,' he went on, 'that makes him unclean. For from within, out of a person's heart, come forth wicked thoughts, sexual immorality, theft, murder, adultery, greed, malice, deceit, indecency, envy, slander, arrogance, foolishness. All these wicked things come from within, and they make a person unclean.' (Mark 7:14–23)

It might appear that Yeshua's words negate Jewish ritual law, yet Messianic Jews contend that Yeshua was here emphasizing the relative importance of ethical commandments, and simultaneously indicating his dissatisfaction with the rabbinic interpretation of biblical law.

Regarding Paul's teaching about the law, it has been suggested that Paul was dismissive of the regulations regarding *kashrut*. Thus in a letter to Timothy, a young Jewish believer, he wrote:

> They (false teachers) forbid marriage and require abstinence from foods which God created to be eaten with thanksgiving by those who have come to trust and to know the truth. For everything created by God is good, and nothing received with thanksgiving needs to be rejected, because the word of God and prayer make it holy. (1Timothy 4:3–5)

Messianic Jews, however, point out that Paul was not saying that anything edible is permissible. Paul was not implying that all foods were permissible as long as a prayer was recited over them; rather, this passage in Timothy should be understood in the same light as Yeshua's teaching. Believers should be more concerned about the spiritual significance of *kashrut* rather than the rabbinic, extra-biblical interpretation of the law.

While having a kosher heart is of primary importance in the life of Messianic Jews, biblical law reminds believers of their holy calling.

Nonetheless, there is considerable divergence among Messianic Jews about which scriptural laws are binding. As Barney Kasdan noted in *God's Appointed Customs*:

> There is . . . a great deal of diversity among believers in Yeshua when it comes to *kashrut*. Many follow what might be described as a 'biblical kosher' approach. This lifestyle shows deference to the biblical dietary laws. Hence, only kosher animals are eaten; the *tareyf* animals are avoided. Pork, shellfish and the unclean fish listed in Leviticus 11 are avoided. A question is often raised as to what to do with the extra-biblical customs the rabbis have included. There is a broad consensus, considering the teachings in the New Testament, that Messianic believers are not bound by the traditions of man. The mixing of milk and meat, for example, while an Orthodox Jewish tradition, is not a biblical law. This means that the laws pertaining to separate dishes, silverware and pots are really not an issue in seeking to live a biblical lifestyle. Of course, there are those who may choose to follow elements of rabbinic tradition . . . A Messianic believer may want to buy meat from a kosher butcher and/or keep separate dishes. Some believers may prefer some modifications. Whatever approach a Messianic believer takes to *kashrut*, it is wise to walk in love and to heed the New Testament's council: 'Whatever you do, whether it's eating or drinking or anything else, do it all so as to bring glory to God.' (1 Corinthians 10: 31)[2]

Mikveh

Immersion was a common practice in ancient times in connection with disease. Hence Leviticus states:

> The Lord said to Moses, 'These are the regulations for the diseased person at the time of his ceremonial cleansing, when he is brought to the priest. The priest is to go outside the camp and examine him. If the person has been healed of his infectious skin disease, the priest shall order that two live clean birds and some cedar wood, scarlet yarn and hyssop be brought for the one to be cleansed . . . Seven times he shall sprinkle the one to be cleansed of the infectious disease and pronounce him clean . . . He must wash his clothes and bathe himself in water, and he will be clean. (Leviticus 14:1–4, 7, 9)

Ritual washing also occurred on other occasions: Exodus 19:10 relates that the people were told that they should wash their clothing before the giving of the Law on Mount Sinai; Leviticus 8 and 16 record that Aaron and his sons were commanded to wash before they ministered in the Tabernacle; Leviticus 15 describes ritual cleansings for various flows of body fluids. While it was possible for immersion to take place in a body of fresh water, such cleansing usually took place in a special pool (*mikveh*). During the

Second Temple period, the practice of immersion in the *mikveh* became common, and was extended to converts to Judaism. According to rabbinic tradition, this custom was instituted before the first century.

Within traditional Judaism the practice of *mikveh* is still followed. However, after the destruction of the Temple in 70 CE, a number of important modifications took place. With the disappearance of the sacrificial system, the priests ceased to have a cultic role in Jewish life. As a result, cleansing for priests and the various healings no longer took place. However, it is common for strictly Orthodox Jewish men to immerse in the *mikveh* in preparation for the Sabbath. Ritual immersion of women also takes place after their menstrual period in accordance with Leviticus, which specifies that a woman shall be separated from her husband for seven days at this time (Leviticus 15:19–24). According to rabbinic interpretation, these seven days are understood as beginning with the end of the woman's menstrual period: thus a total of about twelve days. After this period, a Jewish woman is to go to a *mikveh*. Before immersion, she must bathe to remove any dirt; only then is she able to immerse fully in the *mikveh*.

Another common practice is for converts to Judaism to immerse in a ritual bath. The convert is to be fully immersed in a *mikveh*. During this ritual the following blessings are to be recited:

> Blessed art thou, O Lord our God, king of the universe who has sanctified us by his commandments and commanded us concerning the ritual immersion.
> Blessed art thou, O Lord our God, king of the universe, who has kept us in life, sustained us and brought us to this time.[3]

According to rabbinic tradition, the *mikveh* itself should contain rainwater or water from a natural spring or stream. There must be enough of this water for the full immersion to take place. Additional water from piped sources may also be used if necessary.

Within rabbinic Judaism, the *mikveh* has important symbolic significance: it represents spiritual renewal and dedication to God. Similarly, in the New Testament the process of immersion was understood as symbolizing spiritual rebirth. In the gospel of Matthew, John the Baptist's ministry is understood in this light:

> It was during those days that John the Baptist arrived in the desert of Judah and began proclaiming the message, 'Turn from your sins to God, for the Kingdom of Heaven is near!' This is the man Isaiah was talking about when he said,
> The voice of someone crying out:
>   'In the desert prepare the way of the Lord!
>   Make straight paths for him!'
> John wore clothes of camel's hair with a leather belt around his waist, and his food was locusts and wild honey. People went out to him from Jerusalem, from

all Judah, and from the whole region around the Jordan. Confessing their sins, they were immersed by him in the Jordan River. (Matthew 3:1–6)

Drawing on this theme, Paul declared in Romans:

> Don't you know that those of us who have been immersed into the Messiah Yeshua have been immersed into his death? Through immersion into his death we were buried with him; so that just as through the glory of the Father, the Messiah was raised from the dead, likewise we too might live a new life. (Romans 6:3–4)

Given the traditional significance of immersion and its place in the life of early believers in Yeshua, Messianic Jews continue to follow this practice. Within Messianic Judaism, most Messianic immersions take place at swimming pools or in rivers or oceans. Rather than involving the exposure of one's body, modest dress is deemed appropriate. Within the movement, various practices take place. In some cases, participants immerse themselves in front of witnesses who assist them; frequently individuals also make personal testimonies of their faith in Messiah Yeshua.

Although Messianic immersion services can occur at any time, in some congregations they take place on the afternoon of *Rosh Hashanah* during the ceremony of repentance, as well as before Passover. This ceremony is accompanied by scriptural readings and music; as participants are immersed, the following blessings are recited:

> Blessed art thou, O Lord our God, king of the universe who has sanctified us by his commandments and commanded us concerning the immersion (in the name of the Father, Yeshua the Messiah and the Holy Spirit). Amen.
> Blessed art thou, O Lord our God, king of the universe, who has given us life, sustained us and brought us to this time. Amen.[4]

For Messianic Jews ritual immersion is an act of great importance, yet it does not have the same religious connotations that baptism has within the Gentile Church. For Gentile Christians, baptism is perceived as a means of entering into the body of Christ. Within Messianic Judaism, however, immersion is understood as a religious act symbolizing the believer's commitment to Yeshua: the faithful are to immerse in a *mikveh* as a sign of their acceptance of Messiah Yeshua and the coming of the Kingdom.

Tzizit

The obligation to wear fringes (*tzizit*) on one's garments is based on Numbers 15:37–41:

> The Lord said to Moses, 'Speak to the people of Israel, and bid them to make tassels on the corners of their garments throughout their generations, and to put upon the tassel of each corner a cord of blue; and it shall be to you a tassel to look upon and remember all the commandments of the Lord, to do them, not to follow after your own heart and your own eyes, which you are inclined to go after wantonly. So you shall remember and do all my commandments, and be holy to your God. I am the Lord your God.'

Jews are thus obliged to attach fringes to the four corners of their garments to remind them of the covenant. In the modern world, a special four-cornered garment with fringes attached, known as a *tallit katan*, is worn by Orthodox Jews under the outer clothing. In addition, Orthodox Jews (as well as Jews within the non-Orthodox branches of Judaism) wear a four-cornered prayer shawl with fringes, known as a *tallit gadol*. It is put on before *tefillin* (phylacteries) are worn. After the recitation of a special blessing, the *tallit* is wrapped around the head and then placed around the shoulders. The *tallit* was usually made of wool, with wool fringes attached, but it may also be composed of other fabrics. Today most prayer shawls are made of silk.

Before putting on the *tallit katan*, the following blessing is recited:

> Blessed art thou, O Lord our God, king of the universe, who has sanctified us by his commandments and commanded us concerning the command of the fringes.[5]

Prior to putting on the *tallit gadol*, it is held with both hands and the following blessing recited:

> Blessed art thou, O Lord our God, king of the universe, who has sanctified us by his commandments and commanded us to wrap ourselves in the fringes.[6]

In the gospel of Matthew, an account is given of Yeshua wearing fringes. When it became known that Yeshua was able to heal the faithful, a woman reached out to touch his garment:

> And behold, a woman who had suffered from a haemorrhage for twelve years came up behind him and touched the fringe of his garment; for she said to herself, 'If I only touch his garment, I shall be made well.' Jesus turned, and seeing her he said, 'Take heart, daughter; your faith has made you well.' And instantly the woman was made well. (Matthew 9:20–22)

Given the significance of this commandment in the history of the Jewish people from ancient times to the present, some Messianic Jews feel obliged to fulfil this precept. Yet there is considerable variation within the movement. As Barney Kasdan explained in *God's Appointed Customs*:

There are a variety of practices of this custom among Messianic Jews and Gentiles. There are some who feel called to maintain a daily expression of the fringes that requires the wearing of the *tallit katan*. With the right focus and attitude, this can be a very meaningful expression of faith. More often, Messianic Jews follow the common approach of wearing the regular *tallit* at religious services or special occasions. Many Messianic congregations provide extra *tallitot* for visitors at their *Shabbat* services. Since the age of thirteen is considered the age of accountability, where boys are required to observe the command-ments for themselves, it is a beautiful gesture to give a *tallit* as a gift at a *Bar Mitzvah* . . . The non-Jews also enjoy the spiritual blessings purchased by the Messiah. If a Gentile believer chooses to wear a *tallit*, this can be a beautiful statement of his faith in the God of Israel. In a Messianic Jewish worship service, such a practice can be a positive testimony of the Gentile believer's stand with the Jewish people.[7]

Traditionally women are exempt from fulfilling this precept. Within Con-servative and Reform synagogues, however, a number of women feel obliged to wear prayer shawls, and the same practice has been adopted by some women within the Messianic movement.

Tefillin

The obligation to wear *tefillin* (phylacteries) is based on Deuteronomy 11:13–21:

> And if you will obey my commandments which I command you this day, to love the Lord your God, and to serve him with all your heart and with all your soul, he will give the rain for your land in its season, the early rain and the later rain, that you may gather in your grain, and your wine and your oil. And he will give grass in your fields and for your cattle, and you shall eat and be full. Take heed lest your heart be deceived, and you turn aside and serve other gods, and worship them, and the anger of the Lord be kindled against you, and he shut up the heavens, so that there be no rain, and the land yield no fruit and you perish quickly off the good land which the Lord gives you. You shall therefore lay up these words of mine in your heart and in your soul; and you shall bind them as a sign upon your hand, and they shall be as frontlets between your eyes. And you shall teach them to your children, talking of them when you are sitting in your house, and when you are walking by the way, and when you lie down, and when you rise. And you shall write them upon the doorposts of your house and upon your gates, that your days and the days of your children may be multiplied in the land which the Lord swore to your fathers to give them, as long as the heavens are above the earth.

Tefillin consist of two black leather boxes containing scriptural passages which are bound by black leather straps on the arm and forehead. They are worn by men during the morning prayer, except on the Sabbath and festivals. The Jewish tradition specifies that the container for the head consists of four individual compartments, each containing a parchment scroll with passages from the *Torah* (Exodus 13:1–10, 11–16; Deuteronomy 6:4–9, 11:13–21). The container for the forearm is a single compartment which holds all of these passages. The symbolism of the knots used in attaching the straps is of considerable importance. The container for the head has the Hebrew letter *shin* on the outside; the knot tied on this container represents the Hebrew letter *dalet,* and the end of the strap is the letter *yod.* Together these letters spell out the word *Shaddai* (Almighty). The same name of God is spelled out by the way in which the leather strap of the container of the arm is wound.

The container for the hand is put on first by wrapping it around the left arm. As the knot is tightened, a prayer for this commandment is said:

> Blessed art thou, O Lord our God, king of the universe, who has sanctified us by his commandments and commanded us to put on *tefillin.*[8]

The leather strap is wound around the arm seven times while the remaining part of the strap is wound around the hand.

The following blessing is said before putting on the container for the head:

> Blessed art thou, O Lord our God, king of the universe, who has sanctified us by his commandments and commanded us concerning the command of *tefillin.*[9]

The container for the head is placed upon the head with the straps pulled tight and the remaining length placed over the chest. Then the following blessing is recited:

> Blessed be his name whose glorious kingdom is for ever and ever.[10]

The next step is to tie the remaining strap for the container for the hand around the fingers in symbolic knots. The strap is wound three times around the middle finger, with one loop around the middle part of the finger; one loop should then be made around the middle part of the finger, and two loops closer to the knuckle. The strap is then placed around the ring finger while the following passage from Hosea is recited:

> I will betroth you to me for ever; I will betroth you in righteousness and justice, in love and compassion. I will betroth you in faithfulness, and you will acknowledge the Lord. (Hosea 2: 19–20)[11]

Among Messianic Jews and Gentiles, the practice of putting on *tefillin* varies. Some Messianic Jews follow the traditional procedure for donning *tefillin*, while others believe that the rabbinic rules concerning the laying of *tefillin* need to be changed in modern society. As Kasdan noted in *God's Appointed Customs*:

> The custom of *tefillin* is biblically based as well as spiritually rich. Messianic Jews and like-minded Gentiles may choose to wear *tefillin* if they feel that it would be a blessing to their spiritual life. The details of how to 'lay *tefillin*' need not be changed for a Messianic believer. While believers are not bound by the innumerable rabbinic details, many of the ancient customs make sense for Bible believers as well. Believers can use their liberty in Messiah to make their understanding of this ancient tradition more meaningful. Whatever the expression is, may every believer always fulfil the intent of the *tefillin* by having their minds and hands serving Messiah.[12]

Head covering

Covering the head was an ancient practice within Judaism. Scripture relates that the priests wear a turban:

> Then bring near to you Aaron your brother, and his sons with him, from among the people of Israel to serve me as priests – Aaron and Aaron's sons, Nadab and Abihu, Eleazar and Ithamar. And you shall make holy garments for Aaron your brother for glory and for beauty. And you shall speak to all who have ability, whom I have endowed with an able mind, that they may make: . . . a breastpiece, an ephod, a robe, a coat of chequer work, a turban, and a girdle; they shall make holy garments for Aaron your brother and his sons to serve me as priests. (Exodus 28:1–4)

Such a headcovering symbolized holiness to the Lord. Originally this custom was practised only by priests, but in time it became common for Jewish men to cover their heads. Thus the Babylonian *Talmud* states that one should not walk even six steps without proper head attire.[13] Elsewhere the *Talmud* specifies that a person should wear a headcovering so that the fear of God will be upon him.[14] Despite these injunctions, the rabbis decreed that wearing a headcovering was optional and a matter of custom.[15] As a consequence, it was not until recent times that the wearing of a headcovering became a uniform practice within Judaism. Since the eighteenth century, traditional Jews have worn a variety of headcovering; in Europe the hat was eventually transformed into a smaller headcovering (*kippah*).

Today observant Jewish men wear both hats or *kippahs* at all times; among Conservative and Reform Jews there are a variety of practices. Within Messianic Judaism, some believers feel obliged to wear a *kippah* during all waking hours; others simply wear a *kippah* at religious services. Similarly, some Messianic women observe the practice of wearing a scarf over the head. In all cases, they regard the headcovering as symbolizing submission to God through the Messiah Yeshua. Such outward expression of faith should reflect the dedication of Messianic Jews to Yeshua and their hope for the ultimate fulfilment of God's plan for his chosen people.

PART III

The authenticity of Messianic Judaism

As we have seen, Messianic Jews insist that despite accepting Yeshua as Messiah and Saviour, they remain true to the tradition. Despite the variations in Messianic belief and practice, Jewish believers are adamant that they are fulfilled Jews. The Jewish community, however, has united against the Messianic movement, regarding it as deceptive, disloyal and dangerous. The dispute between Messianic Jews and mainstream Judaism thus focuses on two central questions: Are Messianic Jews in fact Jews? and Is Messianic Judaism a legitimate interpretation of the Jewish faith?

From a Messianic perspective, the answer to these questions is simple. Messianic Jews believe they are fulfilled through belief in the long-awaited redeemer of Israel. No longer under the yoke of the law, they have been saved through the life and death of Messiah Yeshua. For such individuals, both the Hebrew Bible and the New Testament provide a framework for Jewish living in the modern world. Fundamentalistic in orientation, they are committed to living Jewishly in anticipation of the Second Coming. Believing in the eschatological unfolding of history, they see themselves as the vanguard for the realization of God's plan on earth.

Critics of Messianic Judaism, however, insist that the Messianic movement is a betrayal of the Jewish faith. In their view, it is impossible for Jews to accept Jesus as Messiah and Lord. Messianic Judaism, they argue, is a misnomer; rather than being a legitimate form of Judaism, it is nothing other than Christianity in disguise. Further, despite the redefinition of Jewishness within various non-Orthodox branches of the faith, both Orthodox and non-Orthodox Jews dismiss the Messianic reinterpretation of Jewishness. Jewish believers are perceived as sinful apostates, unworthy of being included within the community. In Israel, Messianic Jews are denied entry into the country under the Law of Return. Yet despite such universal rejection, Messianic Jews continue to proclaim their loyalty to the Jewish tradition and to other Jews who have denounced them as furthering the destruction of the Jewish people.

14 Messianic Judaism and the Jewish people

Messianic Jewish theology

As we have seen, Messianic Judaism is grounded in the belief that Yeshua is the long-awaited Messiah. In this respect, Messianic Judaism and the earlier Hebrew Christian movement are based on the same belief system. Nonetheless, Messianic Jews are anxious to point out that there are important distinctions between their views and those of Hebrew Christians. As Dan Juster explained in an interview with David Rausch, the author of *Messianic Judaism*:

> The Hebrew Christian would be a person who sees himself coming from the Jewish ethnic origin and may desire to maintain the identity of himself that he has a Hebrew origin. But at the same time, the Hebrew Christian sees himself having come into the New Covenant. The Old Covenant has passed away. So the direct practice of anything Jewish is contrary to his being part of the new people of God and the body of Christ. The Messianic Jew, on the other hand, holds that the Jew is still called by God. It is not a legalistic thing, but it is a biblical calling to maintain his heritage and practice consistent with extolling fulfilment in Yeshua.[1]

In the view of Messianic Jews, faithfulness to Yeshua is expressed most fully within congregational life. In this regard, David Chernoff stressed the importance of communal fellowship in another interview with David Rausch. Messianic Judaism, he stated, is a much deeper identification than Hebrew Christianity: 'There is no doubt about it that the Messianic synagogue or congregation is at the centre of it [Messianic Judaism] . . . It is the centre of God's movement through the Holy Spirit.'[2] At the Messiah 80 Conference, Paul Liberman stressed the fundamental importance of the community within the movement:

> To some people there is no distinction between being a Messianic Jew and a Hebrew Christian. I think that I see one . . . The distinction comes bottom line down to the issue of congregational worship . . . The Hebrew Christian typically believes that a Messianic congregation is an option, it is no better and no worse than any other option, and (he) says that it is the same to go to a Christian denomination as it is to go to a Messianic congregation . . . Messianic Jews believe more

strongly in the call (particularly of the Abrahamic covenant) to remain Jews and as a practical matter they have come to recognize that history has reflected that within ten years and certainly by a second generation there is an assimilation whereby Jews are no longer identified as Jews and there are practically no third generation Jewish believers who recognize their Jewish heritage. Messianic Jews commonly believe that as a practical matter this just does not work out and is not consistent with the call of the Abrahamic covenant and elsewhere to observe God's pattern of Jews being preserved.[3]

Despite such a desire to differentiate themselves from Hebrew Christianity, Messianic Judaism has nonetheless borrowed a number of important features from both fundamentalist Christianity and the Hebrew Christian movement. For Messianic Jews, the Hebrew Bible as well as the New Testament are literally true. Adopting the stance of biblical literalists, Messianic Jews regard the words of Scripture as the word of God. In this regard, Juster wrote in *Jewish Roots*:

> Messianic Jews accept the full authority and truth of the complete Bible. Whatever Scripture teaches is to be believed and obeyed . . . Basically, the inspiration of the Bible means that God has superintended the biblical writers in such a way that what they wrote conveyed what God desired to convey. That which was taught was all truth and not error . . . It is crucial to understand that the highest authority and court of appeal for all teaching in Messianic Judaism is the Bible . . . As Messianic Jews, we may gain wisdom and insight from our Jewish tradition. The tradition, however, is to be tested by the Bible, which alone is accepted as totally true.[4]

Regarding the doctrine of God, Messianic Jews are united in their belief in the Trinity. Despite the use of the *Shema* in the liturgy, the conviction that God is triune is a central feature of the faith. As Michael Schiffman noted in *Return of the Remnant*:

> Belief in the triune nature of God is not merely held by a group within the Messianic community, but is believed by every Messianic organization of the community: the Union of Messianic Jewish Congregations, the Fellowship of Messianic Congregations and the Messianic Jewish Alliance of America.[5]

For Messianic Jews, the concept of the Trinity sounds overly Gentile; hence, within Messianic Judaism a different terminology is used to depict the same divine reality. Nonetheless, the belief that God is triune is based on the conviction that Yeshua is God. Such a belief, Messianic Jews contend, is scriptural in origin. As Schiffman explained:

> Scripture can be cited to teach the full humanity and full divinity of Yeshua, the divinity and person of the Holy Spirit, and their separateness and unity with the

Father . . . The purpose of the doctrine of the tri-unity was to teach and safeguard
the truth of one God, eternally existing as Father, Son and Holy Spirit.[6]

For Messianic Jews, the belief in the tri-unity of God is not apologetic, but
rather an explanation. Even if one criticizes its language, it is not inconsistent with the *Shema* or any other notion within biblical Judaism. Such a
belief is not polytheistic in character, as some theologians in the past maintained. Nor does it diminish one's sense of Jewishness. 'Jewishness',
Schiffman asserted, 'is heritage. What Messianic Jews believe is based on
God's revelation in his Messiah. The traditional Jewish view of God
without the Messiah is incomplete. The Messiah is the key to understanding the Scripture. He is the fullest revelation of God.'[7]

Given their view of Scripture, Messianic Jews believe that all of the
prophecies in the *Tanakh* relating to Messianic atonement were fulfilled in
Yeshua. Repeatedly they affirm that the Messiah Yeshua came to the Jews,
and his followers transmitted his message to the world. Although the *Torah*
demands a blood sacrifice, the Messiah is able to offer himself as a means of
atonement. Whereas traditional Judaism stresses the importance of performing *halakhic* ritual, Messianic Judaism stresses that human effort is
futile. What is required instead is belief in God's word and acceptance of
the Messiah's atonement for sin. Only in this way can the faithful receive
God's forgiveness and the promise of salvation.

In answer to the question why the world was not changed given
Yeshua's divinely appointed role, Messianic Judaism asserts that this will
be accomplished during the Second Coming. Drawing on the Suffering
Servant passages in the book of Isaiah, Messianic Jews argue that Yeshua
fulfilled this role on earth but he will come again to deliver the world,
defeat Israel's enemies, and establish God's Kingdom on earth. Like the
mainstream fundamentalist churches, many Messianic congregations are
pre-tribulationist in orientation, holding to the view that all believers in
Yeshua will be raptured at the beginning of the Great Tribulation. This will
be a time of intense anti-semitic feeling that will last until the end of days.
During this period, a powerful world leader who advocates peace will be
given unlimited power by the European countries, the United States, and
Israel.

This individual will gain complete political control; he will provide a
solution to the Middle East crisis and thereby win support from Israel
because of his guarantee for the safety of the country. At this stage the
world will be undergoing such misery that all peoples will be willing to
turn to this figure to provide a solution to the world crisis. This charismatic
figure will eventually be joined by a religious leader who is referred to in
the book of Revelation as 'the beast which rises out of the earth'. The aim of
this figure is to direct attention to the world political leader. During the
Great Tribulation, Messianic Jews predict that the world political leader
will consolidate his leadership. According to a number of Messianic Jews,

the last half of the period of tribulation will be before the worst. Crises will occur for the Jewish people and the rest of humanity, including floods, famines, earthquakes and disease.

At this time the world religious leader will declare the world political leader to be divine. Those who refuse to accept this ecumenical religion will be accused of subversive behaviour: both traditional Jews and Christians will be persecuted and killed. Eventually three coalitions of nations will converge on the Middle East and engage in battle with the world political leader. The last struggle between these forces will be in the plain that stretches in north-central Israel. Explaining this eschatology in *Messianic Judaism*, David Rausch wrote:

> One coalition will include Russia and the North, the second will be from the Far East and the third will be an Egyptian–African block. These coalitions battling against the world political leader in command of the Western block would devastate the world except for the fact that the Messiah will come back to earth at this time. All of the coalitions and power blocks will forget their differences and turn to fight against the Messiah, but he will triumph over them. At the Messiah's victory, there will finally be peace and a glorious future for Israel, the Jewish people and the world.[8]

The Jewishness of Messianic Jews

According to Orthodox Judaism, anyone who is born of a Jewish mother or has converted to the faith through Orthodox authorities is to be considered a Jew. Conversion through any other branch of Judaism is regarded as ineffective. Until recently, both Conservative and Reform Judaism accepted the criterion of matrilineal descent (while providing their own procedures for conversion). In the last few years, however, the Reform movement decreed that anyone born of either a Jewish mother or a Jewish father should be considered Jewish. Reconstructionist Judaism has similarly accepted paternal as well as maternal descent as a sufficient condition for determining the status of an individual.

Messianic Judaism, on the other hand, has redefined the definition of Jewishness. Basing its view on scriptural teaching, the movement points out that in ancient times Jewish descent was determined by the father. Thus David Stern argued in *Messianic Jewish Manifesto*:

> It is commonly accepted that the Bible traces Jewishness genetically through the father. According to this theory, Jewishness came to be traced through the mother at a time of historical turmoil when Jewish women were being sold as concubines to Gentiles, so that there could be doubt whether a child's father was Jewish. However, one can make a case that even in the Bible Jewishness depends on the mother. Some in the Reform movement have cut the Gordian knot by accepting as Jewish anyone with either parent Jewish.[9]

In Stern's view, anyone who is born a Jew – whether through maternal or paternal descent, or who has converted to Judaism through any one of the movements within the Jewish world – should be regarded as Jewish. Within the movement, the broadening of the definition of Jewishness to include both matrilineal and patrilineal descent has been universally accepted. In general, if a person is able to claim descent from at least one Jewish grandparent, that individual is regarded as a Jew. However, obviously not everyone who is Jewish is a Messianic Jew.

In considering this issue, David Stern argued that only those Jews who wish to live a demonstrable Messianic Jewish lifestyle within the framework of *Torah* are to be viewed as Messianic Jews. In his view, it is not enough for a believer in Yeshua who happens to be of Jewish descent to be considered a Messianic Jew. What is required is a conscious decision to live as a Jew. In this regard, Stern listed a number of sub-Messianic positions. The first category consists of individuals who are either too Jewish or insufficiently Messianic:

1. Open Jews, Jews who are willing to hear about Yeshua and the Gospel, but don't get saved. They may have good things to say about Yeshua, the New Testament and believers, but they are not willing to take the step of faith to be born again.
2. 'Secret believers' who remain in the Jewish community without confessing publicly their faith in Yeshua . . .
3. Some Jewish believers find themselves uncomfortable in Gentile Christian churches, but are not located near a Messianic Jewish congregation. They don't go to any church but have casual fellowship with like-minded people. Communal aspects of our faith achievable only in a congregational setting get neglected. The person's faith is Messianic, not 'sub-Messianic', but his spiritual growth is stunted by his stand-offishness.[10]

Other positions are designated as too Gentile:

1. Jews who Gentilize themselves in Christian churches, doing all they can to conceal their Jewishness and 'pass' as Gentiles. This phenomenon was more prevalent in the eighteenth and nineteenth centuries, when many Jews considered baptism 'the passport to Western Civilization' . . .
2. Veneer of Jewishness. Often Christian missions to the Jews put on a thin veneer of Jewishness, to the best of their ability, over what is clearly a Gentile Christian approach to faith . . . The problem arises from the missionary's unawareness of how Jewish the Gospel really is and of how to express biblical Messianic faith in genuinely Jewish ways.[11]

For Messianic Jews, however, there is no conflict between living a Jewish lifestyle and accepting Messiah Yeshua. Believing in Yeshua is viewed as the fulfilment of one's Jewish commitment. As Stern explained:

> A Jewish believer in Yeshua is not faced with having to give up some Jewishness
> in order to be more Messianic, or having to give up some of his Messianic faith to
> be more Jewish. Non-Messianic Jews might try to convince him of this, as some
> Gentile Christians, but they would be wrong. The New Testament picture
> throughout is that Jews who believed in Yeshua remained as fully Jewish as they
> ever were.[12]

In defending this position, Messianic Jews point to the fact that the concept
of the Messiah is Jewish; Yeshua himself was Jewish; all of Yeshua's
disciples were Jews; and all of his followers were Jews. The Gospel was
brought by Jews to the non-Jewish world, and Paul too was Jewish.
Further, Messiah Yeshua's sacrificial atonement was rooted in the Jewish
sacrificial system; the Lord's Supper is based on the Jewish Passover;
baptism is a Jewish ritual; and the New Testament is grounded in the
Hebrew Bible.

For these reasons Jewish believers insist that Messianic Jews are the only
truly fulfilled Jews. The basis for this claim is that God's intention for his
chosen people is that they should acknowledge Jesus as Israel's Messiah.
As the American Board of Missions to the Jews explained in *Introducing the
Jewish People to Their Messiah*:

> A Jewish person who accepts Jesus as his Messiah does not convert to another
> religion, but actually returns to the faith of Abraham, Isaac and Jacob fulfilled.[13]

Similarly, Arthur Kac in *The Messiahship of Jesus* declared:

> This means that a Jew who becomes a Christian is not converted in the ordinary
> sense of the term. He does not turn around or change direction; he advances in
> faith from the Old Testament to the New Testament.[14]

Hence Jews should not see the choice between accepting Jesus or
remaining within the fold as an alternative – recognizing Yeshua as Lord
and Saviour should be perceived as a return to the true faith rather than an
abandonment of the tradition. Such an understanding is widespread
within the movement. In a survey of British Messianic Jews undertaken in
1976 by David Hartley, for example, believers were asked if since accepting
Yeshua, they felt more Jewish or less: 4 per cent said they felt less Jewish, 14
per cent said that it made no appreciable difference, but 82 per cent said
they felt more Jewish. Many stated that they felt 'completed' or 'fulfilled';
others replied that they found their real identity or that they had discovered what the Jewish people have been looking for.[15]

In *Messianic Jewish Manifesto*, Stern proclaimed that Messianic Jews must
regard themselves as being 100 per cent Jewish while affirming Jesus'
central role in God's plan for humanity:

We are 100% Jewish, no matter who denies it. And we are 100% Messianic, no matter who denies it. So it was for the first-century Jewish believers, and so it must be today. This is God-determined truth, in the face of all lies, slanders and disinformation of those who would deny us our true identity. Yet it is up to us to make good our claims. We must, in the Messiah, in obedience to God, through the power of his Holy Spirit, create the visible reality that will validate our rhetoric... We will not boast in our Jewish identity, but in the God of the universe who chose to act through a people of whom we are a part. Nor will we boast in our Messianic identity, but in the Messiah who chose from among Jews and Gentiles those who are his, and we are his. And thirdly, we will not boast in our Messianic Jewish identity, but in the Lord who has made us the bridge between the two separated communities of which we are part and given us the work of helping to bring them together.[16]

Messianic Judaism and the Jewish tradition

According to Messianic Jews, Messianic Judaism is the legitimate heir of biblical Judaism. The New Testament, they argue, is the only divine revelation after the *Torah*; hence it is only through the New Testament that the *Tanakh* can be understood. As Walter Riggans explained in *Messianic Judaism and Jewish-Christian Relations*:

> It is the New Testament which actually determines what is true faith in God. Therefore the idea that the faith centred on Jesus is somehow a child of Judaism, in the sense of being essentially derivative, is rejected summarily.[17]

As B. Z. Sobel explained in his sociological study of Messianic Jews, this belief was shared by Hebrew Christian societies throughout the nineteenth and early twentieth centuries:

> The basic contention put forward by the Hebrew Christian movement was that the only legitimate expression of Jewishness was in fact Christianity, in that it constituted the fulfilment of the promise vouchsafed in the Old Testament faith of Israel . . . the assertion is in fact made by Hebrew Christianity that the true tradition has been destroyed or obscured by a fraudulent development, and that modern Judaism is, as it were, living a lie.[18]

Such a contrast has continued within the modern Messianic movement: Messianic Jews similarly contend that by accepting Yeshua as their Messiah they have found true biblical Judaism. In *Everything You Need to Know to Grow a Messianic Yeshiva*, Philip Goble stressed that biblical institutions and observances have been transformed through Yeshua's sacrificial death. Messianic Judaism, he stated, maintains that in the death of Yeshua the *Torah*'s demand for blood sacrifice has been fulfilled. In addition,

Messianic Judaism also preserves the true significance of such Jewish institutions as the high priesthood, the sage, and the prophet and such doctrines as concerning the Messianic King, the Holy Spirit, and salvation.[19]

Messianic Jews thus see themselves as completed Jews, in contrast to the other groups within the Jewish community (Orthodox, Hasidic, Conservative, Reform and Reconstructionist Jews) which are rooted in rabbinic Judaism. Nonetheless, as we have seen, in recent times Messianic leaders have drawn attention to the abiding significance of traditional Jewish customs. Unlike the early Hebrew Christians, Messianic Jews have rediscovered the spiritual insights of traditional Judaism. As David Stern explained in *Messianic Jewish Manifesto*:

> Jewish history is important . . . because Judaism has preserved better application of biblical truth to many specific ethical decision-making situations than the usual Christian arrangements, which tend to be more *ad hoc* and therefore less well designed for preserving wisdom. Moreover, phenomena such as the sanctification of time in festivals and *Shabbat*, and the introduction of holiness into daily life through repeated activities such as laying *tefillin*, reciting prayers in a synagogue, and even seeing the *mezuzah* on the door express in practical ways the immanence of God. Thus modern Jewish history and the Judaism it has produced help us Messianic Jews to understand our faith.[20]

Despite such a recognition of the spiritual significance of traditional Jewish observance, Messianic Jews are faced with the perplexity of determining the extent to which they should observe the *Torah*. In *Messianic Jewish Manifesto*, Stern pointed out that individual Messianic Jews, as well as Messianic Jewish congregations, currently work out their own ways of relating to the teachings and legal rulings produced over more than three millennia by the Jewish people. According to Stern, there are five major approaches to this issue within the movement:

1. Orthodox Jewish law should be observed in its entirety. Such a stand is arguably supported by New Testament teaching. Thus in Matthew 5:17–20 Yeshua declares that he did not come to abolish the *Torah*, and that anyone who disobeys its least commands and teaches others to do so will be counted least in the Kingdom of Heaven. Further, when castigating the religious establishment, Yeshua did not denigrate any part of the *Torah*. Again, in Matthew 23:2–3, Yeshua states that the *Torah* teachers and the Pharisees sit in the seat of Moses, implying that they have authority to determine how the law should be applied. Finally, Paul in Romans 7:12 refers to the *Torah* as holy, just and good. Yet, even those Messianic Jews who insist on the observance of traditional Jewish law are convinced that salvation is based on God's grace and mighty acts rather than strict observance of the *Torah*.

2. It is desirable, though not essential, that Messianic Jews observe traditional Jewish law. Biblical law, they argue, was given by God to the Jewish people and never abrogated; therefore it is obligatory. Further, those who are knowledgeable about Jewish history are aware of the importance of the legal tradition. It has been God's will that the Jewish people be preserved: the law has served as a vital means of ensuring Jewish survival. Added to these arguments is the conviction that by keeping the law, Messianic Jews will be able to identify with fellow Jews.

3. Keeping Jewish law is a totally subjective issue. Whether Messianic Jews obey the law is a matter of individual conscience. The New Testament, the Church and Christianity have nothing to say on this subject. Those who hold to this view insist that obedience to Jewish law is in no way essential for salvation. Rather, salvation is based alone on faith, repentance from sin, and turning to God through Messiah Yeshua.

4. It is actually undesirable for Messianic Jews to observe traditional Jewish law. While it is not prohibited, Messianic Jews should recognize that they are liberated from the law and instead alive in the Spirit.

5. Messianic Jews should not observe Jewish law at all. The fear is that they will regard the *Torah*, rather than trust in Yeshua, as the means of salvation.[21]

Messianic Jews thus approach the Jewish tradition in a variety of ways. Yet while accepting that such individual decision-making is essential to the life of a Messianic Jew, a number of leaders of the movement have been anxious that Messianic Judaism embarks on the task of constructing a legal framework for Messianic living. Discussing the resources for such an endeavour, David Stern wrote:

What might Messianic Jewish halakhists wish to consult as they prepare for their task? . . . the New Testament is one such source, and it should go without saying that the *Tanakh* is another. In addition to the Bible, Messianic Jewish halakhists must know how to deal with the vast amount of halakhic material that has arisen within Judaism. This includes not only the *Mishnah* (220 CE) and the two *Gemaras*, each of which with the *Mishnah* equals a *Talmud* – the Jerusalem *Talmud* (4th century) and the Babylonian *Talmud* (5th century) – but also the *Tosefta* (composed of 2nd–3rd-century codifications similar to the *Mishnah*), the halakhic *midrashim* (*Mekhilta* on Exodus, *Sifra* on Leviticus, *Sifrei* on Numbers and Deuteronomy, all compiled in the fourth or fifth centuries) and the opinions of the *Savoraim* (6th–7th centuries), *Gaonim* (7th–10th centuries), *Poskim* (11th–14th centuries), *Rishonim* (14th–17th centuries) and *Acharonim* (18th–20th centuries) contained in codes, responsa (case law) and other writings . . . other Jewish materials touch on *halakhah* from without rather than from within. For example, there is Jewish philosophy, Jewish ethics (*musar*), and an interesting literature on *taamey ha-mitzvot*, 'the reasons for the commandments'. We should research the Conservative, Reform and Reconstructionist writings on *halakhah*, since these movements have had to explain to their own constituencies why they adopt a view different from that of the Orthodox, and have therefore pioneered some paths we should explore.[22]

Hence, Messianic Jews see themselves as firmly rooted within the Jewish tradition. Dedicated to living in accordance with scriptural teaching, they are open to the insights of the Jewish heritage as it developed over the last 2000 years. Determined to distance themselves from the Gentile Church, they insist that they are faithful Jews, holding firm to the principles of the faith as manifest in the life and teaching of Messiah Yeshua.

Messianic Jewish mission

In the view of Messianic Jews, the Gentile Church has abandoned its Jewish roots. As a consequence, the Messianic movement seeks to recapture the original structure and mission of the Church. Messianic Judaism is thus perceived by its members as a spiritual renaissance, a return to the faith of the followers of Yeshua. In this quest Messianic Jews have been anxious to persuade other Jews to embrace Yeshua as their long-awaited deliverer.

From the very beginning of the movement in the early part of this century, the drive to share the Gospel was a central aim of the movement. Thus Article II of the constitution of the Hebrew Christian Alliance of America stated that the movement seeks:

1. To encourage and strengthen Hebrew Christians and to deepen their faith in the Lord Jesus Christ.
2. To propagate more widely the Gospel of our Lord and Saviour, Jesus Christ, by strengthening existing Jewish missions, and fostering all other agencies to that end.
3. To provide for the evangelical Christian churches of America an authoritative and reliable channel how best to serve the cause of Jewish evangelism.[23]

As Riggans noted in *Messianic Judaism and Jewish–Christian Relations*, the movement believed that if Messianic Judaism desisted from embarking on such a task, this would be a subtle form of anti-semitism: 'The argument used is basically that to withhold from the Jewish people the most precious gift of God to them betrays a conscious or unconscious desire to prevent them receiving that gift.'[24]

According to B. Z. Sobel in *Hebrew Christianity: The Thirteenth Tribe*, only Messianic congregations are able to serve as a base for such Jewish evangelizing. 'If Hebrew Christianity itself can effectively gain converts,' he wrote:

how much more effective could this work be when buttressed by a church that the convert may call his own. This is the one hope that seems to have induced widespread support for the church idea, and the one goal that brooked little argument even from persons who would otherwise have opposed such a development.[25]

Endorsing this approach, Dan Juster stressed in *Jewish Congregations: A New Approach to Jewish Witness* that such a programme of outreach is crucially needed in the modern world:

> This is precisely what has been missing in Jewish outreach for almost 1,850 years. There has been no ongoing lay movement for Jesus in the Jewish community. A Jew is converted, baptized, Christianized and assimilated . . . What is the source of a powerful Spirit-led movement for Jesus in the Jewish community. Certainly it is the planting of Jewish congregations in these communities.[26]

Evangelism of the Jewish people is thus at the heart of the Messianic movement. In the view of David Stern in *Messianic Jewish Manifesto*, the goal of the Messianic community is to praise Yeshua and make him known throughout the world. Such a crusade, however, is not possible unless the movement witnesses to the Jewish community. Without Messianic Judaism, he asserted, the Jewish people will fail to achieve their proper role in history:

> The destiny of Messianic Judaism is to live out the fact that it is simultaneously 100% Messianic and 100% Jewish, rejecting the 'either-or' demanded by many Christians and Jews, and instead, through its very existence and self-expression, bringing reconciliation. It will eventually be centred in Israel, the land God has promised the Jewish people. It will provide the matrix for the growth of true Judaism and true Christianity and for assisting both in fulfilling their rightful aims. It will be the means of evangelizing the Jewish people corporately, as a people.[27]

In *A Case for Messianic Judaism*, James Hutchens similarly argued that Messianic Jews are under an obligation to bear witness of Yeshua's Messiahship to the Jewish people:

> Messianic Jews aren't satisfied merely to be additional caretakers and perpetrators of a heritage, as rich and meaningful as that heritage is . . . Thus, Messianic Judaism is a Missionary Judaism. It seeks to bring men into a covenant relationship to the God of Abraham, Isaac and Jacob, through the atoning sacrifice of Jesus, His Messiah.[28]

Becoming a follower of Yeshua, however, does not lead the Jewish person away from Judaism; rather, such a step involves a return to the true faith. Messianic Judaism, he argued, affirms that a Jew can accept Yeshua and still maintain the distinctive features of Judaism.

Not surprisingly, such attitudes have evoked a bitterly hostile response from the Jewish community. In February 1980, for example, two members of the Jewish Defense League in Los Angeles stole the *Torah* scroll from the local synagogue. The next month members of the Jewish Defense League picketed the congregation and hurled rocks through a window of the building. According to the rabbi who had joined them (Rabbi Kenneth Cohen of Young Israel Congregation), these Messianic Jews were misleading members of the Jewish community and engaging in idol worship. In Toronto a similar incident occurred in the same year where a Messianic youth choir was performing. As Yohanna Chernoff explained in *Born a Jew . . . Die a Jew*, she and Joe Finkelstein had accompanied this group to Toronto. The congregation's leader, Hans Vanderwerff, however, warned the community to expect strong opposition:

> His warning was both expedient and timely. More than two hundred protesters turned out in force, distributing leaflets entitled, 'The Soul Snatchers are at it . . . again.' . . . As Joe stood to introduce *Kol Simcha* to the audience, whistles and jeers came from the back of the room, and more than twenty Jewish protesters stood up and began their loud chanting: 'Jews don't switch! Jews and Jesus don't mix!'[29]

Although the police escorted the protesters out of the meeting, other critics of the movement gained entrance by using forged tickets. During the performance they loudly accused Messianic Jews of being Gentiles masquerading as Jews as well as 'spiritual Nazis'. They whistled, booed, coughed, stamped their feet, and even provoked fights in the aisles.

Continuing her narrative of opposition to the movement, Yohanna Chernoff described further agitation which occurred in the 1980s:

> There were constant bomb threats and death threats; our tires were punctured, our children spat on, and items were stolen from around the synagogue. The antagonists would take down license plate numbers of those attending our services, call their places of business and try to get them fired.[30]

Eventually a major rally took place against the Messianic community in Philadelphia. Large posters were put up throughout the city, including one directly across the street from the entrance to the synagogue. Thousands of protesters descended on the congregation from the local Jewish population:

> Several shiny, black Cadillacs and two 20-foot-long flat-bed trucks rolled up and parked directly across the street from our property . . . While they watched us, we watched the Orthodox rabbis. With their black coats and hats, *pa'ot* (side curls) and beards, they surveyed the crowd of hundreds of onlookers thronging the street. Their assistants hooked the loudspeakers up to their portable electric generators, then tested for sound . . . The march began.[31]

In the past few decades similar reactions have occurred throughout the Jewish community; increasingly groups from across the Jewish religious spectrum have become alarmed by the growth of the Messianic movement. Pre-eminent among anti-Messianic organizations, Jews for Judaism has been actively engaged in countering Messianic missionizing. Established in 1986, it now has branches in Los Angeles, Baltimore, Chicago, Harrisburg, Washington, Philadelphia, New York, Toronto, and Johannesburg, South Africa. Its two primary goals are preventive education and winning back those Jews who have been influenced by missionaries.

In the movement's counter-missionary handbook, *The Jewish Response to Missionaries*, Rabbi Bentzion Kravitz concluded:

> One thing upon which the entire Jewish community and several Christian denominations agree is that 'Hebrew Christian' movements are not a part of Judaism. To be a 'Jew for Jesus' is as absurd as being a 'Christian for Buddha' and as ridiculous as 'kosher pork'; it is an obvious contradiction. To paraphrase Elijah, if you are a follower of Jesus, call yourself a Christian. If you are a Jew, practice Judaism. Don't deceive yourself; you can't be both.[32]

15 Messianic Judaism and its critics

Critique of Messianic Judaism

Critics of Messianic Judaism insist that it is impossible to remain Jewish while accepting Jesus as Messiah and Lord. In their view, the use of terminology such as 'Messianic Jew', 'Hebrew Christian' or 'Jew for Jesus' is a deceptive attempt to represent converted Jews as Jewish. As an example of such deceptive practices, counter-missionaries point out that missionary training manuals encourage the use of the expression 'believer' rather than 'Christian'; 'Messiah' instead of 'Christ'; 'tree' instead of 'cross'; and 'New Covenant' instead of 'New Testament', to promote a more Jewish-sounding message.

The misrepresentation and deception used in the attempt to disguise the seriousness of a Jew's conversion to Christianity is further reflected in the misuse of Jewish symbols and customs, the fabrication of Jewish texts, and the misrepresentation of the background and education of many believers. As Kravitz explained in *The Jewish Response to Missionaries: Counter-Missionary Handbook*:

> Numerous 'Hebrew Christian' leaders dishonestly refer to themselves as 'rabbis' and to their places of worship as 'synagogues'. These tactics are employed in an attempt to render their version of Christianity more palatable to the Jews they seek to convert.[1]

Such superficial attempts to sound Jewish, however, do not disguise the true facts of the situation. Even though Messianic Jews maintain that a person who is born Jewish can never lose his ancestral birthright, Scripture teaches that Jewish status is dependent on belief. Citing the case of Elijah and the prophets of Baal in 1 Kings 18:21, where Elijah declared to the ancient Israelites: 'How long will you waver between two opinions? If the Lord is God, follow him: but if Baal, follow him', Kravitz argued:

> A Jew who follows another religion is Jewish only to the point that he retains a spiritual obligation to repent and to return to Judaism. However, as long as his beliefs are idolatrous and foreign to Judaism, he cannot call himself a Jew.[2]

Regarding the Messianic claim that Yeshua fulfilled scriptural prophecies about the coming of the Messiah, anti-Messianics assert that such proof texts have been misquoted, mistranslated or taken out of context. A typical example of such misunderstanding of Scripture concerns the 'suffering servant' passages in Isaiah. In *The Jew and the Christian Missionary: Jewish Responses to Missionary Christianity*, Gerald Sigal explained:

> Christian missionaries have often wondered why Jews do not accept their contention that the fifty-third chapter of Isaiah is a prophecy of the life and death of Jesus. What Jews find even more amazing and mystifying is how any person who studies this chapter critically can possibly believe it alludes to Jesus. Based on what they thought the Hebrew Scriptures said concerning the Messiah, the New Testament authors restructured the life of the historical Jesus to make it conform to their preconceived ideas. However, neither figurative nor literal fulfilment of all that the New Testament authors claim holds up upon close examination of the text of Isaiah 53.[3]

Critics of Messianic Judaism also reject the claim that spiritual salvation and a personal relationship with God can only come through Yeshua. Here the Messianic argument is that in ancient times Jews needed blood sacrifices to rid themselves of sin. Since the Temple was destroyed in 70 CE, Jews today can find salvation from sin only by believing in Yeshua, who died on the cross and shed his blood as the final sacrifice. Such a conviction, critics assert, is a distortion of scriptural teaching. As Leviticus 4:1 makes clear, sacrifice was required only for unintentional sin; further, numerous biblical passages such as Hosea 14 state that prayer has taken the place of sacrifice. Thus, through repentance, prayer, fasting and observing God's laws, one may attain salvation.

Anti-Messianics also reject the belief that miracles prove the validity of faith in Yeshua. Claims of miracles and of changes in one's life are not unique to any religion – converts to cults and to other religions relate similar events. Yet the Jewish Bible warns that such alleged miracles may in reality be a test from God. A classic example of such an event is found in Deuteronomy 13:1–6:

> If a prophet or a dreamer of dreams arises and gives you a sign or wonder (miracle), and the sign or wonder comes true, saying, 'Let us go after other gods whom you have not known and let us serve them', you shall not listen to the words of that prophet or that dreamer of dreams; for the Lord your God is testing you to find out if you love the Lord your God with all your heart.

Critics of the movement also assert, in contrast to Messianic claims, that the belief in the Trinity is incompatible with Judaism. Opponents of the movement assert that it is forbidden for Jews to accept such a doctrine. The commandment to believe in God's unity is a fundamental precept of the faith. Thus Deuteronomy 6:4 states: 'Hear O Israel, The Lord our God, the Lord is one.' Such a proclamation is an explicit rejection of the notion of a plurality of gods, or any plurality in the Godhead. In contrast with Messianic Jews, who assert that the Deity is a composite unity embracing Yeshua as part of the triune nature of the Godhead, upholders of the tradition insist that there can be no multiplicity in God. In their view the divine creator is a single, incorporeal being who created the universe out of nothing.

Further, opponents of Messianic Judaism point out that Jesus did not fulfil the traditional criteria for Messiahship: he did not restore the kingdom of David to its former glory, gather in the dispersed ones of Israel, restore all the laws of the *Torah* that were in abeyance such as the sacrificial cult, compel Israel to walk in the way of the *Torah*, rebuild the Temple, or usher in a new order in the world and nature. In other words, Jesus did not inaugurate a cataclysmic change in history: universal peace, in which there is neither war nor competition, did not come about on earth. Thus, for opponents of the Messianic movement, Jesus did not fulfil the prophetic Messianic hope in a redeemer who would bring political and spiritual redemption, as well as earthly blessings and moral perfection, to the human race.

In his *Counter-Missionary Handbook*, Kravitz offered a number of concrete recommendations about how to prevent Messianic Jews from converting Jews. In answer to the question whether there is anything that Jews can do to immunize themselves and their families, he stated:

> As with so many facets of life, prevention begins at home. A Jewish home should feel Jewish. Parents can set the tone through their own positive example: by learning about Judaism, by observing its customs, traditions and meaning in ways with which they themselves are comfortable. A formal Jewish education is necessary . . . It is dangerous to give a child the impression that Judaism is a religion of convenience that allows one to pick and choose one's observances. This may leave the child with an impression that there are no consequences for his or her religious actions and that Judaism is both hypocritical and void of spiritual content.[4]

Concerning the question how a parent can know whether his son or daughter is at risk or under a missionary's influence, Kravitz explained:

> Parents might discover pamphlets, New Testament tracts, jewelry representing a particular group, or the Bible of a different faith. Sometimes the son or daughter will give verbal clues, like 'We need to be saved' or 'I'm being given salvation lest I go to hell.' Or the child may open a discussion by saying, 'Did you know that the New Testament (or another book) says such and such?' Just as a parental intuition can detect the onset of an illness before medical symptoms appear, it can frequently detect a spiritual malady.[5]

Turning to the question what should take place if preventive measures are too late and the son or daughter has joined a Messianic congregation, Kravitz emphasized that parents should not over-react:

> The important thing is not to panic, explode, accuse, say *Kaddish* or otherwise provoke the convert into avoidance of you or the issue. A calm demeanour, coupled with open channels of communication mentioned earlier, will often facilitate the start of dialogue. Dialogue is the first step we take in attempting to get a person to reconsider his or her new religion or cult. If parents or other significant family members actively listen, the convert may be more than willing to discuss his or her motivation and reasoning.[6]

However, what if the family recoils in shame? What if the family members disown the convert? According to the *Counter-Missionary Handbook,* if confrontation occurs, dialogue will become difficult or impossible. Creating an argument which polarizes both parties undermines any constructive exchange. It is necessary to acknowledge that a convert's new beliefs are as true to him as one's own are to oneself. Given such a situation, family members must do whatever they can to convince the convert to consider all sides of the issue. Nonetheless, this does not mean that the family has to tolerate the religious practices of the convert:

> If the family tolerates the person's decision to change religion, the convert should also respect the family's wishes. The alien religion should be practised in the appropriate place . . . This arrangement also facilitates a more open atmosphere, more conducive to a willingness on the part of the convert and his or her family to meet with a trained professional. It is important to respect each person's right to an honest mistake.[7]

But what if the convert is not persuaded and continues to adhere to his or her new faith? Is that person lost to Judaism? In Kravitz's view, the situation is not desperate:

> Those of us in the field can tell you hundreds of stories about people who spent years in Christianity or a cult only to return to Judaism. That's why it's important to maintain an open channel of communication and to set a good religious example. Family will always remain family; differences in belief and faith do not change a lifetime biological and emotional relationship. One should never stop hoping that the individual will return.[8]

Former Messianic Jews

In *The Jewish Response to Missionaries: Counter-Missionary Handbook,* Kravitz cited the case of three former Messianic Jews who left the movement and became anxious to warn the community of its pernicious influence. These examples, he argued, illustrate the dangers facing the Jewish community from the growth of Messianic Judaism. Jews for Judaism has also published an account by another former Messianic Jew who had gained prominence in the movement and eventually became a counter-missionary, *From 'Messianic Jew' to Counter-Missionary: The Story of Julius Ciss.* These four testimonies challenge Messianic Judaism's claims to religious authenticity:

Laura's story

Although born Jewish, I was active in Bible studies with Baptist and other evangelical churches for over three years, and went to Christian camps during my summers. For a long time, I was actively involved with Jews for Jesus, handing out tracts (leaflets), attending 'Messianic retreats' and Bible study courses. I felt more comfortable studying with other Jews who also believed in Jesus, or Yeshua, as we called him. Most of the people involved with Jews for Jesus came from the same limited Jewish background as I, and like me were dissatisfied with their previous experiences of Judaism. But now we considered ourselves 'completed Jews'. At Bible study sessions, we studied both the 'New' and 'Old' Testaments. Using the 'Old' to prove that Jesus was indeed the prophesied Messiah, I was very content with my relationship with 'the Lord' and with my involvement in Jews for Jesus.

One day, I handed out a tract to a religious Jewish woman and told her about the spiritual completeness and close relationship one can have with God through belief in Yeshua (Jesus). I showed her many passages in the 'Old' and 'New' Testaments, as she listened to my enthusiastic 'witness'. After I finished, she asked me some basic questions about Jewish holidays and prayers. Her questions caught me off guard. I felt flustered and ashamed that I didn't know the answers. In my frustration, I asked her if she felt that she had a personal relationship with God, something I knew I didn't feel growing up as a Jew. 'Yes', she said, 'why don't you come over to my home for *Shabbat* and decide for yourself whether we Jews have a relationship with God?' She gave me her number and left.

Her many questions pounded in my head. Why didn't I know about those holidays? Had I really given Judaism a chance? I had never met a religiously committed Jew before, and had thought they existed only in books. My 'Hebrew Christian' friends tried to dissuade me from calling this woman. But I felt that, if I really believed in Jesus, I would see that her spirituality was false. I didn't think that anything could get in the way of my relationship with Jesus.

I went to the home of those observant Jews and was overwhelmed by the beauty of *Shabbat*. It seemed that everything they did was related to God. From the blessing of the children to the flickering of the *Havdalah* candle, there was something holy about their Jewish lifestyle. I felt oppressed by my ignorance, and wanted to know more. I prayed to Jesus to show me the way, but in time my commitment began to change. I realized that I didn't need an intermediary to relate to God. The more I studied the *Torah*'s views of the relationship between man and God, the more I realized that the Trinity could not be a biblical concept and the more I felt allied with traditional Judaism. While studying the *Torah* in Hebrew, I discovered numerous mistranslations in the Christian text. Slowly, I returned home to my people.

Through my intense study, I learned the deeper meanings of the Jewish concepts of God, commandments, devotion and prayer. The spirituality that I had longed for in my youth was in my own backyard the whole time. I am married now, and my husband and I have dedicated our lives to God and to the *Torah*. Our children won't need to ask the question I was forced to ask myself: 'Did I really give Judaism a chance?'[9]

Jerry's story

I was raised in a Conservative Jewish home and my parents were Holocaust survivors. As a child, I attended Hebrew school, and observed the holiday traditions. I always felt proud of being Jewish, especially after visiting Israel.

After high school, I attended a major university in Southern California, majoring in engineering. During my years at the university, I came into contact with a number of 'born again Christians'. It was my acquaintance and subsequent study with them that led me to become a 'born again Christian'. I experienced a real personal relationship with God. I was very involved for over four years. I read the Bible every night and attended a fundamentalist church called Calvary Chapel at least twice a week. As I grew in my faith, I started influencing others and even ran my own Bible study group. Since I lived on campus, I joined an organization called Campus Crusade for Christ. I became very involved in that group, attending leadership training classes and 'action group' meetings. Eventually, I ran my own 'action group'. I also appeared on Christian radio and television programs, and even in two Christian movies. I considered myself not only a 'born again Christian', but a 'completed Jew'.

One day, our entire advanced action group went to hear a rabbi from 'Jews for Judaism' lecture about Christianity. The sincerity, commitment and wealth of knowledge of this rabbi impressed us all. But, since we knew that we had the 'truth', we challenged him on numerous theological points. To my amazement, he was able to answer every one. After the lecture, I decided that I would stay and continue talking with this rabbi. We spoke all night . . .

I began to realize that even with my Jewish background I still had a very limited understanding of what it meant to be a Jew. My acceptance of Jesus had been a very one-sided decision. I knew so much of the Christian perspective but relatively little of the Jewish viewpoint. As a Christian I had been very dogmatic; my attitude was, 'I'll listen to what you have to say, but I know that I'm right.' My encounter with this rabbi made me realize that there are two sides to every story.

I started to study and check things out. Christians would ask me, 'Do you think the devil's got a little hold on you?' I would reply that I was only doing what Jesus said: 'Ask and ye shall receive' and 'Seek diligently and ye shall find.' I prayed for guidance, and others prayed with me that I be led on the right path. My course of inquiry turned up countless 'proof texts' from the Christian Bible which were based upon mistranslations or what had been taken out of context.

The more deeply I searched, the more apparent it became to me that I had made a mistake.

At the same time, another part of me was demanding, 'What about all the changes in my life, the miracles I had seen, the gifts of the Holy Spirit?' How was I to ignore all of this? I eventually realized that all of these experiences were not unique to Christianity, but that they happen to people in other religions as well. People's lives have been changed within the realm of Judaism; Christians hardly have a monopoly on God!

I am now practising Judaism in its proper and spiritual way, and feel much closer to God than ever before. I know now what it means to be a Jew. It is important to use the mind that God gave me, and to follow his word as he intended it. I can't see how anyone who would really understand Judaism could ever believe in Jesus; there's just no room for Jesus in the Jewish picture.[10]

Rachel's story

I was born and raised in Tel Aviv, Israel, and had the best education possible. I am fluent in Hebrew and English and knowledgeable about Jewish and Israeli life as well as the Bible stories. When I moved to America at age 20, numerous Christians befriended me and talked to me about Jesus. I studied their Bible with them on a regular basis and eventually became a 'born again Christian'. I joined a 'Messianic synagogue' and for over 5 years considered myself a better Jew than before; I was now a 'Messianic Jew'.

American Jews were always surprised to meet an Israeli who had accepted Christianity, and I used these encounters to share my faith with them. One individual challenged me to meet with Rabbi Bentzion Kravitz of Jews for Judaism. My fluency in Hebrew assured me that he couldn't put anything over on me. Our first meeting lasted for seven hours. We examined all the biblical passages in the Hebrew original, since prior to this, my 'born again' friends and I had studied the Bible in English. I discovered that the English translations which I had used were based upon mistranslations and distortions.

I spent *Shabbat* with Rabbi Kravitz and his family on many occasions, exploring basic concepts of religion, morality and God. My close association with these religiously committed Jews made a tremendous impression on me. I noted the truth in their commitment, their sincerity and closeness to God, something that I had never been exposed to in secular Israeli society. In fact, it was something which I had never wanted to approach. However, because the facts were so convincing, I continued my exploration of Judaism and eventually realized that I had made a big mistake accepting Christianity. I returned to Judaism and this time it has changed my life. I am now delighted with my commitment to Judaism and my belief in one God.[11]

Julius' story

I grew up in a traditional Jewish home. My parents are both Holocaust survivors . . . My parents attended an 'Orthodox' synagogue thus leading me to believe in my younger years that I was an 'Orthodox' Jew. While they did keep a semblance of *Shabbat*, attended synagogue on the High Holidays, and conducted a Passover *seder*, religion was not a vibrant entity in our home. As a result of my sparse religious education, I never had much understanding of the essentials of Judaism . . . Consequently I found little reason to maintain a strong Jewish identity. I did have a sense of being Jewish, but I lacked any kind of vital commitment to this identity, either religiously or socially. It wasn't difficult to make a decision in my adolescent years to begin dating non-Jewish girls. In my fourth year at Toronto's Ontario College of Art, I met a woman named Mary Beth . . . There was only one problem; she informed me on our second date that she was a 'born again' Christian. However, I didn't care, I was already deeply emotionally involved with her . . .

On several occasions, Mary Beth had asked me to go to church with her. I finally consented. However, once I was in the church, everything screamed out that I was in the wrong place. The entire setting was foreign: Gentiles worshipping a foreign 'god' with strange hymns. Being there made me feel like a traitor to my people . . . She was now desperate to find a way to get me to accept Christian religious belief. She discovered a congregation of predominantly Jewish people in Toronto who believed in Jesus . . . Not knowing what to expect, I walked into the meeting hall and sat down. The congregation was addressed by a very pleasant man with a large nose and a face as Jewish as the map of Israel. He wore a *yarmulke* (skullcap) on his bald head, and a *tallit* (prayer shawl). Many of the male congregants that evening were also wearing *yarmulkes* and *tallitot*. Some of the women wore headcoverings, and one lit Sabbath candles while reciting a Hebrew blessing. This was followed by the recitation of *kiddush* blessings over a cup of wine and *Ha-Motzi* over a *challah*; but each blessing ended with the expression '*B'shem Yeshua Ha-Mashiach*' (in the name of Jesus the Messiah) . . .

It was in the environment of this 'Hebrew Christian' church, or 'Messianic Jewish Synagogue', as its leaders preferred to call it, that my interest in Jewish identity was rekindled . . . Through my weekly Bible study group, I was drawn deeper into serious consideration of the belief system offered me by these people because of their ability to use the Old Testament, or as they called it, the '*Tanakh*', to prove repeatedly that Jesus was the Jewish Messiah . . . As a result of this congregation's pervasive use of Jewish symbols, terminology, music, ritual and liturgy, and their distorted celebration of Jewish holidays, I soon began to feel that I had never been more Jewish in my life . . .

However, as time wore on – and despite feeling good about belonging to a congregation of Jews who believed in Jesus – I sensed that something was terribly wrong. I noticed that almost all of the Jewish people who shared my Christian beliefs came from backgrounds which were clearly devoid of any substantial Jewish content . . . What disturbed me most about their obvious lack of Jewish background was beginning to crystallize: the only Jews who appeared to accept Jesus as the Messiah were Jews who were ignorant of Judaism . . . As a result of this awareness, a process of questioning, doubting and probing had begun . . .

Gradually . . . I began to realize that much of what I believed seemed to be making less and less sense. I was not allowing my intellect to think through any of the profound arguments advanced by my friends. I had believed in Jesus, but was now finding that my reason and intellect, my *'pintele Yid'* (spark of Jewish spirituality), and my *neshama* (soul) were crying out to me, 'Julius, stop, listen! You're making a mistake.' After five years of exposure to a variety of people who claimed to be 'fulfilled, Messianic Jews', I was forced to admit that not a single Jew among them had ever known what authentic Judaism was all about . . .

I could no longer continue my commitment to Christianity or my belief in Jesus. What I read . . . completely shattered my faith and left me with a mountain of doubts. Despite having been cautioned that these doubtful thoughts were from the Devil, I had reached the point where I said to myself, 'Devil be damned! I have to listen to my own intellect.' This Christian teaching of doubts being the voice of Satan himself had maintained a powerful hold on me for most of the five years of my involvement in 'Messianic Judaism', just as I am sure it has a hold on many adherents to the Christian faith . . .

Abandoning the 'Hebrew Christian' movement was very difficult, and the difficulty was compounded by the fact that I was leaving behind some of the best friends I had ever had . . . I went to Aish Ha-Torah and to Ohr Somayach, two organizations devoted to exposing Jewish uneducated Jews to the richness and depth of their faith, and there started learning for the first time what Judaism truly was all about. For the first time in my life, I met 'born again' Jews, true Messianic Jews, and I encountered a Jewish life I'd never known. I met Jews who were more than willing to talk about belief in God, and about how to achieve a personal relationship with him. They invited me into their homes and synagogues, and I was able to experience the magnificent sanctity of *Shabbat* and the spiritual depth of Jewish prayer . . . I soon realized that I had missed so much, by simply closing my eyes to my true Jewish heritage . . .

I am now a 'counter-missionary', not by choice but by necessity. Other than a few activists, no one in the Jewish community appears to be addressing the problem of deceptive missionary tactics in the aggressive drive to convert Jews. When I walked into the church with Mary Beth, I knew to what I was being exposed; but when I walked into the 'Messianic Synagogue', I was misled. The people used Hebrew names and Hebrew terminology, sang Hebrew songs, and wore *yarmulkes* and *tallitot*. The leader of the congregation said, 'You're not going to convert and become a Christian. You're a Jew; now you'll be a "completed Jew", a "fulfilled Jew". You're not being asked to believe in Jesus Christ, but to accept "*Yeshua Ha-Mashiach*" as your Messiah instead. You won't be baptized; you'll have a "*Mikvah-Bris*".' The missionaries make the Christian religion look very Jewish, like kosher pork! It troubles me that Jews are falling prey to these false claims. Because of my own misspent years when I could have been living as a Jew, I hate to see others being sold the same false bill of goods, and cheated of their authentic heritage.[12]

16 Messianic Judaism and Israeli law

Jewishness and conversion to another faith

For Messianic Jews the question of Jewish identity is of vital significance. As we have seen, Messianic Jews insist that by accepting Yeshua, they become fulfilled Jews. Critics of Messianic Judaism, however, insist that they thereby forfeit their Jewishness. At the heart of this issue is the question: Who is a Jew? As previously noted, the traditional *halakhic* answer to this question is that a Jew is a person born of a Jewish mother: it is the mother who determines whether a person is a Jew or not. In addition, Orthodox Judaism provides a process of conversion for those who seek to become part of the Jewish community. Yet as we have seen, in recent years Reform Judaism has distanced itself from the tradition by asserting that a person born of a Jewish father is also to be considered Jewish. Hence, either matrilineal or patrilineal descent is seen as a sufficient basis for Jewish identity. Regarding conversion, the various non-Orthodox movements have provided their own mechanism for acceptance into the Jewish faith.

In addition to the biological definition of Jewishness, there exist three other kinds of non-*halakhic* definitions. According to the religious definition of Jewishness, to be a Jew one must be *Torah* observant. On this basis, many within the Jewish community insist that a person who has converted to another religion has violated the religious grounds of being a Jew. Hence such conversion creates a disqualification from being considered Jewish. A similar argument relates to the socio-cultural definition of Jewishness. On this basis being Jewish is construed as primarily a matter of commitment to the Jewish people. If through conversion to another faith a person disassociates herself from the Jewish community, she thereby abandons her Jewishness. Finally, the nationalist definition of Jewishness affirms that by living in Israel or supporting the Zionist cause, a person expresses her Jewishness. There is thus considerable confusion within the Jewish world as to what constitutes the basis of Jewish identity. Nonetheless, it must be stressed that the non-*halakhic* definitions of Jewishness are not recognized by rabbinic authorities. Within the main branches of Judaism, Jewish identity is defined exclusively in terms of biological descent or conversion.

Turning to the issue of apostasy, Jewish law provides a clear basis for determining the status of a convert to another faith. According to the *halakhah*, it is technically impossible for a person born to a Jewish mother or converted to Judaism through the traditional procedure to change his status. Even though a Jew undergoes the process of admission to another faith and formally renounces the Jewish religion, he remains a Jew, even though he is deemed a sinner. In the view of the medieval scholar Nahmanides, this attitude is based on the fact that the covenant between God and Israel was made 'with him that standeth here with us today before the Lord our God and also with him that is not with us here today' (Deuteronomy 29:14).[1]

For an individual who is born a Jew, Jewish identity is thus not a matter of choice: that person remains a Jew regardless of his religious beliefs. However, if a person assumes another faith, he is treated differently from other Jews. Technically such individuals are known as '*mumar*' (from the Hebrew root 'to change') or '*meshummad*' (from the Hebrew root meaning to persecute or force abandonment of faith) or '*apikoros*' ('heretic') or '*poshe'a Yisrael*' ('rebellious Jew'). According to the *halakhah*, an apostate who eventually reverts to Judaism requires no special ritual of acceptance since he never ceased to be a Jew. Nonetheless, some authorities insist that he must confess his sins and repent before a rabbinic court and declare that he will keep Jewish law; other authorities require ritual immersion in a *mikveh*.

In *The Jewish Religion*, Louis Jacobs summarized the traditional position regarding the apostate:

> The question of the status of a Jew converted to a religion other than Judaism did not arise and could not have arisen before the emergence of Judaism's two daughter and rival religions, Christianity and Islam ... the Jew who converted to Christianity or Islam had actually embraced a religion other than Judaism and it might have been held that by so doing he had severed all his connections with Jews and Judaism and had lost his Jewish status according to Jewish law. The homiletical Talmudic saying, 'Even when he has sinned an Israelite is still an Israelite', did not refer to apostasy but simply to a Jewish sinner who, the homily observes, still retains the high title 'Israel' despite his sinfulness. In the Middle Ages, however, perhaps in order to stem the tide of apostasy, the saying was given a completely new turn. Sin being understood as the sin of apostasy, the saying was taken to mean: 'Once a Jew always a Jew', namely, Jewish law does not acknowledge that a Jew's conversion to another religion can be in any way effective in changing his Jewish status.[2]

The Brother Daniel case

When the State of Israel was created in 1948, it became clear that legislation would be needed to determine who had a right to settle in the land. Two laws became the basis for all subsequent legislation: the Law of Return enacted in 1950 and the Nationality Law of 1952. These laws affirm that every Jew has the legal right to settle in the Holy Land as an '*oleh*' (a person who immigrates with the intent to become an Israeli citizen). As David Ben-Gurion, Israel's Prime Minister at the time, declared when the law was introduced into the Knesset:

> This law lays down not that the State accords the right of settlement to Jews abroad but that this right is inherent in every Jew by virtue of his being a Jew if it but be his will to take part in settling the land.[3]

In 1953 a further law was passed, the Rabbinic Courts Jurisdiction Law, which states that marriages and divorces of Jews, as well as other personal religious matters, must be settled in accordance with the *Torah* under the exclusive jurisdiction of rabbinic courts. All areas of personal status were thereby under Orthodox supervision, and the question of who is a Jew was thus to be settled by reference to the *halakhah*. A further law was passed in 1965, the Population Registration Law, which decreed that all Israelis must register with the Ministry of the Interior their nationality and religion.

For Messianic Jews these were of particular significance. Were Messianic Jews to be considered members of other religions? Does becoming a believer in Yeshua constitute a conversion to Christianity? Such questions were raised by a number of significant test cases. The first case which challenged such laws was the Brother Daniel case which concerned a Jewish convert to Christianity. Brother Daniel, Oswald Rufeisen, was born to Polish–Jewish parents; from an early age he was determined to live in Palestine. In 1939 he finished his schooling and embarked on a training scheme for farmers who wished to settle in the Holy Land. However, during the Nazi occupation of Poland, Rufeisen joined the Jewish resistance movement. In 1942 he went into hiding in a convent where he became a Roman Catholic, while maintaining links with his family as well as the Jewish community. After the war, he joined the Carmelite order, becoming a monk.

In 1958 he was transferred to Israel. When he went to the Polish authorities, he stated that he was a Jew who wished to emigrate, and produced his birth certificate to satisfy the authorities of his Jewishness. He was stripped of his Polish nationality and given a Jewish title on his documents. On arrival in Israel, he filled out the immigration papers, listing himself as Jewish by birth but a Roman Catholic by religious conviction. This complex situation, however, was brought to the attention of the Minister of the Interior who asked the government for a ruling, which denied Brother Daniel registration as a Jew. Subsequently he appealed to the Supreme Court which rejected his appeal by a majority of four to one.

The rejection of the Supreme Court was based on two issues: first, that the Law of Return did not include 'apostates' within its definition of who is a Jew; second, since the religious apostates have by definition deserted their Jewish roots and left the community, Brother Daniel could not legitimately be recorded as Jewish. Brother Daniel contested this first point, claiming that he was still a Jew under religious law, basing his view on the *halakhic* ruling that 'Israel – even if he sins – is still Israel.'[4] Although the judges conceded this point, they nonetheless declared that this was irrelevant since the term 'Jew' in the Law of Return does not refer to the 'Jew' of religious law, but to the 'Jew' of secular law. In their view, the Law of Return was established as a secular Zionist Law as opposed to a *halakhic* law. Appeal in this instance was made to the legal fiction of the common man and how he would determine the proper definition of who was a Jew. On this basis, biological descent did not constitute sufficient grounds for determining Jewish status.

The second point, that a Jew who converts to another religion thereby forfeits his claim to Jewish identity, was also contested by Brother Daniel who stressed his ongoing links to the Jewish community. Though Justice Cohn accepted this claim, the other judges were unconvinced. In his ruling, Justice Landau argued that through conversion a Jewish apostate 'cuts himself off from his national past . . . no longer shares a common fate with the Jewish people . . . and erects a barrier against any further identification with the Jewish people'.[5] This case has been decisive for subsequent legal cases, and has critically affected Messianic Jews who have considered settling in Israel.

The Shalit case

Another case which came before the Israeli Supreme Court between 1968 and 1970 was also instrumental in bringing about changes to the Population Registration Law and the Law of Return. Here the question concerned the status of children born of a Jewish father and a non-Jewish mother. Were these offspring to be registered as Israelis? Major Benjamin Shalit was an Israeli by birth, and served in the Israeli army. While stationed in Edinburgh he met a non-Jewish woman whom he married. Later the family settled in Israel, where their children were born.

Because the Population Registration Law demands the registration of each baby, Major Shalit filled out the forms as required, indicating no religious affiliation under the section 'Religion', but entering 'Jewish' under the 'Nationality' section. When the registration official refused to accept this classification, Major Shalit wrote to the Ministry of the Interior. Eventually, Major Shalit took his case to the High Court. After considerable deliberation, the majority of judges found in favour of Major Shalit and his wife, decreeing that the nationality of his children could be registered as Jewish. Nonetheless, the judges refused to be drawn into a discussion about the ultimate criteria for determining who is a Jew. Instead, they sought to reduce their remit to the legal technicalities of the case, namely whether registration officials are bound to accept the father's statements, and if not, whether they are permitted to use other criteria such as the *halakhah.* Their ruling was that the official must accept the father's registration of Jewish nationality for his children.

Nonetheless, the judges conceded that the wider issue of Jewish identity needed to be settled. One of the judges, Mr Justice Berinson, was concerned about the Orthodox refusal to distinguish between the Jewish faith and Jewish nationality. As he explained, this meant that 'the head of the terrorists in Eastern Jerusalem, born of a Jewish woman and a Moslem father, who tried to kill and annihilate the State of Israel, is considered as Jewish by religion and nationality: while the family of a Jewish Major, fighting the wars of Israel, is considered devoid of Jewish nationality'.[6]

As might be expected, this decision led to considerable discussion; as a consequence, the Religious Parties put pressure on the government to reverse the decision. The government acquiesced, and the Knesset enacted new legislation. Although these laws were not retroactive, they prevented the Shalit case from serving as a precedent. Both the Law of Return and the Population Registration Law were amended in 1970 to include the traditional definition of Jewishness in terms of matrilineal descent. The Population Registration Law was amended as follows:

3A (a) No man will be registered as a Jew by nation or by religion if a notice according to this Law or any other registration or public document show that he is not a Jew ...
(b) In regards to this Law and any registration or document made in accordance to this Law the term Jew bears the meaning given this term in article 4B of the Law of Return.
(c) This article is not retroactive.

The Law of Return was also amended:

4A (a) The rights pertaining to a Jew by the Law of Return ... thereby pertain to the children or grandchildren of the spouse of a Jew or ... of a Jew, excepting those (children, grandchildren or spouses) who were Jews and converted to another religion.
4B In regards to this Law a Jew is one who was born of a Jewish mother or converted to Judaism, and has not converted to another religion.[7]

For Messianic Jews, these changes were deeply disturbing – the traditional definition of Jewishness was officially affirmed, and members of other faiths were barred from entering the Holy Land under the Law of Return.

The Dorflinger case

The next important case concerning Jewish status was that of Esther Dorflinger, which was brought before the High Court in 1979. Born in the United States, Esther Dorflinger decided to make *aliyah*. On her arrival in

Israel, she requested status as a new immigrant. The Minister of the Interior, however, refused her request on the grounds that she had accepted another religion. When she petitioned the High Court for a ruling, the Justices ruled against her request. Justice Witkon delivered the main opinion of the Court with Justice Asher. In their view, it was not a question whether Dorflinger felt Jewish or regarded herself as Jewish; rather, there had to be an objective measurement in this case. It was, he believed, for the Court, not the petitioner, to establish such a criterion. Membership or allegiance to another faith, he argued, must guide the Court in such a case. Dorflinger, the Court ruled, lived by a faith and lifestyle which would be considered Christian by any Church.

This decision was particularly important since Dorflinger was not a member of any Christian denomination or congregation. She refused to join a church or to give her assent to any credal statement. Further, she stated to the Court that her faith was the result of a revelation from God, rather than the result of theological education or participation in church services. Only by reading the New Testament had she come to faith in Jesus as the Messiah. As she declared:

> Theology and theological creeds are alien to the pure and simple New Testament faith in Jesus. The identity of Jesus is not simply an issue of theological definitions but one of divine revelation. My understanding of Jesus is not based on theological definitions but on God's revelation to me personally by his Spirit according to his word.[8]

According to Justice Shamgar, by expressing her faith in Jesus, Dorflinger had forfeited her right to be classed as Jewish:

> In so doing she has made use of long and tortuous arguments, regarding the possible tie of a Jew to the belief in the messiahship of Jesus as though we were still in the beginning of the first millennium of the Common Era, as though nothing had happened since then in regards to the formation of religious frameworks and the separation from Judaism of all those who chose the other way . . . However, religious freedom does not mean that the petitioner can force the respondent, who acts on the basis of statutory law, to accept her innovations and definitions that contradict those that are in the law, and to treat her as a Jewess, despite her belonging to another faith.[9]

The Dahaf Report

In 1988 a group of Israeli Messianic Jews sought to determine if there was any public support within Israel for permitting Messianic Jews to make *aliyah* under the Law of Return. From 17 to 24 January 1988 the Dahaf Research Institute conducted a poll of 1189 Israeli citizens. The interviewees were asked about ten categories of potential *olim* (immigrants):

1. A person born to a Jewish mother, who does not believe in the existence of God.
2. A person born to a Jewish mother, who belongs to Hare Krishna, Scientology, or a similar cult.
3. A person born to a Jewish mother, who believes that Yeshua is the Messiah.
4. A person born to a Jewish mother, who does not believe that the *Torah* is the words of the living God.
5. A person born to a Jewish mother, who believes that both the *Torah* and the New Testament are the words of the living God.
6. A person born to a Jewish mother, who was baptized in the framework of a Christian church.
7. A person born to a Jewish mother, who was baptized in the framework of a Messianic Jewish congregation.
8. A person born to a Jewish mother, who believes that Yeshua is the Messiah, considers and feels himself to be Jewish, and was baptized within the framework of a Messianic Jewish congregation.
9. A person born to a Jewish mother, who believes that Yeshua is the Messiah, considers and feels himself to be both Jewish and Christian, and was baptized within the framework of a Christian church.
10. A person born to a Jewish mother, who is faithful to the State of Israel, pays his taxes to the State, serves in the army, celebrates the Jewish holidays, keeps commandments from Israel's tradition, feels that he is a Jew, and believes that Yehsua is the Messiah, but was not baptized into Christianity.[10]

In tabular form, this study reveals the following results concerning the question whether such individuals should be granted immigrant's visas:

Question no.	Has right	Has no right	No response	Total
1	83	13	4	100
10	78	17	5	100
4	73	22	5	100
5	68	27	5	100
7	63	32	5	100
8	61	34	5	100
3	61	35	4	100
2	61	35	4	100
9	54	41	5	100
6	49	46	5	100

This report highlights a number of important points with regard to the perception of Messianic Jews in Israeli society:

An absolute majority of the public (more than 50%) favours granting an immigrant's visa under the Law of Return to all the above mentioned categories, except for the last case. Even in this case, an absolute majority of those expressing an opinion favoured granting the visa . . .

> The two groups which received the highest support rates may be identified as Jews who do not believe in God at all, and persons . . . who keep the Jewish tradition, celebrate the Jewish feasts, and believe that Yeshua is the Messiah . . .[11]

The report concluded that the Israeli public was generally happy to grant *aliyah* rights to a person born of a Jewish mother who believes in Yeshua. Such acceptance was based on the assumption that such an individual lived a Jewish lifestyle, identified with the Jewish people, and was loyal to Israel. Such reassurances were drawn from several observations made in the survey:

1. The very high (78%) support rate given to the believer in Yeshua who pays his taxes, serves in the army, celebrates Jewish festivals, etc., etc. It seems that each point adds more reassurance.
2. A comparison between questions 6 and 9. If all that is known about a person is that he had a Jewish mother and was baptized in a Christian church, only 49% support his right to immigrate. But if it is also know that he considers himself a Jew (even though he explicitly states that he believes Yeshua is the Messiah) then the rate rises to 54%.
3. A comparison of questions 6 and 7. Here the focus is on the context of baptism. If the baptism is in a Christian church framework the support rate is 49%, but if it is in a Messianic Jewish congregational framework the support rate rises to 63%.[12]

Not surprisingly, the Dahaf Report was welcomed by the Israeli Messianic community; it appears that, despite the views of the Orthodox, the general public in Israel is little concerned about the beliefs of Messianic Jews as long as they see themselves as loyal citizens of the State of Israel.

The Beresford case

More recently there has been an important case in Israel concerning a married Messianic couple who sought to settle in Israel. Gary and Shirley Beresford are South Africans born to Jewish mothers who became Jewish believers in the late 1970s. In 1982 they sought to commence the immigration process, but the Israel Agency in South Africa rejected their application once their religious beliefs became known to the authorities. In 1986 the Beresfords went to Israel on visitors' visas and attempted to begin the immigration procedures. During this period they attended a Messianic congregation in Ramat Ha-Sharon near Tel Aviv.

Their application was based on the Law of Return, but the Interior Ministry rejected their appeal on the grounds that the Beresfords were members of a different faith. The couple then petitioned the High Court on the grounds that they were *bona fide* Jews: they pointed out that they had never joined a church, nor were they supporters of a Christian group. Rather, they saw themselves as fulfilled Jews who accepted Yeshua as the Messiah. In 1989 the High Court, consisting of Justices Elon, Barak and Khalima concluded that the Beresfords' beliefs constituted a voluntary and consistent membership of another religion. As Justice Elon stated:

> Messianic Jews attempt to reverse the wheels of history by 2,000 years. But the Jewish people has decided during the 2,000 years of history that (Messianic Jews) do not belong to the Jewish nation . . . and have no right to force themselves on it.[13]

Arguing along similar lines, Justice Barak maintained that since the majority of Jewish people as well as Israelis would regard the beliefs of Messianic Jews as inconsistent with the Jewish faith, the claim of Messianic Jews that they are *bona fide* Jews should be rejected by Israel's legislature.[14]

Anxious about the outcome of this case, the Messianic movement in the United States took out full-page advertisements in the *Jerusalem Post* in support of the Beresfords. In this Open Letter, a number of challenges were made to the High Court. First, Justice Elon's Orthodoxy was described as being out of line with the religious position of most Jews: 'If given the opportunity', the Open Letter stated, 'these same Orthodox factions would disqualify most of the current Jewish nation from Jewish identity. If the Israeli nation does not wish to submit the question of their own Jewish identities to these men, why do they submit ours?'[15]

The Open Letter then turned to Justice Barak's appeal to the majority view:

> Why then is he ignoring the results of the 1988 Dahaf Poll, published in the *Jerusalem Post*, which found that 78% of the Israeli public favoured Messianic Jews coming into Israel under the Law of Return, provided that the *olim* in question were really of Jewish lineage, held to their historic heritage, and served in the IDF when called upon to do so.[16]

Rejecting the authority of rabbinic Judaism, the Open Letter went on to assert that the only legitimate criterion of Jewishness should be based solely on the *Tanakh*. Further, the Open Letter drew attention to the view of Rabbi Akiva, who maintained that the incorrect identification of the Messiah has not served as grounds for dismissal from Jewry. The Open Letter also insisted that the Messianic movement is the direct heir of first-century Messianic Judaism. Hence, the Open Letter argued:

> If a Jew who truly clings to his national identity and the heritage of his faith happens to believe in the way hundreds and thousands of the Jewish people in the first century did, that Yeshua of Nazareth is the Messiah of Israel . . . he is told,

'You are not part of the Israeli nation.' Since even Judge Elon had to admit in his decision that, 'It was true that Messianic Jews were a legitimate Jewish sect in the first century', the Messianic Jewish Alliance of America can only oppose the Court's current stand as discriminatory and inconsistent.[17]

Finally, the Open Letter appealed for the right of Messianic Jews to return under the Law of Return given the threat of future persecution and suffering: 'If our people should ever face another Holocaust is it the intention of the Government of Israel to shut the doors to our homeland on any Jews who do not "qualify" according to the religious standards set by the *datim* (Orthodox)?'[18]

Undeterred, the Beresfords, along with two other families, continued to fight for recognition under the Law of Return. In addition, they applied to be admitted to Israel under the Law of Entry, the ordinary immigration law under which non-Jews are permitted to settle in the Holy Land. The Interior Ministry, however, rejected these applications, and in September 1992 the High Court turned down the request of all these families to enter under the Law of Return. The present situation is that Messianic Jews are not allowed to make *aliyah* under the Law of Return, and the Interior Ministry is not obliged to grant them permanent residence in the country. Recognizing the dangers posed to the movement by such legislation, the Messianic movement recently embarked on a campaign, Operation Joshua, which aims to secure the right of the Messianic community to settle in the Holy Land. Their aim is to obtain a million signatures of protest to the Israeli Supreme Court's decision of 25 December 1989 to deny Messianic Jews the right to immigrate to Israel under the Law of Return.

Messianic Judaism and Jewish status

In response to the complex legislation concerning Jewish status in Israel, Messianic Jews continue to insist that individuals born of a Jewish mother who accept Yeshua as Messiah and Saviour should be regarded as fully Jewish. Basing themselves on rabbinic teaching, they point out that the *Talmud* views apostates as Jewish sinners rather than non-Jews. Hence Henry Knight in *The Role of Messianic Congregations in the Body of Christ* wrote:

> The *Talmud* states that 'an Israelite' (Jew), even though he sin, is still an Israelite (B. San. 44a). Most Orthodox authorities accept that this *halakhic* rule covers the sin of apostasy, so that membership of another religion, or of none at all, does not exclude the Jew from belonging to the community of Israel. This principle, if evenly applied, means that Jews who have embraced the Christian faith are still Jews.[19]

In *Refutations*, another Israeli believer in Israel, Menachem Benhayim, stated:

In an article on 'apostasy' published in the *Encyclopedia Judaica*, the writer notes: 'Previously *halakhic* opinion throughout the ages has always considered the apostate a Jew for all purposes of obligations, ties and possibilities given to a Jew, but denying him some specific legal rights, in particular in the economic sphere, and in the performance of certain honorary symbolic acts.'[20]

In appealing to tradition, Messianic Jews are anxious to illustrate that critics of Messianic Judaism are misguided in seeking to rule them outside the Jewish fold. Such exclusion, either in Israel or the diaspora, is not in accord with the traditional rabbinic understanding of Jewishness.

Nonetheless, as we have seen, the movement has distanced itself from the rabbinic understanding of matrilineal descent. Instead, Messianic Jews argue that Jewish status should be determined on the basis of the biblical understanding of Jewish descent. In *Hebrew Christianity*, Arnold Fruchtenbaum explains in detail what such teaching entails. The biblical definition, he asserted, lies in the Abrahamic covenant in Genesis which was subsequently confirmed through Isaac and Jacob:

> From the Abrahamic covenant a simple definition of Jewishness can be deduced. It lies in the repeated statement that a nation will come through the line of Abraham, Isaac, and Jacob, and thus defines Jewishness in terms of nationality . . . The theology of Judaism teaches that Jewishness is determined by the mother; if the mother is Jewish, then the children are Jewish. But . . . this is a departure from the biblical norm and is therefore rejected by Hebrew Christianity. In the Scriptures it is not the mother who determines Jewishness but the father; consequently the genealogies of both the Old and New Testaments list the names of the men and not the women, except in cases where a mother was notable in Jewish history . . . If the Scriptures are used as the objective standard, then the definition of a Gentile is equally simple. A Gentile is simply anyone who is not a descendant of Abraham, Isaac and Jacob. In short, a Gentile is anyone who is not a Jew.[21]

Like Fruchtenbaum, Dan Juster contended in *Jewish Roots* that Jewish status must be understood in biblical terms. According to *halakhah*, he noted, a person is Jewish if born of a Jewish mother. However, he stated:

> the major problem with this position is its contradiction of the Scriptural indications that Jewish descent was carried through the father. The covenant was originally made with Abraham. The father clearly determined the religious identity of his family. The covenant sign of circumcision was applied to the male sexual member, indicating that this was a covenant applying to physical descendants through the father.[22]

On this basis, Juster concluded that a person is of Jewish descent as long as he or she identifies as a Jew, and is circumcised if he is a male.[23]

In a similar vein, David Stern in *Messianic Jewish Manifesto* pointed out that the Bible traces Jewishness genetically through the father. According to this theory, he wrote, Jewishness came to be traced through the mother at a time of historical turmoil when Jewish women were being sold as concubines to Gentiles, so that there could be doubt whether a child's father was Jewish.[24] Like Fruchtenbaum and Juster, Stern contended that the biblical definition must hence serve as the basis for determining Jewish status rather than the traditional rabbinic understanding of maternal descent.

Messianic Jews thus believe that Jewish descent serves as the fundamental criterion of Jewishness. In general it is accepted that an individual is Jewish if he or she has one Jewish grandparent. As David Chernoff explained in *An Introduction to Messianic Judaism* in answer to the question who is a Jew:

> Obviously, this is a question that has been debated for centuries. One cannot be considered Jewish strictly on the basis of religion, because most Jewish people today are not religious. The same applies to any definition of a Jew based on culture, as well. According to rabbinic Judaism, to be considered a Jew, one must have Jewish parents (in particular a Jewish mother).
>
> This rabbinic definition is not biblically correct. The scriptural definition of a Jew is three-fold; first of all we are a nation and a people; to be considered Jewish one must be a physical descendant of Abraham through Isaac and Jacob (Genesis 12:1–3). Secondly, the biblical lineage is patrilineal, i.e. carried through the father, not matrilineal or carried through the mother . . . Finally, the Scriptures indicate that if either parent is Jewish or if a grandparent is Jewish (i.e. if there is a significant Jewish heritage), one can identify himself or herself as being Jewish and can claim himself as part of God's chosen people.[25]

Turning to Israel's contention that Messianic Jews are members of another faith and therefore do not qualify for admission under the Law of Return, Jewish believers insist that such categorization is based on a fundamental misunderstanding of Messianic Judaism. As Stern explained in *Messianic Jewish Manifesto*:

> There is no conflict whatever between being Messianic and being Jewish. Believing in Yeshua, the Jewish Messiah, is one of the most Jewish things a Jew can do. A Jewish believer in Yeshua is not faced with having to give up some Jewishness in order to be more Messianic, or having to give up some of his Messianic faith to be more Jewish. Non-Messianic Jews might try to convince him of this, as might some Gentile Christians, but they would be wrong . . . we are 100% Jewish, no matter who denies it. And we are 100% Messianic, no matter who denies it. So it was for the first-century Jewish believers, and so it must be today. This is the God-determined truth, in the face of all lies, slanders and disinformation of those who would deny us our true identity.[26]

17 Models of Messianic Judaism

Orthodox exclusivism

According to Orthodox Judaism, only those born of a Jewish mother (or individuals converted under Orthodox auspices) are Jews. Hence, members of the Messianic movement who have Jewish mothers are Jewish even though they are perceived as apostates. Messianic Jews born of a Jewish mother are therefore Jews by status, yet as apostates they are excluded from all the privileges of the Jewish community including synagogue membership as well as membership of Jewish communal organizations. Even though some traditionalists have argued that only a fundamental misunderstanding of rabbinic sources allows Jews to retain Jewish identity while accepting Christianity, the majority view is that Messianic Jews – by their acceptance of another religion – have relinquished their communal ties to other Jews, but have not lost their fundamental Jewish identity.

Although Israel has barred Messianic Jews who have Jewish mothers from entering Israel under the Law of Return, this does not mean that within the Orthodox community such individuals are not perceived as Jewish. Rather, the Israel Supreme Court has gone beyond Jewish religious law in declaring that a Jew who accepts another religion violates the commonsense sociological boundaries of inclusion within the Jewish community. For Orthodox Jews then, only those born of matrilineal descent or properly converted through specified Orthodox legal procedures can be deemed Jewish even if they have been converted by non-Orthodox Jewish subgroups. Yet, according to Orthodox Judaism, some Messianic Jews are part of the Jewish world even though they are sinful apostates.

While this understanding of Jewishness does allow some Messianic Jews to be included within the Jewish community, it explicitly rejects the Messianic conception of Jewishness. As noted previously, Messianic Jews argue on biblical grounds that Jewish status should be based on patrilineal, rather than matrilineal, descent. As a result, they contend that a person is Jewish if he or she has one Jewish grandparent. Orthodox Judaism bars such individuals from inclusion within the Jewish community.

It should be noted that this model of Jewishness not only excludes Messianic Jews of patrilineal descent but also many individuals who are perceived as Jewish within the non-Orthodox branches of Judaism. Both the Reform and Reconstructionist movements accept as Jews those born of a Jewish father; such classification is adamantly rejected by the Orthodox. In addition, Orthodox Judaism rejects any form of conversion other than its own. As a result, Conservative, Reform and Reconstructionist converts and the children of female converts are regarded as non-Jews. Thus, Orthodox Judaism includes some Messianic Jews within the Jewish community while regarding individuals born of patrilineal descent and non-Orthodox converts as non-Jews.

Turning to the question of Jewish authenticity, Messianic Judaism would be regarded as totally unacceptable: despite the claims of Jewish believers that by accepting Yeshua they have become completed Jews, Orthodox Judaism categorically rejects any form of Jewish Christianity as part of the Jewish tradition. From a theological point of view, Messianic Judaism is viewed as fundamentally distinct from traditional Judaism because of the centrality of Jesus. As we have seen, Messianic Judaism is essentially Christological in character: Jesus is understood as the long-awaited Messiah who has come to redeem the world. In addition, Messianic Jews embrace many of the central tenets of the Christian faith including the doctrine of the Incarnation, the Trinity, and the Atonement – for Messianic Jews, the world has been transformed through Jesus' death and resurrection. According to Orthodoxy, such Christological notions fall outside the boundaries of Jewish religious belief.

Furthermore, Orthodox Jews regard Messianic Judaism's conviction that the New Testament is part of God's revelation as a fundamental deviation from the Jewish faith. Within Orthodoxy, the belief that the Written *Torah* (consisting of the Five Books of Moses) and the the Oral *Torah* constitute God's sole revelation to the Jewish people is a cardinal principle. As the medieval Jewish philosopher Moses Maimonides explained in his formulation of the Thirteen Principles of the Jewish Faith:

> The *Torah* was revealed from heaven. This implies our belief that the whole of the *Torah* found in our hands this day is the *Torah* that was handed down by Moses, and that it is all of divine origin. By this I mean that the whole of the *Torah* came unto him from before God in a manner which is metaphorically called 'speaking'; but the real nature of that communication is unknown to everybody except to Moses (peace to him!) to whom it came.[1]

Within this context the New Testament is regarded as nothing more than a collection of non-canonical writings which falsely depict Jesus as the Saviour of humankind.

Messianic Judaism's view of the rabbinic tradition constitutes a further basis for rejection. As we have seen, Messianic Jews have distanced themselves from the rabbinic interpretation of Scripture. Repeatedly Messianic Jewish writers stress that the movement must free itself from the shackles of Orthodox *halakhah* in seeking to understand God's will for his people. What is required instead is a new basis for Jewish legalism. As David Stern explained in *Messianic Jewish Manifesto*:

> A Messianic Jew who realizes that the *Torah* still is in force under the New Covenant ought to be full of questions. How is the *Torah* to be applied? What is the *halakhah* under the New Covenant? What ought to be done, and what ought not to be done in particular situations? One can imagine creating a body of New Testament case law much like the *Talmud*, the Codes and Responsa of Judaism. It would take into consideration Jewish *halakhah,* which has, after all, dealt with nearly every sector of human existence; yet everything would have to be re-examined in the light of New Covenant truth.[2]

Not surprisingly, such an enterprise which consciously distances itself from rabbinic Judaism is regarded with dismay by the Orthodox. According to traditionalists, there is only one legitimate form of the faith: Orthodox Judaism. Any deviation from *Torah*-observant Judaism as practised by Jews through the centuries is heresy, no matter what its practitioners believe. In this connection it should be noted that this is true, not only of Messianic Judaism, but of all the non-Orthodox Jewish movements which currently exist in the modern world. Hence, not only is Messianic Judaism an illegitimate interpretation of Judaism, so too is Conservative Judaism, Reform Judaism, Reconstructionist Judaism, and Humanistic Judaism. The Orthodox model thus not only excludes Messianic Judaism from the circle of authentic Judaism, but also excludes all other branches of Judaism in contemporary society. Although Orthodox Jews are particularly vehement about the inauthenticity of Messianic Judaism, other Jewish movements are similarly regarded as illegitimate interpretations of the tradition.

Non-Orthodox exclusivism

Given the theological presuppositions of Orthodoxy, it is understandable why Orthodox Jews categorically deny legitimacy to Messianic Jews. Yet non-Orthodox attitudes are more difficult to comprehend given the multi-dimensional character of contemporary Jewish life. As we have noted, there is no general agreement among the different non-Orthodox movements about Jewish status. Conservative Jews, for example, do not accept the doctrine of patrilineal descent as espoused by Reform and Reconstructionist Jews. For Conservative Jews, a significant number of individuals who are perceived as Jews within the Reform and Reconstructionist movements are regarded as non-Jews. The picture for Reform and Reconstructionist Jews, however, is markedly different. There is thus no general agreement among these groups as to the criterion for Jewishness.

The attitude of Humanistic Judaism further complicates the situation.

According to Humanistic Judaism, people are Jewish simply if they identify as Jews:

> We the members of the International Federation of Secular Humanistic Jews, believe that the survival of the Jewish people depends on a broad view of Jewish identity. We welcome into the Jewish people all men and women who sincerely desire to share the Jewish experience regardless of their ancestry. We challenge the assumption that the Jews are primarily or exclusively a religious community and that religious convictions or behaviour are essential to full membership in the Jewish people . . . In response to the destructive definition of a Jew now proclaimed by some Orthodox authorities, and in the name of the historic experience of the Jewish people, we therefore affirm that a Jew is a person of Jewish descent or any person who declares himself or herself to be a Jew and who identifies with the history, ethical values, culture, civilization, community and fate of the Jewish people.[3]

For Humanistic Jews, Jewishness is thus a matter of personal choice rather than descent. A person is Jewish if he or she seeks to identify with the Jewish heritage.

It is clear then that there is no common ground between the various branches of non-Orthodox Judaism regarding Jewish status. Conservative Judaism insists on the Orthodox criterion of matrilineal descent and retains the traditional process of conversion, whereas Reform and Reconstructionist Jews accept both matrilineal and patrilineal descent and have formulated their own conversion procedures. Humanistic Jews, on the other hand, have abandoned the notion of descent altogether and advocate instead a definition of Jewishness based on individual choice.

This confusion about Jewish status is made even greater by Reform Judaism's attitude toward apostates. In a *responsum* about the status of a 'completed Jew' in the Jewish community, the Central Conference of American Rabbis adopted an even stricter stance than the Orthdodox: in answer to the question: 'There are a number of individuals in the community who consider themselves as "completed Jews" or "Messianic Jews"; they accept Jesus as their saviour, but, nevertheless, still feel Jewish "in their hearts"; how should the congregation view such individuals?', the movement stated:

> For us in the Jewish community anyone who claims that Jesus is their saviour is no longer a Jew and is an apostate. Through that belief she has placed herself outside the Jewish community. Whether she cares to define herself as a Christian or as 'fulfilled Jew', 'Messianic Jew', or any other designation is irrelevant; to us she is clearly a Christian . . . We would, therefore, be stricter with her than with individuals who were forced into a position of becoming Christian. For us such a modern willing apostate is a non-Jew. In this we would disagree with the *Talmud* and later tradition.[4]

Within the non-Orthodox community, therefore, there is no common ground concerning the question: Who is a Jew? Instead the Conservative, Reform, Reconstructionist and Humanistic Jews are deeply divided over the issue of Jewish status.

Turning to belief and practice, the divisions between these movements are equally great. Orthodox Judaism, on the one hand, while embracing a variety of different groupings (including Hasidism, Traditional Orthodoxy, and Modern Orthodoxy) adheres to a firm belief in *Torah MiSinai* (the doctrine that Moses received the Five Books of Moses on Mount Sinai). As a consequence, the 613 commandments contained in the Pentateuch are regarded as binding on all Jews; together with their interpretation in the Oral Law, this legislation provides a framework for everyday Jewish living. In addition, the description of God and his action in the world in Scripture is accepted as true. Hence, Orthodox Jews, whatever their orientation, strictly adhere to traditional belief and practice as embraced by Jews through the centuries.

There is, however, a great theological divide between Orthodox and non-Orthodox Jews. Non-Orthodox Judaism arose in response to Jewish participation in mainstream, secular civilization. Increasingly, Western European Jews were uncomfortable with the traditional services; later in the mid-nineteenth century, an attempt was made to study the tradition with no religious presuppositions. On the basis of the findings of biblical scholars, many Jews were unable to believe that the entire written and oral *Torah* were handed down to Moses on Mount Sinai.

Conservative Judaism is largely an American phenomenon. It arose in reaction to what were perceived as the radical excesses of the Reform movement; standing midway between the certainties of Orthodoxy and the liberties of Reform, it views the Jewish tradition in dynamic terms. Conservative Jews assert that the tradition has changed through the centuries; hence, the ultimate source of authority must be the Jewish people themselves. In the light of history, some aspects of the Jewish heritage are viewed as permanent, whereas others are seen as meaningful only at certain periods. Today Conservative Judaism covers a wide variety of beliefs, and considerable tensions exist between members of the Rabbinical Assembly, the official association for Conservative rabbis.

Moving across the Jewish religious spectrum, Reform Judaism represents an even more radical departure from the tradition. In the early nineteenth century, Reformers were initially embarrassed by the Jewish liturgy; as a consequence they championed a new form of service more in line with modern ideas. As time passed, Reformers sought to modify both belief and practice. As in Conservative Judaism, there are many shades of opinion. At the end of the nineteenth century, Reformers sought to distance themselves from Jewish traditionalism, yet in recent years there has been a dramatic return to the Jewish heritage. Nonetheless, Reform Jews have abandoned many of the central tenets of the faith. In many ways modern Reform Jews live lives that are almost identical to those of their Gentile neighbours: they eat the same food, wear the same clothes, share the same worldly aspirations, and enjoy the same amusements. Their lives are very different from those of their ancestors in the Jewish villages of Europe.

In addition to these three major movements, Reconstructionist Judaism emerged in this century under the influence of the Jewish thinker Mordecai Kaplan. According to Kaplan, Jews in the past believed in a supernatural God who revealed himself to the Jewish people and provided a means of salvation. Yet in his view, such belief is no longer viable; instead, he maintained, Jews must divest themselves of belief in the supernatural. In response to his call for a reconstruction of the Jewish tradition, the Jewish Reconstructionist Foundation in New York was established in 1935 and began to publish the magazine, the *Reconstructionist*. In 1954 a congregational organization was created, and the Reconstructionist Rabbinical College was opened in 1968.

The central principle of Reconstructionism is that Judaism is an evolving religious civilization. Because of this continual development, ideas about God, humanity, sin, miracles, laws, prayer and the afterlife have all undergone considerable change over the centuries. In Kaplan's view, Judaism is therefore more than a religious denomination; it is a total civilization embracing art, music, language, folk ways and customs, whose purpose is to ensure the survival of the Jewish nation. Within this framework, Reconstructionists have generally adopted a humanistic and naturalistic understanding of the nature of the Divine while embracing many of the practices and customs of the Jewish tradition.

An even more radical departure from Orthodoxy has been undertaken in recent years by Humanistic Jews. Under the leadership of Sherwin Wine, Humanistic Judaism emerged in the 1960s as a non-theistic interpretation of the Jewish faith. Distancing itself from all other branches of Judaism, this new movement extols the humanistic dimensions of the faith. On the basis of this ideology, Jewish holidays and lifecycle events have been reinterpreted so as to emphasize their humanistic characteristics. In addition, Humanistic Jews insist that traditional Jewish beliefs must be reformulated in the light of scientific knowledge. Promoting a secular lifestyle, this new conception of Judaism seeks to adjust the Jewish tradition to modernity.

These modern Jewish movements thus embrace a wide range of theological and ideological perspectives. There is simply no consensus among non-Orthodox Jews concerning the central tenets of the faith, neither is there any agreement about Jewish observance. Instead, the various branches of non-Orthodox Judaism embrace a totally heterogeneous range of viewpoints. Nonetheless, these disparate branches of modern Judaism are united in their rejection of Messianic Judaism as an authentic expression of the Jewish faith. Even though the adherents of these branches of the tradition differ over the most fundamental features of the Jewish religion, even including belief in God, they have joined together in excluding

Messianic Judaism from the range of legitimate interpretations of the Jewish heritage.

For Messianic Jews, such a rejection is baffling. Why, they ask, should they be perceived as the sole inauthentic Jewish movement in contemporary society given that they believe in God, view the *Torah* as divinely revealed, and remain loyal to Israel? In their view, such exclusion is due to prejudice and misunderstanding. If Conservative Jews deny the belief in *Torah MiSinai,* Reform Jews reject the authority of the Law, Reconstructionist Jews adopt a non-theistic interpretation of the faith, and Humanistic Jews cease to use the word 'God' in their liturgy, why should Messianic Jews alone be universally vilified? As Carol Harris-Shapiro explained in *Messianic Judaism*:

> This exclusion rankles Messianic Jews, who seek to have not only their status but their legitimacy in the community affirmed . . . After all, the American Jewish community is rife with well-accepted 'heretical' Jews. Liberal Jews, who deny the Divine authorship of *Torah* and the authority of the Oral Law, wholly secular Jews, even Jews who follow Eastern beliefs are not systematically removed from Jewish life, but are in fact still welcomed into the community. Why, in the twentieth century, have the barriers fallen to include all Jews but themselves?[5]

Despite such protests, non-Orthodox Jews adamantly affirm that Messianic Judaism is a deceptive form of Christianity which should be exposed, denounced, and rejected. In *Passing Over Easter: Constructing the Boundaries of Messianic Judaism*, Shoshana Feher pointed out that the entire Jewish community regards Messianic Jews as the lowest form of Christian life:

> Whether they call themselves Hebrew Christians, Messianic Jews, or Jews for Jesus, in the eyes of the normative Jewish community they are Christians all the same, 'the worst of the *Goyim*.' These self-identified Jews have become a symbolic threat to the Jewish community. Of all the proselytizers, Christians who identify as Jews are held in the lowest esteem because of their attempt to merge Judaism with Christianity, an attempt that the collective Jewish psyche, with all its scars and prejudices, finds repugnant.[6]

The pluralist model

A very different approach to the issue of Jewish authenticity is espoused by thinkers who advocate a more tolerant view of the Messianic movement. Given the multi-dimensional character of modern Jewish life, they contend that Messianic Judaism should be regarded as one among many interpretations of the Jewish faith. The central difficulty with the non-Orthodox exclusion of Messianic Jews, they point out, is that the various non-Orthodox movements are themselves deeply divided over the central principles of Judaism. As we have seen, many Humanistic, Reconstructionist, Reform and Conservative Jews seek to redefine the concept of God; these movements even include adherents who have totally abandoned a belief in a supernatural Deity. In the view of Jewish pluralists, this state of affairs makes it absurd to exclude the Messianic movement from the Jewish community.

The same applies across the range of religious beliefs. Doctrines concerning creation, revelation, divine action, omniscience, omnipotence, providence and salvation have been either redefined or abandoned by many members of all these movements. In addition, the multifarious laws in the *Code of Jewish Law* have been largely neglected by the various non-Orthodox movements. No longer is Jewry united by belief and practice: instead the various branches of the modern Judaish establishment have radically separated themselves from their past. In the light of such an abandonment of the tradition, pluralists maintain that the exclusion of Messianic Judaism from the circle of legitimate expressions of the Jewish heritage is totally inconsistent.

The situation is accurately described by Carol Harris-Shapiro in her study of Messianic Judaism. She observed:

> The present-day Jewish community contains a goodly number of 'heretics' from one Jewish perspective or another . . . If one were to follow the great rabbi and philosopher Maimonides' definiton, anyone who could not affirm one of his thirteen articles of faith, such as the resurrection of the dead, would be excluded from the Jewish community. If one were to follow a commonly accepted premodern definition, anyone who violates the Sabbath publicly is considered an ideological, deliberate heretic, and is not to be counted in the community of Israel. Both definitions would neatly decimate the American Jewish population. Given the cost, it is not surprising that American Jews of all movements are loathe to clearly identify boundary-crossers.
>
> The exception, of course, is the Messianic Jews; the Jewish community is uniquely united in their condemnation of Messianic Judaism. The traditional allowances made by Orthodox Jews are not extended to Messianic Jews; unlike liberal Jews, Messianic Jews are not considered as 'captive children' unintentionally violating Judaism. The core value of freedom of thought held by liberal Jews that enables them to accept secular Jews or Jews incorporating Eastern practices stops cold at Messianic Jewish theology; a Jew can believe almost anything but Jesus as Lord.[7]

What are the factors that have led to this strange state of affairs? According to Carol Harris-Shapiro, the rejection of Messianic Jews by the Jewish community is due to a number of deep-seated factors. First, the history of Christian anti-semitism has profoundly affected Jewish consciousness. As a consequence, Jews who believe in Jesus, in contrast to those who follow Eastern meditation or Buddhist spirituality, are perceived as traitors to the

Jewish people. Also, while it is possible for Jews to be liberal or secular without losing their distinctive identity, accepting Jesus is different. In making observation, Harris-Shapiro cited the view of Stuart Charmé:

> To embrace the radioactive core of goyishness – Jesus – violates the final taboo of Jewishness and brings immediate condemnation. Belief in Jesus as Messiah is not simply a heretical belief, as it may have been in the first century; it has become the equivalent to an act of ethno-cultural suicide.[8]

A second factor contributing to the hostility toward Messianic Jews is the general perception within the community that evangelical Christianity of any form, including Messianic Judaism, is an expression of the Religious Right. For many Jews, this ideology is associated with the Ku Klux Klan, with institutionalized racism, with the fire-bombing of abortion clinics and with a serious threat to the separation of Church and State. There is a social agenda as well. The Religious Right is loosely connected in the mind of the Jewish liberal establishment with Southern rednecks, with ill-educated, isolated country communities, with lower-class obesity and with funda-mentalist preachers declaring that all Jews will burn in hell:

> When this unattractive spiritual imperialism is given a Jewish face, when a Jew puts her trust in one who sounds and behaves Jewishly, only to discover the evangelical Christian beneath, it is experienced as a deep treachery, a type of religious 'Invasion of the Body Snatchers'.[9]

Such subliminal reactions to Messianic Judaism are to be found across the Jewish religious spectrum. Messianic Jews are regarded as having committed the ultimate ethnic and religious betrayal. Yet, as we have seen, Messianic Jews themselves do not see their acceptance of Yeshua as a form of treachery. They enthusiastically embrace Jewish identity which they inculcate in their children at home and in synagogues. They remain loyal to the Jewish people, even though they are universally rejected and condemned. They are vociferous supporters of the State of Israel. By their very way of life, they continually challenge the claim that accepting Yeshua as Messiah is equivalent to abandoning Jewishness.

Jewish pluralists understand why there should be such a visceral rejection of Messianic Jews. Despite modern ecumenical efforts, Christian-ity in its various manifestations is still seen to symbolize centuries of oppression, persecution and murder. Moreover, the assocation of Messianic Judaism with Christian evangelical fundamentalism causes considerable unease among Jews who have, in general, embraced the liberal values of Anglo-American society. Nonetheless, Jewish pluralists insist that given the multi-dimensional character of contemporary Jewish life, the rejection of Messianic Judaism from *Klal Yisrael* (the body of Israel) makes little sense. If non-theistic as well as non-halakhically observant forms of Judaism are acceptable, why, they ask, should Messianic Jews, who are observant believers, be denied recognition within the Jewish community?

Pluralists would argue that what is now required is a new vision of Judaism as a multi-faceted religious system. In the distant past, the Jewish tradition was largely monolithic in character. Over the centuries the development of Orthodox Judaism rested on a common core of shared belief and practice – biblical and rabbinic teaching about the nature of God and his action in the world constituted the foundation of the faith and the community was united in its observance of *Torah*. The Enlightenment in the eighteenth century, however, had a profound impact on Jewish life; no longer were Jews compelled to live an isolated existence in ghettos and shtetls. Instead, they were increasingly accepted as free citizens in the countries where they lived.

The result of this was fragmentation into a number of sub-groups with conflicting orientations and ideologies. This shattering of the monolithic system of Judaism has become the hallmark of contemporary Jewish life. In this light, Jewish pluralists argue, Messianic Judaism should be seen merely as one among many expressions of the Jewish faith. Alongside Hasidism, Orthodox Judaism, Conservative Judaism, Reform Judaism, Reconstructionist Judaism, and Humanistic Judaism, Messianic Judaism offers a pathway through the Jewish heritage. Admittedly, unlike the other branches of Judaism, this movement is firmly rooted in the belief that Yeshua is the long-awaited redeemer of Israel. Yet such a belief is in principle no more radical than the Reconstructionist and Humanistic rejection of a supernatural deity. Indeed, as we have seen, in many respects Messianic Jews are more theistically oriented and more *Torah*-observant even than their counterparts within the Conservative and Reform movements.

For Jewish pluralists, this new conception of modern Jewish life can best be represented by the image of a seven-branched *menorah*. Today there no longer exists one monolithic form of Judaism; instead there are seven distinctly different Judaisms, each with its own ideology. These branches of the Jewish faith converge as well as diverge from each other at central points: they are united at the base, but separate in their expressions of the Jewish faith:

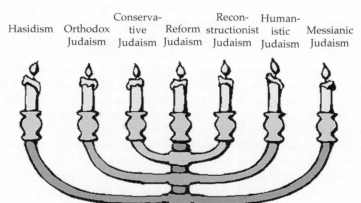

Jewish pluralists recognize that most Jews would be appalled by the inclusion of Messianic Judaism within the Jewish fold. However, they believe that the advantage of their model is that it comes to terms with the multi-dimensional character of modern Jewish life. No longer are the Jews a community with a shared pattern of belief and practice, and it is therefore illogical to rule out new expressions of Judaism given the pluriform nature of the contemporary Jewish community. To depict Messianic Judaism as demonic and dangerous suggests that the Jewish community shares a common set of religious values from which Messianic Jews have distanced themselves. But this is patently not the case.

Like Jewish pluralists, Messianic Jews themselves are well aware of the deep fissures within the Jewish community, and similarly regard their exclusion from Jewish life as utterly inconsistent. As Harris-Shapiro noted:

> In order to show that they are as acceptable as the next Jew, Messianic believers shout that the uniform of authenticity, which the Jewish community clutches about itself to ward off the cold winds of change, has been blown off long ago. 'At least we believe in God!', declares the Messianic Jew to the secular Jew. 'At least we believe the *Torah* is God's word!' declares the Messianic Jew to the liberal Jew. By examining the most extreme case, one of the only groups of Jewish origin that have clearly been cited as out of the pale, one can see that in fundamental ways most American Jews, if not all, are 'out of the pale'. We are not 'pure'; we self-consciously search, we innovate, we profane, we cover core secular values with Jewishness. We weave Judaisms out of the traditions of our forebears and the values of contemporary society, actively construing identities while calling this creativity 'Jewish continuity'.[10]

Jewish pluralists know that it will not be easy for the Jewish community to come face to face with itself and to recognize that Messianic Judaism is no more inauthentic than other forms of contemporary Jewish life. Many Jews will need to overcome subconscious feelings of antipathy towards rural values as well as hostility to evangelical fundamentalism. Yet, paradoxically, Jewish pluralists argue, Messianic Judaism can evoke from the Jewish community a greater awareness of the need for acceptance and tolerance in the modern age. Rather than engaging in bitter and acrimonious criticism of one another's religious viewpoints, the Jewish people need a new framework for harmonious living, one which will serve as a remedy for the bitter divisions that have split the community into warring factions since the Enlightenment. On the principle that it is always better to listen to people than to spit on them, the pluralists argue for an open model. In accordance with this, the seven-branched *menorah* in which all denominations, including Messianic Judaism, are represented, is the only reasonable starting point for inter-community relations in the twenty-first century.

Notes

Introduction
1. Dan and Lavinia Cohn-Sherbok, *The American Jew*, Grand Rapids, Michigan, Eerdmans, 1995, pp. 323–5.
2. *Ibid.*, p. 322.

Chapter 1: Early Jewish Christianity
1. Irenaeus, *Adversus Haereses*, i, p. 26.
2. Eusebius, *Ecclesiastical History*, iii, p. 20.
3. Eusebius, *Ecclesiastical History*, iv, p. 5.
4. Epiphanius, *Panarion*, xxxix, p. 7.
5. Epiphanius, *Panarion*, xxx, p. 18.
6. Origen, *Contra Celsum*, v, p. 61.
7. J. Parkes, 'The Conflict of the Church and the Synagogue', pp. 397–400, cited in H. Schonfield, *The History of Jewish Christianity*, London, Duckworth, 1936, p. 107.
8. *Panarion*, xxx.
9. Milman, *History of the Jews*, Vol. ii, p. 277, in Schonfield, *op. cit.*, pp. 138–9.
10. Schonfield, *op. cit.*, p. 159.
11. *Ibid.*, p. 161.
12. *Ibid.*, p. 166.
13. *Ibid.*, p. 180.
14. *Encyclopedia Judaica*, Jerusalem, Keter, 1972, Vol. 3, p. 106.
15. Schonfield, *op. cit.*, p. 206.
16. *Ibid.*, pp. 213–14.

Chapter 2: The emergence of Hebrew Christianity
1. Ruth Fleischer, *So Great a Cloud of Witnesses*, privately published, 1996, pp. iv–v.
2. Gidney, 'Biographies of Eminent Hebrew Christians', No. IV, cited in Schonfield, *op. cit.*, p. 219.
3. Schonfield, *op. cit.*, p. 221.
4. *Ibid.*, p. 222.
5. Kai Kjaer-Hansen, *Joseph Rabinowitz and the Messianic Movement*, Grand Rapids, Michigan, 1995, pp. 93–4.
6. *Ibid.*, pp. 152–3.
7. *Ibid.*, pp. 103–7.
8. Schonfield, *op. cit.*, p. 228.
9. *Ibid.*, pp. 234–5.
10. *Ibid.*, p. 234.
11. *Ibid.*, p. 235.
12. Ibid., pp. 235–6.
13. Arthur Kuldell, 'Letter to the Editor', *Hebrew Christian Alliance of America Quarterly*, Vol. 6:1, pp. 38–40.

Chapter 3: The Hebrew Christian Alliance of America
1. Robert I. Winer, *The Calling: The History of the Messianic Jewish Alliance of America*, Wynnewood, Pennsylvania, 1990, pp. 94–5.
2. *Report of the First General Conference of the Hebrew Christian Alliance of America*, 1915, p. 22.
3. Arthur Kuldell, 'The Spiritual Aims of the HCAA', *Hebrew Christian Alliance Quarterly*, Vol. 1:1, 1917, pp. 22–5.
4. *Papers, Addresses and Proceedings of the Second General Conference of the Hebrew Christian Alliance of America*, 1916, pp. 3–4.
5. *Ibid.*, pp. 20–3.
6. *Organ of the New York Jewish Evangelization Society*, Vol. 10:120, 1919, pp. 266–8, 288.

7. *Ibid.*
8. *Organ of the New York Jewish Evangelization Society*, Vol. 11:124,1920, pp. 75–8.
9. Sabbati Rohold, 'Another Voice', *Hebrew Christian Alliance Quarterly*, Vol. 4:2, 1920, pp. 39–40.
10. *Ibid.*
11. *Ibid.*
12. Winer, *op. cit.*, pp. 101–5.
13. *Ibid.*, p. 20.
14. Maurice Ruben, 'Resumé by Host of Conference', *Hebrew Christian Alliance Quarterly*, Vol 1:3, 4, 1917, pp. 102–5.
15. Winer, *op. cit.*, pp. 107–8..
16. Max Reich, 'The Forged Protocols', *Hebrew Christian Alliance Quarterly*, Vol. 5:1, 1921, p. 5.
17. Max Reich, 'Israel', *Hebrew Christian Alliance Quarterly*, Vol. 6:2, 1922, p. 45.
18. Mark Levy, 'Hebrew Christian Unity and the International Conference', *Hebrew Christian Alliance Quarterly*, Vol. 7:6, 1924, pp. 162–4.
19. Schonfield, *op. cit.*, pp. 238–9.
20. Mark Levy, 'The International Hebrew Christian Alliance, Its Feasibility – Its Function', *Report of the First International Hebrew Christian Alliance Conference*, London, 1925, p. 60.
21. *Ibid.*, p. 116.

Chapter 4: Missions to the Jews in the early twentieth century
1. Mitchell Glaser, *The Rise and Fall of Jewish Missions within the PCUSA*, Chicago, 1989, in Fleischer, *op. cit.*, p. 5.
2. David Bronstein, Jr, *Peniel Portrait*, Chicago, 1943, pp. 63–4.
3. *Ibid.*, pp. 66–7.
4. Joseph Hoffman Cohn, *I Have Fought a Good Fight*, New York, 1953, pp. 201–3.
5. Martin Parsons, *Pilgrimage in Partnership*, Bramcote, 1982, pp. 42–3.
6. Robert Allen, *Arnold Frank of Hamburg*, London, p. 179.
7. Schonfield, *op. cit.*, p. 234–5.

8. *Ibid.*, p. 233.
9. *Ibid.*, p. 234.
10. John Stuart Conning, *Our Jewish Neighbours*, New York, 1927, pp. 5–6.
11. Mitchell Glaser, *The Rise and Fall of Missions Within the PCUSA*, Chicago, 1989, p. 22, cited in Fleischer, *op. cit.*, p. 64.
12. *Ibid.*

Chapter 5: Growth of the Messianic movement
1. Jacob Peltz, 'Notes of the General Secretary', *Hebrew Christian Alliance Quarterly*, Vol. 17:3, 1932, pp. 3–4.
2. Elias Newman, 'The Beginning of a Great Task,' *Hebrew Christian Alliance Quarterly*, Vol. 17:1, 1932, pp. 25–33.
3. 'Minutes of the Seventeenth Annual Conference of the HCAA', *Hebrew Christian Alliance Quarterly*, Vol. 16:3, 1931, p. 37.
4. Editorial, *Hebrew Christian Alliance Quarterly*, Vol. 18:1, 1933, pp. 3–4.
5. 'Minutes of the Nineteenth Annual Conference of the HCAA', *Hebrew Christian Alliance Quarterly*, Vol. 18:2, 1933, p. 36.
6. Winer, *op. cit.*, pp. 32–3.
7. Morris Zeidman, 'Notes by the Hon. General Secretary,' *Hebrew Christian Alliance Quarterly*, Vol. 23:1, 1938, pp. 13–14.
8. Annie Zeidman, 'How Can Hebrew Christian Children Remain Hebrew and Christian?', *Hebrew Christian Alliance Quarterly*, Vol. 23:2, 1938, pp. 20–4.
9. Max Reich, 'The Future of Hebrew Christianity', *Hebrew Christian Alliance Quarterly*, Vol. 23:3, 1938, pp. 1–3.
10. Winer, *op. cit.*, p. 40.
11. *Ibid.*
12. *Ibid.*
13. *Ibid.*, p. 42.
14. Arnold Fruchtenbaum, *Hebrew Christianity: Its Theology, History and Philosophy*, Tustin, California, 1992, pp. 79–80.
15. *Minutes of the Biennial Conference of*

the Hebrew Christian Alliance of
America, 1967, pp. 2–4.
16. Winer, *op. cit.*, p. 73.
17. Yohanna Chernoff, *Born a Jew . . .
Die a Jew*, Hagerstown,
Maryland,1996, pp. 113–14.
18. *Ibid.*, pp. 117–18.
19. *Ibid.*, p. 125.

**Chapter 6: Messianic Judaism in
transition**
1. Juliene G. Lipson, *Jews for Jesus: An
Anthropological Study*, New York,
1990, p. 62.
2. *Ibid.*, pp. 70–1.
3. *Ibid.*, p. 73.
4. *Ibid.*, p. 74.
5. Yohanna Chernoff, *op. cit.*, p. 100.
6. Winer, *op. cit.*, p. 46.
7. *Ibid.*, p. 47.
8. Paul Liberman, 'Toward Our
Destiny', *American Messianic Jew*,
Vol. 67:4, 1982, p. 3.
9. Robert C. Coote, 'How Kosher Can
Christianity Get?', *Eternity*,
September, 1975.
10. John Fischer, 'If It Be of God',
Chicago, MJAA, 1977.
11. Winer, *op. cit.*, p. 53.
12. Jerome and Ruth Fleischer, 'Letter
to the Editor', *American Messianic
Jew*, Vol. 61:3, 1976, pp. 3–6.
13. Winer, *op. cit.*, p. 54.
14. Rachmiel Frydland, 'Let There Be
No Strife, I Pray Thee', *American
Messianic Jew*, Vol. 61:1, 1976,
pp. 3–6.
15. *Ibid.*
16. *Ibid.*

**Chapter 7: Contemporary Messianic
Judaism**
1. Winer, *op. cit.*, pp. 62–3.
2. 'The Proposed Articles of Faith for
the Hebrew Christian Church',
Hebrew Christian Alliance Quarterly,
Vol. 18:1, 1933, pp. 30–1.
3. Ruth Fleischer, *op. cit.*, p. 104.
4. Winer, *op. cit.*, p. 65.
5. Paul Liberman, *The Fig Tree
Blossoms*, Harrison, Arkansas,
1976, p. 2.

6. Union of Messianic Jewish Congregations' By-Laws, 1979, p. 1.
7. *By-Laws*, Appendix I.
8. Ruth Fleischer, *op. cit.*, p. 106.
9. *Ibid.*
10. D. Rausch, *Messianic Judaism: Its
History, Theology and Polity*,
Lewiston, New York, 1982, p. 230.
11. Marc H. Tanenbaum, 'No, They
Have Forsaken the Faith',
Christianity Today, Vol. 26, 24 April
1981, p. 25.
12. A. James Rudin and Marcia R.
Rudin, 'Onward (Hebrew)
Christian Soldiers', *Present Tense:
The Magazine of World Jewish
Affairs*, Vol. 4, Summer, 1977, p. 18.
13. A. James Rudin and Marcia R.
Rudin, 'Countering the Cults',
New York Times, 26 September
1980.
14. Rausch, *op. cit.*, pp. 236–7.
15. *Ibid.*, pp. 237–8.
16. *Ibid.*, p. 239.
17. *Ibid.*
18. *Ibid.*, p. 244.
19. *Ibid.*, p. 245.
20. Michael Schiffman, *Return of the
Remnant*, Baltimore, Maryland,
1996.
21. *Ibid.*, p. 128.
22. *Ibid.*, p. 130.
23. *Ibid.*, pp. 142–3.

Chapter 8: Sabbath
1. Jeremiah Greenberg, *Messianic
Shabbat Siddur: A Messianic Prayer
Book for Use in Sabbath Services and
at Home*, Gaithersburg, Maryland,
1997, p. 6.
2. *Ibid.*, p. 36.
3. *Ibid.*, p. 38.
4. *Ibid.*, p. 8.
5. *Ibid.*, p. 10.
6. *Ibid.*, p. 38.
7. John Fischer and David Bronstein,
Siddur for Messianic Jews, Palm
Harbor, Florida, 1988, p. 9.
8. Greenberg, *op. cit.*, p. 4.
9. *Ibid.*, p. 14.
10. *Ibid.*, p. 16.
11. *Ibid.*, p. 40.

12. *Ibid.*, p. 46.
13. *Ibid.*, p. 50.
14. *Ibid.*
15. *Ibid.*, p. 58.
16. Fischer and Bronstein, *op. cit.*, pp. 83–5.
17. *Ibid.*, p. 87.
18. Greenberg, *op. cit.*, p. 64.
19. *Ibid.*
20. *Ibid.*, p. 66.
21. *Ibid.*
22. *Ibid.*, p. 70.
23. *Ibid.*
24. *Ibid.*, p. 72.
25. *Ibid.*
26. Fischer and Bronstein, *op. cit.*, p. 99.
27. Greenberg, *op. cit.*, p. 76.
28. *Ibid.*, p. 78.
29. Fischer and Bronstein, *op. cit.*, pp. 105–7.
30. *Ibid.*, pp. 109–10.
31. *Ibid.*, pp. 117–19.
32. Greenberg, *op. cit.*, p. 86.
33. *Ibid.*, p. 88.
34. *Ibid.*, p. 90.
35. *Ibid.*
36. *Ibid.*
37. *Ibid.*

Chapter 9: Pilgrim festivals
1. *The Messianic Passover Haggadah*, Baltimore, Maryland, 1998, p. 5.
2. *Ibid.*, pp. 6–7.
3. *Ibid.*, p. 8.
4. *Ibid.*, p. 13.
5. *Ibid.*, pp. 13–14.
6. *Ibid.*, p. 16.
7. *Ibid.*, p. 25.
8. *Ibid.*, p. 26.
9. *Ibid.*, p. 27.
10. *Ibid.*
11. *Ibid.*, pp. 28–9.
12. *Ibid.*, p. 29.
13. Barney Kasdan, *God's Appointed Times: A Practical Guide for Understanding and Celebrating the Biblical Holidays*, Baltimore, Maryland, 1993, p. 42.
14. John Fischer, *Messianic Services for the Festivals and Holy Days*, Palm Harbor, Florida, 1992, p. 217.

15. Kasdan, *op. cit.*, p. 57.
16. *Ibid.*
17. Fischer, *op. cit.*, p. 227.
18. Kasdan, *op. cit.*, p. 102.
19. Fischer, *op. cit.*, p. 143.
20. Kasdan, *op. cit.*, p. 102.

Chapter 10: New Year and Day of Atonement
1. Fischer, *op. cit.*, p. 13.
2. *Ibid.*, pp. 29–31.
3. *Ibid.*, p. 41.
4. *Ibid.*, pp. 41–3.
5. *Ibid.*, pp. 49–51.
6. *Ibid.*, p. 57.
7. *Ibid.*
8. *Ibid.*, p. 59.
9. *Ibid.*, p. 61.
10. *Ibid.*, p. 63.
11. *Ibid.*, p. 73.
12. *Ibid.*
13. *Ibid.*, p. 75.
14. *Ibid.*, p. 83.
15. *Ibid.*, pp. 83–7.
16. *Ibid.*, pp. 89–91.
17. *Ibid.*, p. 91.
18. *Ibid.*, pp. 103–5.
19. *Ibid.*, p. 115.
20. *Ibid.*
21. *Ibid.*, pp. 115–16.

Chapter 11: Festivals of joy
1. Fischer, *op. cit.*, p. 57.
2. *Ibid.*, pp. 157–61.
3. *Ibid.*, p. 167.
4. *Ibid.*
5. *Ibid.*, p. 171.
6. *Ibid.*, p. 241.
7. *Ibid.*, p. 249.
8. *Ibid.*, p. 251.
9. *Ibid.*
10. *Ibid.*, p. 253.
11. *Ibid.*
12. *Ibid.*, pp. 187–97.
13. *Ibid.*, p. 199.
14. *Ibid.*, pp. 257–9.

Chapter 12: Life cycle events
1. Fischer, *op. cit.*, p. 261.
2. *Ibid.*
3. *Ibid.*, p. 263.
4. *Ibid.*

5. *Ibid.*
6. *Ibid.*, p. 265.
7. *Ibid.*, pp. 265–7.
8. Barney Kasdan, *God's Appointed Customs*, Grand Rapids, Michigan, 1996, p. 24.
9. *Ibid.*
10. *Ibid.*, p. 25.
11. *Ibid.*
12. *Ibid.*
13. *Ibid.*, pp. 25–6.
14. *Ibid.*, p. 35.
15. *Ibid.*
16. *Ibid.*
17. *Ibid.*
18. *Ibid.*
19. *Ibid.*, p. 36.
20. *Ibid.*
21. Fischer, *op. cit.*, p. 269.
22. *Ibid.*, pp. 269–71.
23. Kasdan, *op. cit.*, p. 65.
24. *Ibid.*
25. *Ibid.*
26. *Ibid.*, p. 66.
27. *Ibid.*
28. *Ibid.*, p. 67.
29. *Ibid.*
30. *Ibid.*, p. 68.
31. *Ibid.*
32. *Ibid.*
33. *Ibid.*, pp. 69–70.
34. Fischer and Bronstein, *op. cit.*, p. 29.

Chapter 13: Personal lifestyle

1. Kasden, *op. cit.*, p. 96.
2. *Ibid.*, p. 110.
3. *Ibid.*, p. 115.
4. *Ibid.*, pp. 121–2.
5. *Ibid.*, p. 126.
6. *Ibid.*, p. 126.
7. *Ibid.*, pp. 129–30.
8. *Ibid.*, p. 144.
9. *Ibid.*
10. *Ibid.*
11. *Ibid.*, p. 145.
12. *Ibid.*, p. 148.
13. *Kiddushin* 31a.
14. *Shabbat* 156b.
15. *Nedarim* 30b.

Chapter 14: Messianic Judaism and the Jewish people

1. Rausch, *op. cit.*, p. 118.
2. *Ibid.*, p. 119.
3. *Ibid.*, p. 120.
4. Juster, *op. cit.*, pp. 157–63.
5. Schiffman, *op. cit.*, p. 93.
6. *Ibid.*, pp. 102–3.
7. *Ibid.*, p. 103.
8. Rausch, *op. cit.*, p. 129.
9. David Stern, *Messianic Jewish Manifesto*, Clarksville, Maryland, 1997, pp. 16–17.
10. *Ibid.*, pp. 22–3.
11. *Ibid.*, p. 23.
12. *Ibid.*, p. 24.
13. American Board of Missions to the Jews, *Introducing the Jewish People to Their Messiah*, 1979, p. 5.
14. Arthur W. Kac, *The Messiahship of Jesus*, Chicago, 1980, p. 99.
15. Walter Riggans, 'Messianic Judaism and Jewish–Christian Relations: A Case Study in the Field of Religious Identity', unpublished doctoral thesis, University of Birmingham, 1991, p. 258.
16. Stern, *op. cit.*, p. 27.
17. Riggans, *op. cit.*, p. 245.
18. *Ibid.*, pp. 245–6.
19. Philip E. Goble, *Everything You Need to Know to Grow a Messianic Yeshiva*, Pasadena, California, 1981, p. 21.
20. Stern, *op. cit.*, p. 61.
21. *Ibid.*, pp. 140–3.
22. *Ibid.*, pp. 162–3.
23. *Report of the First General Conference of the Hebrew Christian Alliance of America*, 1915, p. 22.
24. Riggans, *op. cit.*, p. 88.
25. B. Z. Sobel, *Hebrew Christianity: The Thirteenth Tribe*, New York, 1974, pp. 234ff.
26. Dan Juster, *Jewish Congregations: A New Approach to Jewish Witness*, 1984, pp. 9–11, in Riggans, *op. cit.*, p. 89.
27. Stern, *op. cit.*, pp. 4–5.
28. James Hutchens, 'A Case for Messianic Judaism', unpublished

doctoral thesis, Fuller Theological Seminary, 1974, p. 277.

29. Yohanna Chernoff, *Born a Jew . . . Die a Jew: The Story of Martin Chernoff*, Hagerstown, Maryland, 1996, p. 201.
30. *Ibid.*, p. 215.
31. *Ibid.*, p. 219.
32. Bentzion Kravitz, *The Jewish Response to Missionaries: Counter-Missionary Handbook*, Beverly Hills, California, 1996, p. 16.

Chapter 15: Messianic Judaism and its critics

1. Kravitz, *op. cit.*, p. 9.
2. *Ibid.*, p. 9.
3. Gerald Sigal, *The Jew and the Christian Missionary: A Jewish Response to Missionary Christianity*, New York, 1981, p. 36.
4. Kravitz, *op. cit.*, p. 23.
5. *Ibid.*, pp. 23–4.
6. *Ibid.*
7. *Ibid.*, p. 25.
8. *Ibid.*
9. *Ibid.*, pp. 26–7.
10. *Ibid.*, pp. 27–8.
11. *Ibid.*, p. 29.
12. Julius Ciss, *From 'Messianic Jew' to Counter-Missionary*, Baltimore, Maryland, 1991, pp. 2–26.

Chapter 16: Messianic Judaism and Israeli law

1. *Encyclopedia Judaica*, Jerusalem, Keter, 1971, Vol. 1, p. 212.
2. Louis Jacobs, *The Jewish Religion*, Oxford, 1995, p. 99.
3. Riggans, *op. cit.*, p. 325.
4. *Sanhedrin* 44a.
5. Riggans, *op. cit.*, p. 330.
6. *Ibid.*, p. 332.
7. *Ibid.*, pp. 326–7.
8. *Ibid.*, p. 334.

9. *Ibid.*, p. 335.
10. *Ibid.*, p. 335–6.
11. *Ibid.*, p. 336–7.
12. *Ibid.*, p. 338.
13. *Ibid.*, p. 340.
14. *Ibid.*
15. *Ibid.*, p. 341.
16. *Ibid.*
17. *Ibid.*, p. 342.
18. *Ibid.*, p. 343.
19. *Ibid.*, p. 358.
20. *Ibid.*
21. Fruchtenbaum, *op. cit.*, pp. 7–9.
22. Dan Juster, *Jewish Roots*, Shippensburg, Pennsylvania, 1995, p. 191.
23. *Ibid.*, p. 192.
24. Stern, *op. cit.*, pp. 16–17.
25. David Chernoff, *An Introduction to Messianic Judaism*, Havertown, Pennsylvania, 1990, p. 10.
26. Stern, *op. cit.*, pp. 24–7.

Chapter 17: Models of Messianic Judaism

1. Dan Cohn-Sherbok, *The Jewish Faith*, London, SPCK, 1993, p. 67.
2. Stern, *op. cit.*, p. 158.
3. Dan Cohn-Sherbok, *Modern Judaism*, London, Macmillan, 1996, p. 157.
4. Walter Jacob, *Contemporary American Reform Responsa*, New York, 1987, pp. 109–12.
5. Carol Harris-Shapiro, *Messianic Judaism*, Boston, Beacon, 1998, pp. 169–70.
6. Shoshana Feher, *Passing over Easter: Constructing the Boundaries of Messianic Judaism*, Walnut Creek, California, 1998, pp. 41–2.
7. Harris-Shapiro, *op. cit.*, p. 174.
8. *Ibid.*, p. 177.
9. *Ibid.*
10. *Ibid.*, p. 189.

Bibliography

Anderson, A. E., 'Messianic Explosion', *Jewish Exponent*, 8 August 1996.

Beiser, V., 'For the Love of Jesus: The Ominous Rise of Messianic Judaism', *Jerusalem Report*, 26 January 1995.

Bennet, R., *Saga: Israel and the Demise of Nations*, Jerusalem, 1993.

Beresford, G. and S., *The Unpromised Land: The Struggle of Messianic Jews*, Baltimore, Maryland, 1994.

Berger, D. and Wyschogrod, M., *Jews and 'Jewish Christianity'*, New York, 1978.

Berkowitz, A. and D., *Torah Rediscovered*, Littleton, Colorado, 1996.

Berkowitz, A. and D., *Take Hold*, Littleton, Colorado, 1998.

Borowitz, E. B., 'Apostasy from Judaism Today', *Modern Theology*, No. 11, 1995.

Bosky, Avner, '30 Messianic Congregations Flourishing in Israel', *Messianic Times*, Vol. 1, No. 1, 1990.

British Messianic Jewish Alliance, *Survey of UK Messianic Groups*, Ramsgate, 1997.

Bronstein, David, Jr, *Peniel Portrait*, Chicago, 1943.

Burnet, K., *Why Pray for Israel?*, Basingstoke, Hants, 1983.

Charmé, S. L., 'Heretics, Infidels and Apostates: Menace, Problem or Symptom?', *Judaism*, No. 36, 1987.

Charry, E. T., 'Christian Jews and the Law', *Modern Theology*, No. 11, 1995.

Chernoff, D., *Yeshua the Messiah*, Havertown, Pennsylvania, 1989.

Chernoff, D., *An Introduction to Messianic Judaism*, Philadelphia, 1990.

Chernoff, Y., 'The Seventies – A Decade of Discovery', *American Messianic Jew*, No. 4, San Francisco, 1980.

Chernoff, Y., *Born a Jew . . . Die a Jew*, Hagerstown, Maryland, 1996.

Cohen, A., 'More Jewish Than Ever – We've Found the Messiah', *Christianity Today*, 1 February 1974.

Cohn, Joseph Hoffman, *I Have Fought a Good Fight*, New York, 1953.

Cohn-Sherbok, Dan, *The Jewish Faith*, London, 1993.

Cohn-Sherbok, Dan, *Modern Judaism*, London, 1996.

Cohn-Sherbok, Dan and Lavinia, *The American Jew*, Grand Rapids, Michigan, 1995.

Conning, John Stuart, *Our Jewish Neighbors*, New York, 1927.

Dahaf Research Institute, 'The Dahaf Report on Israeli Public Opinion Concerning Messianic Jewish Aliya', Tel Aviv, 1988.

Danielou, J., *The Theology of Jewish Christianity*, London, 1964.

Dewitz, L., 'Why Messianic Jews?', *Hebrew Christian*, Vol. 53, No. 1, Ramsgate, 1980.

Edelstein, A., 'Jews Who Choose Jesus', *Moment*, No. 19, 1994.

Ellwood, R. S., *One Way: The Jesus Movement and Its Meaning*, Englewood Cliffs, New Jersey, 1973.

Endelman, T. (ed.), *Jewish Apostasy in the Modern World*, New York, 1987.

Evans, M., *Messianic Judaism? Young Lions of Judah*, New Jersey, 1974.

Everitt, D. J., *Jewish–Christian Missions to the Jews: 1820–1935*, Ann Arbor, Michigan, 1989.

Feher, S., *Passing over Easter, Constructing the Boundaries of Messianic Judaism*, Walnut Creek, California, 1998.

Finkelstein, J., 'Jewish Identity', *American Messianic Jewish Quarterly*, No. 3, Chicago, 1976.

Fischer, J., 'Why a Messianic Movement?', *American Messianic Jewish Quarterly*, No. 4, Chicago, 1976.

Fischer, J., *Sharing Israel's Messiah*, Highland Park, Illinois, 1978.

Fischer, J., 'Messianic Jews are Still Jews', *Christianity Today*, 24 April 1981.

Fischer, J., *The Olive Tree Connection*, Downers Grove, Illinois, 1983.

Fischer, J., *A Messianic Synagogue*, Palm Harbor, Florida, 1986.

Fischer, J., *Messianic Services for the Festivals and Holy Days*, Palm Harbor, Florida, 1992.

Fischer, J. and Bronstein, D., *Siddur for Messianic Jews*, Palm Harbor, Florida, 1988.

Fleischer, R., *So Great a Cloud of Witnesses*, privately published, 1996.

Forta, Arye, 'The New Christian Mission to the Jews: How Shall We Respond?', *L'eyla*, No. 25, 1988.

Friedman, E., 'What Is a Jew? The Father Daniel Case', *Southern Cross*, 2 January 1963.

Friedman, E., *Jewish Identity*, New York, 1987.

Friedman, T., 'Who Is Not a Jew?: The Halachic Status of an Apostate', *Conservative Judaism*, No. 41, 1988/9.

Fruchtenbaum, A., *Israelology: The Missing Link in Systematic Theology*, Tustin, California, 1989.

Fruchtenbaum, A., *Hebrew Christianity: Its Theology, History and Philosophy*, Tustin, California, 1992.

Fruchtenbaum, A. R., *Jesus Was a Jew*, Nashville, Tennessee, 1974.

Frydland, R., 'Messianic Rabbinic Dialogue', *American Messianic Jewish Quarterly*, No. 3, Chicago, 1979.

Galanter, M., 'A Dissent on Brother Daniel', *Commentary*, July 1963.

Gartenhaus, J., *Famous Hebrew Christians*, Chattanooga, Tennessee, 1979.

Gidney, W. T., *The History of the London Society for Promoting Christianity Amongst the Jews*, London, 1908.

Goble, P., *Everything You Need to Know to Grow a Messianic Synagogue*, Pasadena, California, 1974.

Goble, P., 'Messianic Judaism: A Biblical Apologetic with a View to Liturgical Reform', unpublished doctoral thesis, Fuller Theological Seminary, 1975.

Goble, P. 'Reaching Jews through Messianic Synagogues', *Evangelical Missions Quarterly*, Vol. 11, No. 2, 1975.

Goble, P., *Everything You Need to Know to Grow a Messianic Yeshiva*, Pasadena, California, 1981.

Goldberg, L., 'The Messianic Jew', *Christianity Today*, 1 February 1974.

Goldberg, L., 'Messianic Jews', *American Messianic Jewish Quarterly*, No. 3, 1979.

Greenberg, J., *Messianic Shabbat Siddur*, Gaithersburg, Maryland, 1997.

Harris-Shapiro, C., *Messianic Judaism*, Boston, Beacon, 1999.

Hutchens, J., 'A Case for Messianic Judaism', unpublished doctoral thesis, Fuller Theological Seminary, 1974.

Jacob, W. (ed.), *Contemporary American Reform Responsa*, New York, 1987.

Jacobs, Louis, *The Jewish Religion*, Oxford, 1995.

Juster, D., 'The *Torah* and Messianic Judaism', *Evangelical Beacon*, 14 October 1975.

Juster, D., *Jewishness and Jesus*, Downers Grove, Illinois, 1977.

Juster, D., 'Messianic Jews', *American Messianic Jewish Quarterly*, No. 2, 1979.

Juster, D., *Jewish Roots*, Shippensburg, Pennsylvania, 1995.

Juster, D. and Fischer, J., 'Messianic Jews: Message and Motive', *United Evangelical Action*, No. 35, 1976.

Kac, Arthur W., *The Messiahship of Jesus*, Chicago, 1980.

Kahn, G., 'Conservative Bodies Debate Membership of a "Messianic Jew"', *The Forward*, No. 1, 12 April 1996.

Kaplan, Aryeh, *The Real Messiah? A Jewish Response to Missionaries*, New York, 1985.

Kasdan, B., *God's Appointed Times: A Practical Guide for Understanding and Celebrating the Biblical Holidays,* Baltimore, Maryland, 1993.

Kasdan, B., *God's Appointed Customs: A Messianic Jewish Guide to the Biblical Lifecycle and Lifestyle,* Baltimore, Maryland, 1996.

Kjaer-Hanson, Kai (ed.), *The Death of the Messiah,* Baltimore, Maryland, 1994.

Kjaer-Hanson, Kai, *Jospeh Rabinowicz and the Messianic Movement,* Grand Rapids, Michigan, 1995.

Kohn, R., 'Hebrew Christianity and Messianic Judaism on the Church–Sect Continuum', unpublished doctoral thesis, McMaster University, 1985.

Kohn, R., 'Hebrew Christians and Modern Judaism', *Religion Today,* Autumn, 1986.

Kravitz, B., *The Jewish Response to Missionaries,* Los Angeles, 1996.

Lapides, L., 'Do We Need the Fellowship of Messianic Congregations?', *Mishkan,* No. 6–7, 1987.

Lascelle, R., *That They Might Be Saved,* Fairfield, Ohio, 1992.

Levine, D., *In That Day,* Lake Mary, Florida, 1998.

Liberman, P., *The Fig Tree Blossoms,* Harrison, Arkansas, 1981.

Lipson, J., *Jews for Jesus: An Anthropological Study,* New York, 1990.

Lowenthal, J., *The Last Chance for the Church to Love the Jewish People,* Mukilteo, Washington, 1998.

Maoz, B., 'The Beresfords: A Reply to David Stern', *Hebrew Christian,* September–November 1990.

Novak, D., 'Response to Michael Wyschogrod', *Modern Theology,* No. 11, 1995.

Parsons, Martin, *Pilgrimage in Partnership,* Bramcote, 1982.

Phillips, M., *The Bible and the Supernatural and the Jews,* Camp Hill, Pennsylvania, 1970.

Pruter, K., *Jewish Christians in the United States: A Bibliography,* New York, 1987.

Rausch, D., *Messianic Judaism: Its History, Theology and Polity,* Lewiston, New York, 1982.

Riggans, W., 'Messianic Judaism and Jewish–Christian Relations: A Case Study in the Field of Religious Identity', unpublished doctoral thesis, University of Birmingham, 1991.

Rosen, M. and C., *Y'Shua: The Jewish Way to Say Jesus,* Chicago, 1982.

Rosenfarb, J., *Talmud, Torah and Messianic Jews,* Virginia Beach, Virginia, 1989.

Roth, S., *Something for Nothing: The Spiritual Rebirth of a Jew,* Plainfield, New Jersey, 1976.

Rubin, B., *You Bring the Bagels I'll Bring the Gospel: Sharing the Messiah with Your Jewish Neighbour,* Baltimore, Maryland, 1997.

Rudolf, D. (ed.), *The Voice of the Lord: Messianic Daily Devotional,* Baltimore, Maryland, 1998.

Schiffman, M., 'Aliyah for Messianic Jews', *Hebrew Christian,* June–August 1989.

Schiffman, M., *Return of the Remnant: The Rebirth of Messianic Judaism,* Baltimore, Maryland, 1996.

Schonfield, H., *The History of Jewish Christianity,* London, 1936.

Sidey, K., 'Messianic Jews Seek Visibility, Respect', *Christianity Today,* No. 43, 1990.

Sigal, G., *The Jew and the Christian Missionary,* New York, 1981.

Silberling, K., 'Women in Leadership', *Messianic Times,* No. 5, 1995.

Silberling, M., *Dancing for Joy,* Baltimore, Maryland, 1995.

Sobel, B. Z., *Hebrew Christianity: The Thirteenth Tribe,* New York, 1974.

Stern, D., *Jewish New Testament,* Clarksville, Maryland, 1989.

Stern, D., *Messianic Jewish Manifesto,* Clarksville, Maryland, 1997.

Telchin, S., *Betrayed,* London, 1981.

Telchin, S., *Abandoned,* London, 1998.

Winer, R., *The Calling: The History of the Messianic Jewish Alliance of America 1915–1990,* Wynnewood, Pennsylvania, 1990.

Wyschogrod, M., 'Letter to a Friend', *Modern Theology,* No. 11, 1995.

Wyschogrod, M., 'Response to the Respondents', *Modern Theology,* No. 11, 1995.

Glossary

Acharonim: Rabbinic scholars of the eighteenth to twentieth centuries.

Adon Olam: Prayer ('Lord of the world').

Adonai hu Ha-Elohim: Prayer ('The Lord he is God').

Adversos Judaeos tradition: Anti-Jewish tradition.

Afikomen: Middle *matzah*.

Al Ha-Nissim: Prayer ('For the miracles').

Al Het: Prayer ('For the sin').

Alenu: Prayer at the end of the service ('It is our duty').

Aliyah: Immigration to Israel.

Amidah: Prayer ('standing').

Apikoros: Heretic.

Ashkenazic: Originating in Eastern Europe.

Ashrey Yoshevey Veysecho: Prayer.

Auto da fé: Public ceremony at which the sentences of the Inquisition were announced.

Avinu Malkenu: Prayer ('Our father our king').

Bar Mitzvah: Male adolescent ceremony ('son of the commandment').

Baruchu: Prayer ('bless').

Bat: Daughter.

Bat Mitzvah: Female adolescent ceremony ('daughter of the commandment').

Bekhorot: Tractate of the *Mishnah* ('firstlings').

Ben: Son.

Bimah: Platform ('elevated place').

Brit Chadasha: New Testament.

Brit Milah: Circumcision.

B'shem Yeshua Ha-Mashiach: Prayer ('In the name of Yeshua the Messiah').

Challah: Sabbath loaf of bread.

Chametz: Leavened bread.

Cohen: Priest.

Dalet: Hebrew letter.

Davening: Praying.

Dayenu: Prayer ('It would have satisfied us').

Dreydel: Spinning top.

Eliahu Ha-Navi: Song ('Elijah the Prophet').

Elul: Sixth month.

Eretz Yisrael: Land of Israel.

Erev Shabbat: Evening of the Sabbath.

Etrog: Citron.

Gemara: Rabbinic discussions on the *Mishnah*.

Greggers: Noisemakers.

Ha-Elohim: Prayer ('The Lord').

Haftarah: Prophetic reading.

Haggadah: Passover prayer book.

Halakhah: Jewish law.

Hallel: Group of psalms ('praise').

Hamentashen: Pastries filled with poppy seed.

Ha-Motzi: Prayer over bread.

Hanukkah: Festival of Lights ('dedication').

Haroset: Passover paste made of *matzah* meal, wine, spice and fruit.

Hasidism: Mystical Jewish movement founded in the eighteenth century.

Havdalah: Service at the end of the Sabbath ('differentiation').

Havenu, shalom aleichem: Sabbath song ('Come, peace upon us').

Hoshanah Rabbah: Seventh day of *Sukkot*.

Huppah: Marriage canopy.

Kaddish: Prayer for the dead.

Kapparot: Day of Atonement ritual ('atonements').

Kashrut: Dietary laws.

Kedushah: Prayer ('holiness').

Ketubbah: Marriage document.

Kiddush: Prayer recited over a cup of wine to consecrate the Sabbath or a festival ('sanctification').

Kippah: Headcovering.

Kittle: Robe.

Kol Nidre: Prayer ('all vows').

Kosher: Ritually fit.

Lekah Dodi: Sabbath hymn ('Come my beloved').

Lulav: Palm branches.

Magen Avot: Prayer ('shield of fathers').

Malkhuyyot: Prayers ('kingdoms').

Maoz Tsur: Prayer ('fortress, rock (of salvation)').

Maror: Bitter herbs.

Matzah: Unleavened bread.

Megillah: Scroll.

Mekhilta: *Midrash* on Exodus.

Menorah: Candelabrum.

Meshummad: Apostate.

Mezuzah: Box fixed to the doorpost of a Jewish home ('doorpost').

Midrashim: Rabbinic commentaries on Scripture.

Mikveh: Ritual bath.

Minyan: Quorum.

Mishnah: Compendium of the Oral *Torah* ('teaching').

Mitzvah: Commandment.

Mohar: Payment by the groom.

Mohel: Person who performs circumcisions.

Mumar: Apostate.

Musaf: Additional service ('additional sacrifice').

Neshama: Soul.

Nisan: Seventh month.

Nissuin: Second stage of the marriage procedure.

Oleh: Immigrant.

Omer: First sheaf cut during the barley harvest ('sheaf').

Oz M'Lifnai B'reshit: Prayer.

Paot: Side curls.

Parnasim: Leaders of the community ('providers').

Pidyon Ha-Ben: Redemption of the Firstborn.

Pintele Yid: Spark of Jewish spirituality.

Poshe'a Yisrael: Rebellious Jew.

Poskim: Rabbinic scholars of the eleventh and twelfth centuries.

Purim: Feast of Esther ('lots').

Rishon: Advent.

Rishonim: Rabbinic scholars of the fourteenth to seventeenth centuries.

Rosh Hashanah: New Year.

Rosh Hodesh: New Moon ('head of the month').

Ruach Ha-Shem: Spirit of God.

Sandak: Godfather.

Sanhedrin: Central rabbinical court.

Savoraim: Rabbinic scholars of the sixth and seventh centuries.

Seder: Passover evening meal ('order').

Sephardic: Originating in Spain or North Africa.

Sevarim: Three notes sounded on a *shofar*.

Shabbat: Sabbath.

Shaddai: Almighty.

Shammash: Additional candle on the *Hanukkah menorah* ('beadle').

Shavuot: Festival of Weeks ('weeks').

Sheheheyanu: Prayer ('Who brought us').

Shehitah: Ritual slaughter.

Sheloshim: Thirty days of mourning ('thirty').

Shema: Prayer ('Hear O Israel').

Shemini Atseret: Final day of *Sukkot* ('eighth day of solemn assembly').

Sheol: Realm of the dead.

Shin: Hebrew letter.

Shittuf: Partnership.

Shivah: Seven days of mourning ('seven').

Shofar: Ram's horn.

Shofarot: Prayers ('Rams' horns').

Shul: Synagogue.

Shulkhan Arukh: Code of Jewish Law ('arranged table').

Siddur: Jewish Prayer Book ('order').

Sifra: *Midrash* on Leviticus.

Sifrei: *Midrash* on Numbers and Deuteronomy.

Simhat Torah: Holy day on which the annual completion of the reading of the *Torah* is celebrated ('rejoicing in the law').

Sukkah: Booth.

Sukkot: Festival of booths.

Taamey Ha-Mitzvot: Reasons for the commandments.

Tahanun: Prayer ('supplication').

Tallit Gadol: Prayer shawl.

Tallit Katan: Small prayer shawl.

Talmud: Collection of the legal discussions based on the *Mishnah* ('study').

Tareyf: Food which is not kosher.

Targum: Aramaic translation of the Bible ('interpreter').

Tashlikh: New Year custom ('thou shalt cast').

Tefillin: Phylacteries.

Tekiah: Long note sounded on a *shofar*.

Tenaim: Betrothal document.

Tenakh: Bible.

Teruot: Nine notes sounded on a *shofar*.

Torah: Five Books of Moses ('law').

Tosefta: Additions to the *Mishnah* ('addition').

Tzimmes: Food made with carrots and honey.

Tzizit: Fringes.

U-Netanneh Tokef: Prayer.

Yaaleh-Ve-Yavo: Prayer.

Yarmulke: Skullcap.

Yeshiva: Rabbinical seminary.

Yigdal: Prayer ('May he be magnified').

Yizkor: Memorial service ('He shall remember').

Yod: Hebrew letter.

Yom Ha-Mashiach: Day of the Messiah.

Yom Kippur: Day of Atonement.

Zikhronot: Prayers ('remembrances').

Zohar: Medieval mystical work.

Index

AAJE (American Association for Jewish
    Evangelism) 46, 67
Aaronic Blessing 99, 115, 117, 122, 123, 124,
    129, 137, 142
ABMJ , *see* American Board of Missions to
    the Jews
Abner of Burgos 8
Abu'l Faraj, Gregory 10
Adat ha-Tikvah 67–8
Adler, Jeff 76
Adon Olam 99, 115, 117, 122
Advent (*Rishon*) 133–7
Ahasuerus 130
Ahazat Zion Synagogue 79
Aish Ha-Torah 190
Akiva, Rabbi 106, 199
Al Ha-Nissim 128
Al Het 120–1
Albright, William F. 219
Alcala, Alfonso d' 12
Alenu 93, 97–8, 112, 114, 122, 123, 127, 133,
    134
Alexander, Michael Solomon 15–16
Alfonsi, Petrus (Moses Sephardi) 7–8
American Association for Jewish Evange-
    lism (AAJE) 46, 67
American Baptist Home Mission Society 38
American Board of Missions to the Jews
    15, 38, 40, 42, 46, 48, 56, 174
American, Conservative and General Asso-
    ciation of Regular Baptists 47
American Episcopal Church 45
American European Mission 42
American Jewish Committee 79, 80
American Messianic Fellowship 46
American Messianic Jew, The 68
Amidah 92–3, 94, 112, 113, 119, 122, 123, 125,
    128, 129, 130, 131, 134
Anacletus II, Pope 9
anti-semitism 47, 50, 171, 210–11
    see also persecutions
apostasy 191–2, 200–1
articles of faith, *see* faith
Ashrey Yoshevey Veysecho 132

Assemblies of God 67, 84
Association of Torah-Observant Messianics
    1, 77–8
Aston, J. D. 42
atonement 171, 174
Atonement, Day of, *see Yom Kippur*
Avinu Malkenu 115, 121–2

baptism 161, 174
    see also immersion
Baptist churches 38, 47
bar Kochba, Simeon 1, 5
Bar Mitzvah 78, 148, 149–50, 163
Barak, Justice 199
Barbican Mission to the Jews 38, 48
Barnabas 3–4
Baron, David 14, 15
Baruchu 91–2, 113, 115, 119, 122, 125, 129,
    130, 131, 134, 149
Bat Mitzvah 78, 148, 149–50
beliefs
    statements, of, *see* faith
    see also Messianic Judaism
Ben-Gurion, David 193
Bendor-Samuel, Elijah 36
Benedictus Christianus 8
Benhayim, Menachem 200–1
Beni Abraham association 16
Benjamin, Bishop of Jerusalem 5
Beresford, Gary and Shirley 198–200
Berinson, Justice 195
Betelheim, Bernard 15
Beth Emanuel congregation 67–8
Beth Messiah 64, 67–8, 81
Beth Messiah Synagogue (Washington)
    67–8
Bethany Neighbourhood Centre 38–9
Bible / *Tanakh* 171, 175, 177
    translations of, and 'proof texts' 187–8
    see also New Testament; *Torah*
bible study 55, 60, 66, 67, 78
    see also education
biblical literalism 170
Birnbaum, Solomon 36, 44

Blecher, Arthur C. 80–1
booths, *see sukkah/Sukkot*
Box, G. H. 25
Brinker, Rudolf 41
Brit Chadasha 116, 125–6
   see also New Testament
British Society for Promoting Christianity
   among the Jews 14
British Society for the Propagation of the
   Gospel among the Jews 38
Bronstein family 44
Bronstein, David 39–40, 59, 67
Bronstein, Esther 39, 67
Brotman, Manny 57, 58, 64, 66, 67, 76
Brotsky, Ed 55–6
Budoff, Barry 76
Buksbazen, Victor 44, 46
burial 154

calendar 131
Calvinism 43
candles 90–1, 99–100, 113, 117, 128, 129,
   133–4, 138–9
Carpenter, H. C. 41
Carthagena, Don Alfonso de 9
Central Conference of American Rabbis
   206
Chair of Elijah 143, 144
Chanukkah, see Hanukkah
charismatic worship 66–7, 82–3, 87
Charmé, Stuart 211
Chernoff, David 64, 67, 74–5, 169, 202
Chernoff, Hope 64
Chernoff, Joel 64, 67
Chernoff, Martin 55, 59, 64, 65, 66, 67, 73–4,
   76
Chernoff, Yohanna 58–9, 63, 67, 180
Chicago Hebrew Mission 38, 46
children
   ceremonies concerning 140–50
   participation in services 125
Children of Abraham 15
choice, religion and 184
Christian and Missionary Alliance 38
Christian missions to Jews 14–15, 16,
   38–48, 60
   HCAA and 49–51
   missionaries' training 44, 48
Christian opposition to Messianic Judaism
   24, 68–9, 81–2
Christian persecution of Jews 6, 7, 8, 10–12,
   211
Christian Witness to Israel 48
Christiani, Pablo 8
Christianity/Christians
   early 1, 3–7, 13, 87
   fundamentalist 61, 170, 171, 211, 213

Hasidic 55
   Jewish 6–14, 45–6
Christmas x, 83, 133
Christoffersen, Miss 42
Church's Ministry Amongst the Jews 42,
   48
circumcision 33, 45, 75, 78, 142–5
Ciss, Julius 186, 188–90
class attitudes 211
cleansing, ritual 117, 159–61
Clement IV, Pope 8
clothing 77, 83, 161–3, 165–6
   see also tallit
CMJ (Church's Ministry Amongst the Jews)
   42, 48
cohen 145–8
Cohen, Kenneth 79, 180
Cohen, Philip 24–5, 45
Cohn, Joseph Hoffman 40–1, 44, 46
Cohn, Justice 194
Cohn, Leopold 15, 40–1, 44, 46
confirmation 78, 148
Congregation of the Messiah Within Israel
   55
Conservative Judaism 125, 148–9, 151, 163,
   165, 172, 177–8, 205, 206–7, 208–9, 212
Constantine 6, 33, 87
conversion 3–4, 6, 160
   forced 7
   and Jewishness 172, 173, 191–2, 203, 204
   Messianic Judaic belief concerning 174
   of minors 80
   preventive measures against 184–5
Coote, Robert C. 68
counting of the *omer* 105–7, 138
Craig, Samuel 42
cremation 154

Dahaf Research Institute and Report
   196–8, 199
dance x, xi, 61, 66, 78, 84
Daniel, Brother (Oswald Rufeisen) 193–4
davening 67
Davis, George 47
Davis, Rose 47
Dayenu 104
death
   beliefs concerning 112, 113, 153–4
   customs and rituals following 154–5
Delitzsch, Franz 44
descent, matrilineal/patrilineal, and definitions of Jewishness 172–3, 191,
   201–2
dietary laws (*kashrut*) 45, 61, 77, 78, 157–9
Domitian 5
Donin, Nicholas 8
Dorflinger, Esther 195–6

drama 60, 62, 65, 130
dual covenant theology 47
Duff-Forbes, Lawrence 55–6

East London Mission to the Jews 38
Easter x, 33, 83
Edersheim, Alfred 15
education 44, 48, 55, 75
  of Messianic Jews 82, 85
Einspruch, Henry and Marie 46–7
Eliahu ha-Navi 100
Elon, Justice 199
embalming 154
Enlightenment, the 212
Ephraim, Bishop of Jerusalem 5
Epiphanius 5–7
Episcopal Jews' Chapel Abrahamic Society
  16
Esther 130
Evangelical Free Church 84
evangelism 61–2, 84, 178–80, 181, 182,
    184–90
  and right-wing views 211, 213
  YHCA and 64–5
  see also Christian missions
*Everything You Need to Know to Grow a
    Messianic Synagogue* 67
*Everything You Need to Know to Grow a
    Messianic Yeshiva* 175

faith, statements of 18–19, 21–4, 61, 72–3,
    204
fasting 117, 138, 183
Feher, Shoshana 209
Fellowship of Christian Testimonies to the
    Jews 68–9
Fellowship of Messianic Congregations 1,
    77
Ferdinand V of Castile (the Catholic) 10
festivals, *see* Christmas; Easter; Jewish
    festivals
Finkelstein, Debbie 64
Finkelstein, Joseph 64, 66, 76, 180
first-born, redemption of 145–8
First Hebrew Christian Church (Chicago)
    39, 55, 59, 67–8
Fischer, John 68 (n. 10), 76
Fleischer, Jerome 55, 69–70
Fleischer, Ruth 69–70, 77
FMC (Fellowship of Messianic Congrega-
    tions) 1, 77
food laws , *see* dietary laws
forgiveness 117
Frank, Arnold 42–3, 44
Frank, Jacob 13
Frederic William IV of Prussia 15
free speech 62

Frey, Joseph Samuel 14
Friends of Israel Gospel Ministry 68
Friends of Israel Missionary and Relief
    Society 46
fringes (*tzizit*) 77, 161–3
Fruchtenbaum, Arnold 56, 66, 76, 77, 201,
    202
Frydland, Rachmiel 44, 54, 68, 70–1
fundamentalism 61, 167, 170, 171, 211, 213

Gannon, Ray 67
Gartenhaus, Jacob 46, 47
Gemaras 177
Germanus, Johannes Isaac Levita 12
Geronimo de Santa Fe 8
Gershom ben Judah 150
Ghennassia, Paul 48
Ginsburg, Solomon 15
Gitlin, Moses 42
Glass, Arthur 55
Glass, Emma Finestone 55
Goble, Philip 67, 175–6
Goldberg, Louis 48
Golding, B. B. 15
Gorodishz, Peter 36
Gospels 5, 12, 129
Grace after Meals 130, 131
Gracia de Santa Maria, Don Gonzalo 9–10
Greenbaum, Emmanuel 30, 38–9, 49–50
Grun, Paulus 24, 45

Ha-Elohim 108
Hadrian 5
Haftarah 96, 115–16, 123, 125, 129, 149,
    150
Haggadah 78, 102, 103
halakhah (Jewish law) 77–8, 176–8, 191, 192,
    200–2, 204–5
  Israeli law and 193
Halevi, Solomon 9
Hallel 105, 109, 128, 129, 130, 131, 132, 138
Haman 130
Hanukkah 58, 78, 127–9
Harris-Shapiro, Carol 209, 210, 211, 213
Hartley, David 174
Hasidism 55, 151, 207, 212
hats, *see* head coverings
Havdalah 90, 99–100
HCAA , *see* Hebrew Christian Alliance of
    America
head coverings 67, 83, 165–6
Hebrew 44, 47, 48
Hebrew Christian Alliance of America 26,
    27–37, 38, 44, 49–54, 65–6, 68, 178
  aims 27–8, 178
  Women's Auxiliary 36
  youth movement 57–9, 60, 64–6

see also Messianic Jewish Alliance of
America
Hebrew Christian Alliance of Great Britain
16–17, 36–7
Hebrew Christian Alliance Quarterly, The 30,
34, 57, 68
Hebrew Christian churches 39, 54–6, 59,
67–8, 75
Hebrew Christian Prayer Union 16
Hebrew Christian Synagogue of
Philadelphia 35
Hebrew Christian Testimony to Israel 14,
15, 38, 48
Hegesippus 5
Hellyer, H. L. 38–9
Herschell, Ridley 14
Heydt, Henry 44
Hillel II 131
Hitler, Adolf 50, 51
holidays, Jewish , *see* Jewish festivals
Holocaust, the 46, 47, 52
Home Mission Board of the Southern
Baptist Church 38
Hoshanah Rabbah 111
Humanistic Judaism 205, 206–7, 208–9, 212
humour 61
Hutchens, James 179
hymns 64, 128

IAMCS, *see* International Alliance of
Messianic Congregations and
Synagogues
'If It Be of God' 68
IHCA, *see* International Hebrew Christian
Alliance
immersion, ritual 117, 159–61
Independence Day 137–9
Inquisition 10–11
Institutum Judaicum Delitzschianum 44
intermarriage 83, 85, 151
International Alliance of Messianic Congre-
gations and Synagogues 1, 74–5, 77
International Board of Jewish Missions 46
International Federation of Messianic Jews
1, 78
International Federation of Secular
Humanistic Jews 206
International Hebrew Christian Alliance
36–7, 51, 53, 54, 72
Irenaeus 4
Irish Presbyterian Mission 42, 43
Irosolimitano, Dominico 12
Isabella the Catholic, Queen of Castile 10
Israel 63–4, 211
and *Hanukkah* 128
IHCA and 54
Independence Day 137–9

law and cases concerning Jewishness
and right of settlement 167, 192–200,
203

Jacobs, Leslie 76
Jacobs, Louis 192
James (apostle) 3, 4
James II of Aragon 8
Jehiel, Rabbi 8
Jerry's story 187–8
Jerusalem 5, 15–16, 18
Jerusalem Church (Hamburg) 42, 43
Jesus, *see* Yeshua
Jesus People movement / Jesus movement
48, 58–9, 60, 66
Jewish Defense League 62–3, 79, 180
Jewish festivals / holidays 67, 75, 78, 83, 87,
101
see also individual festivals
Jewish identity 56, 60, 61, 62, 64, 70–1,
174–5
see also Jewish lifestyle; Jewishness
Jewish law, *see halakhah;* Noachide laws
Jewish lifestyle 67, 156–66
HCAA and 65, 66–8
Messianic Judaism and 77–9
Jewish Missions of America 60
Jewish Missions of the United Lutheran
Church of America 38
Jewish observance 19–21, 67, 77–8
Jewish Christians and 11, 33, 45–6
in Messianic Judaism 77–8, 83, 84, 87–166
Jewish Reconstructionist Foundation 208
Jewishness / Jewish status, definitions of
167, 171, 172–5, 182–3, 191–2, 200–7
Israeli law and cases concerning 167,
192–200, 203
see also Jewish identity
Jews for Jesus 46, 60–3, 64–5
Jews for Judaism 186
JMA (Jewish Missions of America) 60
Jocz family 41, 44
Jocz, Jacob 44
John (apostle) 4
John the Baptist 160–1
John, Bishop of Jerusalem 5
John of Valladolid 8
Jonas, Giovanni Baptista 12
Joseph, Bishop of Jerusalem 5
Joshua ben Joseph ibn Vives al-Lorqui 8
Judaism
Christian missionaries and 44
and Christianity 87
education in 44, 48, 55, 75
groups within 167, 176, 205–13 (*see also
individual groups*)
see also Jewish observance

Judas, Bishop of Jerusalem 5
Julian, Archbishop of Toledo 7
Julius' story 188–90
    see also Ciss, Julius
Juster, Daniel 67, 74, 76, 77, 80–1, 169, 170, 180, 201, 202
Justus I, Bishop of Jerusalem 5
Justus II, Bishop of Jerusalem 5

Kac, Arthur 52, 53–4, 57, 174
Kaddish 93, 97, 114, 117, 123, 125, 129, 132, 134, 155
Kaminsky, Ida 67
Kaminsky, Morris 55, 67
Kaplan, Mordecai 46, 148, 208
kapparot 117
Kasdan, Barney 159, 162–3, 165
kashrut (dietary laws) 45, 61, 77, 78, 157–9
Kedushah 94, 119, 123
ketubbah 151, 153
Khalima, Justice 199
Kiddush 67, 78, 83, 89, 91, 102, 113, 118, 127, 148, 149
kippah 67, 83, 165–6
Klayman, Elliot 76
Knight, Henry 200
Kol Nidre 118–19
Kol Simcha 66
kosher food, *see kashrut*
Kravitz, Bentzion 181, 182, 184–6, 188
Kuldell, Arthur 26, 27, 29–30

Lancaster School of the Bible 44
Landau, Justice 194
Landsman, Joseph 30, 44
language, *see* terminology
Laura's story 186–7
Lederer Foundation 46–7
Leo de Benedicto Christiano 8
Leventhal, Barry 66, 76
Levertoff, Paul 55
Levi, Bishop of Jerusalem 5
Levi, Nathan Benjamin 13
Levison, Leon 37, 51, 72–3
Levy, Mark John 24, 26, 27, 29, 33–4, 36, 45, 65, 75
Lewek, Joseph 29
Liberman, Paul 65, 75–6, 169–70
Lichtenstein, A. 29
Lichtenstein, I. 24
Lights, Festival of, *see Hanukkah*
Lindhagen, Th. 25
liturgy 19–21
London City Mission 38
London Society for Promoting Christianity Amongst the Jews 14, 15, 38, 48
Long Island Council of Churches 81

Lopez, Rodrigo 12
Lord's Prayer 155
Lord's Supper 174
Los Angeles Bible Institute 44
Lowenthal, Isidor 15
LSPCJ , *see* London Society for Promoting Christianity Amongst the Jews
Lucky, Theodore 24, 25, 45–6
lulav 109, 110
Luther, Martin 11–12

McCoombe, Lawrence 81–2
Machlin, A. B. 46
Magath, Julius 29
Maimonides, Moses 18, 112, 204
Malkhuyyot 112
Maoz Tsur 128, 129
Marcus, Bishop of Jerusalem 5
Marranos 10–11
marriage 83, 150–3
    Israeli law and 193
Matthias, Bishop of Jerusalem 5
media 62
Mehemet Effendi 13
menorah 78, 138–9
menstruation 160
Messiah
    beliefs concerning 167, 171–2, 183
    criteria for 184
    see also Yeshua
Messiah 75 Conference 68, 73–4, 76
Messiah 79 Conference 76
Messianic age, belief in advent of 43
Messianic Jewish Alliance of America 65, 66, 68, 74–5, 77
    see also Hebrew Christian Alliance of America
Messianic Jewish congregations 67–8, 73–5, 82–5
    composition of membership 82, 83
    conference attendance 79
    forerunners 1, 18–26, 33–4, 55, 75
    importance as fellowship 169
    leaders of 82–3
    places and times of worship 84
    variation among 87
    see also Messianic Judaism
Messianic Jewish Manifesto 174–5, 176–8, 202, 205
Messianic Judaism 67–8, 69–71, 75–9, 209–10, 211–13
    beliefs 69–71, 75–7, 81, 82–3, 89, 167, 169–78, 182–4, 202, 204
    and definitions of Jewishness 191, 200–2, 203
    early Christianity and 1, 3–7, 87
    evangelism 84, 178–80, 181, 182, 184–90

and Hebrew Christian movement
    169–70, 178–9
Israeli law and cases 167, 193–200, 203
Jewish observance and services 77–8,
    84, 87–166
opposition to 24, 68–70, 79–82, 167, 171,
    180–1, 182–90, 209, 210–12
responses to criticism 69–71, 80–1
see also Messianic Jewish congregations
Messianic pretenders 13
Messianic Testimony to Israel, *see* Hebrew
    Christian Testimony to Israel
Meyer, A. M. 17
Meyer, Louis 26
mezuzah 156–7, 176
midrashim 44, 177
mikveh 117, 159–61
Mildmay Mission to the Jews 38, 42, 48
Million Testaments Campaign 47
minors, conversion of 80
minyan 143
miracles 183
Mishnah 44, 145, 177
missions, *see* Christian missions;
    evangelism
MJAA, *see* Messianic Jewish Alliance of
    America
mohar 150, 151
mohel 143
Moody Bible Institute 35–6, 44, 48, 55
Moses ha-Cohen 8
Moses Sephardi (Petrus Alfonsi) 7–8
Mountain Lake Conference 26, 27
mourning 154–5
musaf 112
music x, xi, 60, 62, 64, 65, 66, 67, 78, 84, 85,
    161
    see also shofar; songs

Nahmanides 8, 192
naming ceremonies 140–2
Nathan Benjamin Levi 13
National Conference of Messianic Leaders
    74
Nazarenes 3–5, 6–7, 13
Nazism 42–3, 46, 47, 50–1, 52
Neilah 123
New Covenant Mission 27, 38
New Moon (*Rosh Hodesh*) 131–3
New Testament 5, 15, 21, 96, 132–3, 134–6,
    157, 174, 175, 177, 204
    see also Brit Chadasha; Gospels
New Year (*Rosh Hashanah*) 78, 112–17, 161
New York Evangelization Committee of the
    Presbyterian Church in the USA 38
New York Jewish Evangelization Society
    30–1

Newgewirtz, D. J. 36
Newman, Elias 49
Noachide laws 3–4
Nunez Coronel, Paul 12

Ohr Somayach 190
omer 105–7, 138
Origen 6
Orthodox Judaism 148, 149, 151, 154, 167,
    172, 178, 203–5, 207, 212
    and conversion 191
Oz M'Lifnai B'reshit 122, 123

palm branches (*lulav*) 109, 110
Parsons, Martin 41–2
Passover 33, 58, 78, 101–6, 161, 174
    Yeshua and 131
Paul (apostle) 3–4, 40, 143–4, 158
Paul de Santa Maria (Solomon Halevi) 9
PCUSA, *see* Presbyterian Church
Peltz, Jacob 49
Peniel Centre 39, 40, 55
Pentecost (Feast of Weeks), *see* Shavuot
Pentecost (Whitsun) 107–8
persecutions of Jews by Christians 6, 7, 8,
    10–12, 211
Pesach, see Passover
Peter (apostle) 3
Petrus Leonis 8–9
Pfefferkorn, Johannes 11
Pfeifer, Joseph 57
Philip, Bishop of Jerusalem 5
phylacteries (*tefillin*) 67, 156, 162, 163–5,
    176
Pidyon Ha-Ben (redemption of the first-
    born) 145–8
Pierleoni family 8–9
pilgrim festivals 101
    see also individual festivals
plays, *see* drama
pluralism 209, 211–13
polytheism 171
prayer x, xi, 58, 183
    see also charismatic worship
prayer shawl, *see tallit*
Prayer Union of Israel 36
preaching 83, 126, 129, 132
Presbyterian Church (USA) 38–40, 47–8,
    54, 84
Presbyterianism 43
priests/priesthood 160, 165, 176
    see also cohen
'Protocols of the Learned Elders of Zion'
    35
publicity 62, 63, 64–5
Purim 78, 130

Rabbinical Assembly 207
Rabinowitz, Joseph 1, 18–24, 32, 33, 43, 65, 72
  articles of faith 18–19, 21–4
Rachel's story 188
racism 47, 50, 171, 210–11
  see also persecutions
Raphael, Mark 12
Rausch, David 169, 172
reconciliation 117
Reconstructionist, The 208
Reconstructionist Judaism 172, 177–8, 204, 205, 206–7, 208–9, 212
redemption of the first-born 145–8
Reform Judaism 125, 148, 151, 154, 163, 165, 172, 177–8, 191, 204, 205, 206–9, 212
Reich, Max 35, 44, 52
religion, choice and 184
religious consciousness, changing 58–9
Religious Right 211
repentance 113, 161, 183
Reuchlin, Johann 11
revivalism 66–8
Riccio, Paulo 12
Rich, Lawrence 67
Riggans, Walter 175, 178
Rishon (Advent) 133–7
Rohold, Sabbati 17, 29, 30, 32
Rosen, Marie 60
Rosen, Moishe 46, 48, 56, 60–1, 62, 63
Rosenthal, Marvin 68, 70
Rosh Hashanah (New Year) 78, 112–17, 161
Rosh Hodesh (New Moon) 131–3
Ruben, Maurice 27, 29, 34
Rudin, A. James 80
Rudin, Marcia R. 80
Rufeisen, Oswald (Brother Daniel) 193–4

Sabbath observance and services 19–21, 33, 45, 55, 61, 67, 78, 83, 84, 87, 89–100, 163, 176
  Yom Kippur and 118
sacrifice 171, 174, 175, 183
salvation 183
sandak (godfather) 143, 145
Sanhedrin 131
Scattered Nation, The 17
Schereschewsky, Samuel Isaac 15
Schiffman, Michael 82–5, 170–1
Schönberger, C. A. 14
Schor, Samuel 36
Schwartz, C. 16, 17
Scriptures 21
Second Coming 167, 171–2
seder 78, 101–6
  Yeshua and 131

self-examination 112
Sendyk, Mr 42
Seneca, Bishop of Jerusalem 5
sermons 126, 129, 132
services, *see* Jewish observance
Shabbat, see Sabbath
Shabbatai Zevi 13
Shabbatean sects 13
Shalit, Benjamin 194–5
Shamgar, Justice 196
Shavuot (Pentecost / Feast of Weeks) 33, 78, 107–8
shawl, *see tallit*
Sheheheyanu 149
Shema 20–1, 92, 93, 113, 115, 122, 123, 125, 129, 130, 131, 149, 156, 184
  trinitarianism and 170, 171
Shemini Atseret 111, 125
Sheskin, Sandra 64, 67
shittuf 79–80
shivah 154, 155
shofar 112, 113, 114, 116, 124, 131, 133, 138
Shofarot 112, 114
Shushan Purim 130
Sigal, Gerald 183
Simeon bar Kochba 1, 5
Simhat Torah 111, 125–7
Simon bar Yona (apostle) 3
Simon, Matthew H. 81
Sitenhof, Benjamin, and family 43, 44
Six Day War 1, 63
skullcaps 67
Sobel, B. Z. 175, 178–9
songs 59, 60, 62, 66
  see also hymns
Spanish Inquisition 10–11
Stern, David 172–5, 176–8, 179, 202, 205
Stern, H. A. 16
Stone, Nathan 44
sukkah 78, 109, 110
Sukkot (Feast of Tabernacles) 33, 78, 109–11, 125
synagogue services, *see* Jewish observance

Tabernacles, Feast of 33, 78, 109–11, 125
Tahanun 138
tallit (prayer shawl) 67, 83, 91, 117, 162–3
Talmud 112, 130, 157, 165, 177
  Christian missionaries and 44
Tanenbaum, Marc H. 79–80
Targums 44
Tashlikh 112–13
tefillin (phylacteries) 67, 156, 162, 163–5, 176
Tenakh, *see* Bible
terminology 68, 182
  see also under Yeshua / Jesus

theatre, *see* drama
theology 47, 170–1, 183–4
    see also beliefs *under* Messianic Judaism
Timothy (companion of Paul) 143
Titus (companion of Paul) 143
Tobias, Bishop of Jerusalem 5
Toland, John 13
tolerance 62, 209, 211–13
Torah 164, 175, 204
    and Jewishness 191
    Messianic Judaism and 93, 94–6, 97,
        109, 111, 115, 116, 123, 125–7, 129, 132,
        134, 140, 149–50, 176–7, 205
Torah MiSinai 207, 209
Tosefta 177
training, *see* education
Tremellius, John Immanuel 12
Tribulation, the Great 171–2
trinitarianism 170–1, 183–4, 187
True Light, The 36
turbans 165
tzizit, see fringes

U-Netanneh Tokef 112, 122
UJMC (Union of Messianic Jewish Congre-
    gations) 1, 74, 76–7
universalism 47

Vanderwerff, Hans 180

washing, ritual 117, 159–61
wedding ceremony 151–3
Weeks, Feast of, *see Shavuot*
Weisenberg, Margaret 53
William Rufus 7
Wine, Sherwin 208
Winer, Robert 64
Witkon, Justice 196
Wolff, Joseph 15
women
    and head coverings 165–6
    and prayer shawls 163
    roles and status 67, 83, 90–1
World Council of Churches 48
worship, *see* Jewish observance; prayer

Yaaleh-Ve-Yavo 131
yeshivas 55, 130
Yeshua / Jesus
    and criteria for Messiahship 184
    and Jewish observance 87, 89, 90, 128,
        131, 143, 146, 149, 158, 162, 176
    and Jewishness 174
    resurrection, and the festival of the
        counting of the omer 106
    use of names of 58, 68
    see also Messiah
YHCA, *see* Young Hebrew Christian
    Alliance
YHCYO (Young Hebrew Christian Youth
    Organization) 57
Yiddish 44, 47, 48, 61
Yigdal 98–9
Yizkor 123, 138
YMJA (Young Messianic Jewish Alliance of
    America) 58, 75
Yocz, Paul 44
Yom Ha-Maschiach 134, 137
Yom Kippur (Day of Atonement) 33, 70–1,
        78, 112, 117–24
    Rosh Hodesh and 131
Young Hebrew Christian Alliance 57–9, 64,
    66
Young Hebrew Christian Reporter 57
Young Hebrew Christian Youth Organiza-
    tion 57
Young Messianic Jewish Alliance of
    America 58, 75

Zaccheus, Bishop of Jerusalem 5
Zacker, John 34–5, 65
Zamora, Alfonso de 12
Zeckhausen, Harry 29
Zeidman, Annie 51–2
Zeidman, Morris 51
Zikhronot 112
Zion Society for Israel 38
Zion's Freund 42
Zutrau, Morris 39